Canadian Foreign Policy, 1945–2000

Major Documents and Speeches

Canadian Foreign Policy, 1945–2000

Major Documents and Speeches

Edited by

Arthur E. Blanchette

The Golden Dog Press

Ottawa-Canada-2000

ISBN 0-919614-89-2

Canadian Cataloguing in Publication Data

Main entry under title:
  Canadian foreign policy, 1945–2000: major documents and speeches

(Rideau series ; 1)
Includes bibliographical references and index.
ISBN 0-919614-89-2

    1. Canada — Foreign relations — 1945-   -Sources. I. Blanchette, Arthur E. II. Series.

FC602.C6348 2000   327.71   C00-931881-X

Cover design by The Dundurn Group of Toronto.

Typesetting by Carleton Production Centre of Nepean.

Printed in Canada.

Published by:
    The Golden Dog Press is an imprint of Haymax Inc.,
    P.O. Box 393, Kemptville, Ont., K0G 1J0 Canada

The Golden Dog Press wishes to express its appreciation to the Canada Council and the Ontario Arts Council for the support these Councils have extended to its publishing programme.

To Alix and Marc

Contents

List of Documents

Documents are numbered by chapter (before the period) and then numbered sequentially within their chapter (after the period). Thus, Doc. 2.12 is the twelfth document in chapter 2.

Preface

This volume documenting the highlights of Canada's external relations from 1945 to 2000 complements the four-volume series on Canadian Foreign Policy launched by Carleton University Press in 1971.[1]

A selection of documents concentrating fifty years of Canadian foreign policy into a volume of this size is a task of compression that many will consider restrictive and arbitrary. Dr. Mackay, editor of Volume I, made this point in 1971 in the first of the series and this editor could not agree more. Nevertheless, it is hoped that this book will serve a useful purpose as a handy compendium of the achievements, the great moments, of Canada's approach to the world during the last half of the 20th century.

A number of conclusions can be drawn from this survey. The first, and probably most striking, is that the fundamentals of Canada's foreign policy established between the years 1945 and 1965, especially between 1945 and 1955, are still very much with us today. The decade between 1945 and 1955 was an especially creative one, during which Canada played a constructive and leading role in world affairs. It was a time when our influence was high and our views were heeded.

Canada's shift towards an outward-looking approach to the world during and after the Second World War led to a role of active participation in the foundation of the UN's economic and political system, the General Agreement on Tariffs and Trade (GATT), and the Universal Declaration of Human Rights. Our part in the creation of NATO stands out, as does our influence in the launching of peacekeeping, both within and outside the UN. Canadian views on disarmament, the Colombo Plan, the Law of the Sea, were influential and produced lasting results.

In terms of foreign policy, relations with the United States

---

[1] These volumes are: (1) *Canadian Foreign Policy 1945-1954* by R.A. MacKay, Carleton Library No. 51, published in 1971; and (2) by the current editor *Canadian Foreign Policy* 1955-1965, 1966-1976, and 1977-1992, Carleton Library Nos. 103, 118, and 183, published in 1977, 1981, and 1994, respectively. They are referred to henceforth as R.A.M., and A.E.B. I, II, and III.

became a good deal closer after the Second World War, notably in the financial, trade and defence sectors. Currently they represent the highest priority in our external relations. Highlights of the period were such developments as NORAD, the Automotive Pact of the 1960s, the Free Trade Agreement of the 1980s. Energy and fisheries problems became pressing. Long-standing environmental issues related to air and water quality continued to confront us and a new one regarding water exports emerged.

Concomitantly, relations with the countries of the Pacific Rim, notably Japan and Korea, among others intensified, especially towards the end of the period under review.

Prominent new actors have appeared on the foreign policy stage: the Provinces. While the provinces, in constitutional terms, always had legitimate interests in some aspects of external relations, notably trade and immigration, there is no doubt that those involved in our early post-war international activities would be astonished by the extent to which the provincial role has grown and become increasingly influential. Indeed, in some sectors, it is impossible to conduct our foreign policy without them.

Many other issues came to the fore towards the end of the 20th century that our foreign affairs pioneers could not have foreseen, for instance, narcotics, money-laundering, land mines, the economic and financial globalization of the world, cyber crimes with international repercussions. These aspects of current international relations require increasing attention today.

Several of our prime ministers and foreign ministers made their mark in the foreign policy field. It was Louis St. Laurent, actively supported by the Department of External Affairs, who launched Canada on its creative outward-looking post-war course.[2] L.B. Pearson's name is forever associated with peacekeeping, as is Howard Green's with disarmament. John Diefenbaker and Joe Clark were vocal and effective against *apartheid*. Paul Martin Sr. was an active minister in the UN context, particularly in promoting its enlarged membership and peacekeeping, as well as in developing the Law of the Sea. Pierre Trudeau got off to a lively start with new approaches to foreign policy and defence. His government established relations with Beijing and the Vatican and also paid a good deal of attention to aid and development. Brian Mulroney played a crucial role in the creation of the Free Trade Agree-

---

[2] See A.E.B. I, pp. xxi–xxiii, for background; also *Bout de papier* (Volume 16, No. 3, autumn 1999, pp. 21–27), for an account, by the current editor, of the life and times in DEA at mid-century. *Bout de papier* is published quarterly by the Professional Association of Foreign Service Officers, Ottawa.

ment with the United States, and the NAFTA. Jean Chrétien will be remembered for his trade-oriented *Team Canada* initiatives and Lloyd Axworthy for his quest for human security. A generation after his father, the current Finance Minister, Paul Martin Jr. is a leader in global finance and monetary affairs.

List of Abbreviations

Abbreviations for main sources

PM	Prime Minister
FM	Foreign Minister
SSEA	Secretary of State for External Affairs
MFAIT	Minister of Foreign Affairs and International Trade (see note below)
DEA	Department of External Affairs
DFAIT	Department of Foreign Affairs and International Trade
DND	Department of National Defence
DOF	Department of Finance
PCO	Privy Council Office
PMO	Prime Minister's Office
CIDA	Canadian International Development Agency
HC	House of Commons
SSEA	Secretary of State for External Affairs
SCEAIT	Standing Committee on External Affairs and International Trade (House of Commons)
SCEAND	Standing Committee on External Affairs and National Defence (House of Commons) (see note below)
SS	Statements and Speeches (DEA and DFA)
CTS	Canada Treaty Series

Note: In the early 1980s, by legislation, the Department of External Affairs absorbed the Foreign Trade Service of the former Department of Trade and Commerce. In 1993, the recently-elected Chrétien government renamed it the Department of Foreign Affairs and International Trade (DFAIT). These changes apply to the House of Commons Standing Committee also.

Acknowledgments

It is impossible to produce a volume of this sort without a good deal of help. Two colleagues, Ross Francis, a former High Commissioner to Malaysia and Ambassador to Finland, and Vernon G. Turner, formerly Ambassador to Israel and to the Soviet Union, read all chapter and section headings. Their comments were particularly pertinent and I am indebted to them for their advice and help. The Library of the Department of Foreign Affairs was again extremely competent and helpful. Christina Thiele, Carleton Production Centre, an outstanding typesetter, put order into a rather chaotic script. Finally, without the interest and encouragement of Michael Gnarowski, an old and valued friend, publication of this book would not have been possible.

All documents in this volume are in the public domain. However, the views expressed in chapter and section headings are personal and do not necessarily reflect those of the Department of Foreign Affairs, of which I was a member for many years.

Arthur Blanchette

Ottawa, September, 2000

Introduction

1. From Pre-War Isolationism to Post-War International Commitment

DURING THE PERIOD BETWEEN THE FIRST AND SECOND WORLD WARS, Canada's approach to world affairs had been that of a small power, recently emerged from colonial status and beset by extremely serious economic problems resulting from the Depression of the 1930s. Bread-and-butter issues at home understandably commanded more attention than problems preoccupying the world abroad.

Canadian participation in the Second World War profoundly altered the equation. We had made notable contributions towards winning the war in manpower, supplies, industrial output, finances.

We also had ideas about how the new world order should be organized and we were prepared to take an active part in helping to organize it.

The Foundations of Canadian Policy in World Affairs   Doc. 1

ADDRESS BY SSEA LOUIS ST. LAURENT, INAUGURATING THE GRAY FOUNDATION LEC-
TURESHIP AT UNIVERSITY OF TORONTO, JANUARY 13, 1947.

The Gray Foundation was begun by a legacy from a former student of the University of Toronto, John Gray, who was killed in the Second World War. John Gray and his brother Duncan, when students at the university, spent their vacations with a family in Quebec in order to achieve a better understanding of French Canada.

The purpose of the Foundation is to promote mutual understanding between French and English-speaking Canada.

I The Need to Examine the Basis of Canadian External Policy

From what we know of Duncan and John Gray it is clear that they had a high ideal for this country. So also did the thousands of young men from this and other universities who turned from the peaceful and constructive pursuits which are the normal interests of our youth and went willingly to war. I think we may now inquire what it is in the ethos of this nation which we cherish so greatly and which we must protect and nourish. In particular, we must consider the role in world affairs which they would wish us to play.

During the war in which they fought, there was won for this nation an enviable reputation as a military power. There now rests with us the opportunity to show the same degree of competence, the same readiness to accept responsibilities, the same sense of purpose in the conduct of our international affairs.

For this reason I propose to make this lecture an enquiry into the foundations of Canadian policy in world affairs, I think this is in keeping with the purposes of the Gray Lectureship. We Canadians of English and French origin have embarked on the joint task of building a nation. One aspect of our common enterprise is our external relations. The subject is one of special interest to me because of my present responsibilities in the Government.

The founder of this lectureship has said: "If we discover and dwell upon what binds us together, we shall accept our differences as the members of a true family accept their differences without losing sight for a moment of the things which hold them together in a vital unity." It is in keeping with this spirit that I propose to discuss the background of our external policy.

A policy of world affairs, to be truly effective, must have its foundations laid upon general principles which have been tested in the life of the nation and which have secured the broad support of large groups of the population. It is true that differences of opinion about foreign policy must continually be reviewed in discussion and debate inside and outside of Parliament. Such discussions, however, can result in constructive conclusions only if they take place against the background of a large measure of agreement on fundamentals.

It may be objected that we are not old enough as a nation to have worked out such agreed principles. But let us not forget that much of which forms the basis of our agreement in that respect is the result of circumstances over which we have had little if any control. The century old struggles between France and England, their rivalry in the New World, the Battle of the Plains of Abraham, the Treaty of Paris of 1763, the revolt of the Thirteen Colonies, the wave of liberal thinking unleashed by the French Revolution, the geography, the climate, the kind of natural resources of our country all tended to create conditions for our ancestors and tend to create conditions for our own generation which lead to almost inevitable results. They have forced French-speaking and English-speaking men and women to live side by side as members of the same community. They have inspired them to work together to obtain an ever increasing measure of self-government; they have tempered the resistance of the metropolitan government to this healthy development; they have made natural and easy the creation of an economy productive of large surpluses of certain kinds of commodities and lacking in certain other kinds and dependent in an extraordinary degree upon exchange and trade to get some benefit out

2

of the surpluses and to secure the commodities not available from our own production.

We are now within close range of two significant anniversaries in the life of this nation. It is almost exactly a century since the decision was taken that the affairs of this part of the world should be conducted upon the principles of responsible government. For a hundred years, therefore, French-speaking and English-speaking people living in the valley of the St. Lawrence River and the Great Lakes, together with their fellow countrymen elsewhere across this continent, have been engaged upon the experiment of building, on their own responsibility and under their own direction, a modern nation. It is, as it had to be, a nation constructed on the foundation of two cultures and two languages.

A century ago the Canadian people in winning responsible government staked their future on the political principles which had been defined in Lord Durham's famous report. They staked their future equally on a denial of Durham's assertion that the country could not survive with two cultures. They said that this could be a free country, notwithstanding that it had also to be a country with both English and French culture. For a hundred years now they have been shown to be right.

The second anniversary of which I would remind you is that of "Confederation" eighty years ago. It was then that the challenge was accepted to build into a single state the scattered communities which stretched across the northern half of this continent. We have therefore been working together on this task of nation building for some considerable time. It is not too soon to look back and determine what principles have had to be and have become generally acceptable throughout this country in the conduct of our relations abroad. When we have defined these principles, we may examine the manner in which we have habitually embodied them in our relations with other states where our associations are especially close. We may also consider them with respect to the international organizations of which we are or have been members.

II The Basic Principles

a) National Unity

The first general principle upon which I think we are agreed is that our external policies shall not destroy our unity. No policy can be regarded as wise which divides the people whose effort and resources must put it into effect.

This consideration applies not only to the two main cultural groups in our country. It applies equally to sectionalism of any kind. We dare not fashion a policy which is based on the particular interests of any economic group, or any class or of any section in this country. We must be on guard especially against the claims of extravagant regionalism no matter where they have their origin.

Our history has shown this to be a consideration in our external policy of which we, more even than others, must be perpetually conscious. The role of this country in world affairs will prosper only as we maintain this principle, for a disunited Canada will be a powerless one.

b) Political Liberty

Second amongst the ideas which shape our external policy I will place the conception of political liberty. This is an inheritance from both our French and English background, and through these parent states it has come to us from the whole rich culture of western Europe. It is a patrimony which we ourselves have enlarged by working out on our own soil the transition from colony to free community. These are days in which the vocabulary of political thought has been so debased that there are many familiar coins that one hesitates to lay on the counter.

I make no apology, however, for speaking to a Canadian audience of political liberty because I know that this phrase has content for us. I know, also, that we are all conscious of the danger to our own political institutions when freedom is attacked in other parts of the world. In the complex series of events which twice in a generation has led us into war, we have been profoundly influenced in our decisions by the peril which threatened the democracies of western Europe. From our joint political inheritance, as well as from our common experience, we have come as a people to distrust and dislike governments which rule by force and which suppress free comment on their activities. We know that stability is lacking where consent is absent. We believe that the greatest safeguard against the aggressive policies of any government is the freely expressed judgment of its own people. This does not mean that we have even sought to interfere in the affairs of others, or to meddle in situations which were obviously outside our interest or beyond our control. It does mean, however, that we have consistently sought and found our friends amongst those of like political traditions. It means equally that we have realized that a threat to the liberty of western Europe, where our political ideas were nurtured, was a threat to our own way of life. This realization has perhaps not been comprehended or expressed by every group and every individual in the country with as much clarity and coherence as, looking back on the events, we should like. I have no doubt, however, that for the young men of our universities who fought in this war, it was a part of our national inheritance which they well understood.

c) The Rule of Law in National and International Affairs

In the third place respect for the rule of law has become an integral part of our external as of our domestic policy. The supremacy of law in our own political system is so familiar that we are in constant danger of taking it for granted. We know, however, that historically the development of this principle is a necessary antecedent to self-government.

4

Introduction

The first great victory on the road to freedom was the establishment in early modern times of the principle that both governments and peoples were subject to the impartial administration of the courts. Only then could the further step be taken by which the people gave their consent to the laws by which they were governed.

Within the past decade we have been reminded by the hideous example of the fascist states of the evil which befalls a nation when the government sets itself above the law. Beneath the spurious efficiency of such a state, we have perceived the helpless plight of individuals who have been deprived of the primary right of an impartial administration of the law. We have seen also the chaos which is brought to world-affairs when lawlessness is practised in the field of international relations. The development of an international code of law is still in its early stages. The past decade has done much to delay and distort this growth. I feel sure, however, that we in this country are agreed that the freedom of nations depends upon the rule of law amongst states. We have shown this concretely in our willingness to accept the decisions of international tribunals, courts of arbitration and other bodies of a judicial nature, in which we have participated. There can be no doubt that the Canadian people unanimously support this principle.

d) The Values of a Christian Civilization

No foreign policy is consistent nor coherent over a period of years unless it is based upon some conception human values. I know that we live in an age when it is fashionable to speak in terms only of hard realism in the conduct of international affairs. I realize also that at best the practice of any policy is a poor approximation of ideals upon which it may be based. I am sure, however, that in our national life we are continually influenced by the conceptions of good and evil which emerged from Hebrew and Greek civilization, and which have been transformed and transmitted through the Christian traditions of the Western World. These are values which lay emphasis on the importance of the individual, on the place of moral principles in the conduct of human relations, on standards of judgment which transcend mere material well-being. They have ever influenced our national life we have built a modern state from East to West across this continent. I am equally convinced that on the basis of this common experience we shall discern the same values in world affairs, and that we shall seek to protect and nurture them.

e) The Acceptance of International Responsibility in Keeping with our Conception of our Role in World Affairs

There is a fifth basic principle which I should like also to mention before considering the background of our relations with particular countries. That is willingness to accept international responsibilities. I know that there are many in this country who feel that in the past we have played too small a part in the development of international political organizations. The growth in this country of a sense of political responsibility on an international scale has perhaps been less rapid than some of us would like. It the nevertheless been a perceptible growth; and again and again on the major questions of participation in international organizations, both in peace and war, we have taken the decision to be present. If there is one conclusion that our common experience has led us to accept, it is that security for this country lies in the development of a firm structure of international organization.

I have been speaking of certain general principles which I think underlie the conduct of our external policy. These are principles which have been defined and articulated in the practice of relations with other countries over many decades. In this application of our principles, too, we have reached certain general conclusions on which we are all agreed, and which serves as a guide to policy.

III The Practical Application

a) The Commonwealth Which We Ourselves Have Fashioned for
   Achieving the Ends We Desire in World Affairs

We have never attempted to define in precise terms our relations with the Commonwealth. They are nevertheless a basic consideration in the external policy of this country. In discussing them 1 will recall two aspects of this relationship concerning which I am sure there will be no disagreement. In the first place the Commonwealth is a form of political association which is unique. There has never been anything like it before in history.

There is no parallel to it in the contemporary world. It is the only case on record of a Colonial Empire being transformed to an association of free nations by experiment, by compromise, by political evolution. I have no doubt that, whatever its future, it will be regarded by the historians of another age as one of the great constructive political achievements of our time. The other fact that I would call to your mind is that the Commonwealth is in a very real sense an achievement in which Canadians can take special pride. We Canadians perhaps more than other of its members, have contributed to its development. We have regarded it as an instrument which, in co-operation with like-minded people, we could use for our common purposes. It has, therefore, the vitality of a living, functioning organism which has been and which can continue to be used for good, according to the wisdom and foresight of our policies.

It is now only twenty years since, the term "Commonwealth" came into popular use as a result of the Declaration which was adopted by the Conference of 1926. Even in that short period the meaning of the word has changed. There are already important differences between the Commonwealth of today and that described in Lord Balfour's famous statement. Even while this change was taking place however, there has been further compelling demonstration of the fact that we are members in an association of free nations, capable of common action in an emergency, greater and more striking than that of any formal military or diplomatic alliance that the world lids ever known. Even though they are not precisely defined, the principles on which we act in regard to the Commonwealth may be clearly discerned. We seek to preserve it as an instrument through which we, with others who share our objectives, can co-operate for our common good in peace as in war. On the other hand, we should continue to resist, as in the past, efforts to reduce to formal terms or specific commitments this association which has demonstrated its vitality through the common understanding upon which it is based. We should likewise oppose developments in our Commonwealth relations which might be inconsistent with our desire to participate fully in the task of building an effective international organization on a wider scale.

Within the Commonwealth, our relations with the United Kingdom have, of course, a very special value and significance. We shall no t forget in our history, the imaginative collaboration of British and Canadian leaders who, a century ago, laid the common political foundations for the modern Commonwealth. Nor can we fail to be influenced by the fact that-our political institutions are those of the British Isles, and that we now share with other parliamentary democracies the responsibility for preserving and developing this system. We shall not forget either the peril in which we shared, together with other Commonwealth countries, but especially with the United Kingdom during the dark days of 1940. This was an episode which threw in dramatic relief the measure to which we have common interests and the degree to which we are alike concerned m the establishment of a world order based on principles of freedom.

b) The United States — The Settlement of International Affairs by
   Negotiation and Compromise

It is not customary in this country for us to think in terms of having a policy in regard to the United States. Like farmers whose lands have a common concession line, we think of ourselves as settling, from day to day, questions that arise between us, without dignifying the process by the word "policy." We have travelled so much of the road together in close agreement that by comparison the occasions on which our paths may have diverged seems insignificant.

There has, however, been more to our relations with the United States than mere empirical neighbourliness. For the century during which we have been building this nation, we have kept company with an adjoining state vastly more powerful, more self-confident, more wealthy than we. It is a state with purposes and ambitions parallel to ours. One by one, the major areas of disagreement have been reduced. Our common border has long since been defined to our mutual satisfaction. The people of this country have taken a final decision to remain outside the United States. There is no longer any body of opinion in this country which looks towards annexation. The people of the United States on their part, have come to a parallel conclusion that they will not extend their boundaries beyond their present limits on this continent. On both sides the fact has been accepted that there shall he a free. and independent federation in the northern part of this continent. None of this has been achieved, however, without reflection and forethought, nor will it be maintained without constant watchfulness. I do not say this because I think there is the slightest intention on either side to move away from the present happy state of our relations. I say it merely because even the simplest relationship between human beings requires the constructive action of both parties. The relationship between a great and powerful nation and its smaller neighbour, at best, is far from simple. It calls for constant and imaginative attention on both sides.

Defined more precisely, our policy in regard to the United States has come with the passage of years to have two main characteristics. On the one hand, we have sought by negotiation, by arbitration by compromise, to settle upon the basis of mutual satisfaction the problems that have arisen between us. As I suggested a moment ago, this has been far more than the unimaginative clearing away of parochial questions. It has succeeded precisely because it is based on the determination of both nations to conduct their affairs, as a matter of policy, on this basis. The other aspect of our relations with the United States which I shall emphasize is our readiness to accept our responsibility as a North American nation in enterprises which are for the welfare of this. continent. In support of this assertion, there is a long and creditable record of joint activity. In making it, however, I must add that it has never been the opinion of any considerable number of people in Canada that this continent could live unto itself. We have seen our own interests in the wider context of the western world. We have realized also that regionalism of any kind would not provide the answer to problems or world security. But we know that peoples who live side by side on the same continent cannot disregard each other's interests, and we have always been willing to consider the possibility of common action for constructive ends.

c) France — A Tradition of Common Interests

We have never forgotten that France is one of the fountainheads of our cultural life. We realize that she forms an integral part of the framework of our international life. We have so much in common that, despite the differences between the French political system and our own, we cannot doubt for a Moment that our objects in world affairs are similar. We in this country have always believed in the greatness of France, even at times when her future seemed most obscure.

8

Introduction

During the war, we were confident that France played a major role in her own liberation. We gave our support to those leaders of the French people whom the French themselves were prepared to follow. We are aware of the heavy burden which invasion twice in a generation has laid upon France. We shall support her recovery not merely out of sympathy, but because we know that her integrity is a matter of great consequence to us.

d) The Support of Constructive International Organization

I shall not endeavour to discuss in detail the question of our relationship with other states. Rather, I shall turn now to our attitude towards international organizations. As I suggested when I was discussing the general principles which underlie our policy we have been ready to take our part in constructive international action. We have, of course, been forced to keep in mind the limitations upon the influence of any secondary power. No society of nations can prosper if it does not have the support of those who hold the major share of the world's military and economic power. There is little point in a country of our stature recommending international action, if those who must carry the major burden of whatever action is taken are not in sympathy. We know, however, that the development of international organizations on a broad scale is of the very greatest importance to us and we have been willing to play our role when it was apparent that significant and effective action was contemplated.

We have already given good evidence of this willingness by the record of our international activities since the war. We sent a strong delegation to the Conference at San Francisco, and I had every reason to be gratified with the delegations which accompanied me to the first part of the General Assembly in London and second part in New York. We were elected to membership in the Economic and Social Council, and have tried to show by the attention we have paid to that body the measure of importance we attached to its creation.

We have taken part in the formation of the World Bank and Fund, of the Provisional International Civil Aviation Organization, of the World Health Organization, of UNESCO, of the International Refugee Organization, of the Food and Agriculture Organization and of the projected International Trade Organization. We have continued to support the International Labour Organization, as we did before the war. We have played a prominent part in the work of the Atomic Energy Commission and of the Peace Conference in Paris.

This list is not exhaustive, but it indicates the measure of our activity. We have not found it easy to provide delegates and advisers for all the conferences which the task of creating a new structure of world organizations has required. I think, however, that we may take pride in the work of our representatives, and that if you had observed them at any of these gatherings, you would have seen them doing competent energetic and constructive work. I think you would find, also, that they had regularly won the respect and confidence of their colleagues from other countries.

In economic as well as political affairs we have put our shoulder to the wheel of post-war reconstruction. Our contribution to UNRRA was more than 150 million dollars, and Canadian food and equipment have been shipped into devastated areas all over the world. We supplied goods freely to our allies during the war under Mutual Aid Legislation, and we have since provided export credits on a vast scale to help in rebuilding the economic life of Europe and of China. We have done this as a matter of policy, because we believe that the economic reconstruction of the world must go hand in hand with the political reconstruction. We are aware, too, that economic revival is a matter of great importance to us. We are dependent on markets abroad for the large quantities of staple products we produce and cannot consume, and we are dependent on supplies from abroad of commodities which are essential to our well-being. It seems to me axiomatic, therefore, that we should give our support to every international organization which contributes to the economic and political stability of the world.

e) The Development of an Effective Diplomatic Service

Seen in the light of these historic developments, the recent expansion of the diplomatic service of this country is a natural development. We are preparing ourselves to fulfil the growing responsibilities in world affairs which we have accepted as a modern state. We wish the Commonwealth to be an effective instrument of co-operation and we have, therefore, appointed High Commissioners in the capitals of every Commonwealth country. I am glad to say that within recent weeks this process has been completed with the appointment of a High Commissioner to India, who will soon be appointed, we may experience the same informal and helpful co-operation which has been characteristic of our relations with the Commonwealth countries.

We have also multiplied rapidly our diplomatic representation in foreign countries. Before very long, we shall have provided ourselves with diplomatic representation in the capitals of every major country in the world. We have not taken this step merely through a desire to follow a conventional practice, or to advertise ourselves abroad. We have done so because our geography, our climate, our natural resources have so conditioned our economy that the continued prosperity and well-being of our own people can best be served by the prosperity and well-being of the whole world. We have thus a useful part to play in world affairs, useful to ourselves through being useful to others, and to play that part we must have our own spokesmen amongst our neighbours.

It is not only in our foreign service that this expansion is taking place. We are trying also to construct a Department in Ottawa which will build upon the activities of our representatives abroad. Our own

Introduction

national interests compel us to take a creditable part in the international conferences which are now determining the nature of the post-war world. We are, therefore, constructing a service which can provide strong and well informed advisers for the delegations which we must send to these gatherings. This is no easy task. It will, of course, make demands upon our financial resources. I am strengthened, however, in my determination to recommend the continuation of this policy because it is no transitory experiment. It is the natural result of a long historic process, and I feel that it will be supported by all sections of our people.

And that is as it should be. Canadian policy in its external relations should not be allowed to become a matter of party political controversy at home. Of course the government in office must take full responsibility for each one of its actions as well as in Canada's external relations as in the conduct of purely domestic Canadian affairs. But in its external relations the Government in office should ever strive to speak and to act on behalf on the whole of Canada and in such manner as to have the support of all the Canadian peoples regardless of party affiliations at home.

IV Conclusion

A few moments no I said that we must play 'a role in world affairs in keeping with the ideals and sacrifices of the young men of this University, and of this country who went to war.' However great or small that role may be, we must play it creditably. We must act with maturity and consistency, and with a sense of responsibility. For this reason I return in conclusion to the point at which I began. We must act as a united people. By that I mean a people who, through reflection and discussion, have arrived at a common understanding of our interests and our purposes. In this Lectureship you have at your disposal an instrument which can help us greatly to achieve this end. You may be confident that, as you plan the Gray lecture from year to year, you will be contributing to that mature conception of our national interest which is the characteristic of a united people.

A former High Commissioner for the United Kingdom in Canada, Mr. Malcolm MacDonald, speaking to a Canadian audience before his departure, referred to Canada as "a unity, a harmony, a nation — a people with national sentiment pursuing national aims." He added these words; "there is a sanity, a wisdom, a true statesmanship about the Canadian outlook and policy in international affairs which is uncommon."

These are words of great praise. In repeating them to you may I add a comment about them which I have made previously: "May Canada never be less deserving of them than she has been during these few recent troubled years."

Canadian Foreign Policy 1945-2000

1

The United Nations

1. Establishment

THE ATLANTIC CHARTER, that is, the declaration of war aims issued by Prime Minister Churchill and President Roosevelt during their shipboard meeting off Newfoundland in 1941, had foreshadowed the establishment of a system of general world security.

It was not, however, until the Moscow Conference of the United Kingdom, the United States, and the Soviet Union in 1943 that the Soviet Union expressly agreed. The United States took the lead and called a meeting of the Big Three and China at Dumbarton Oaks on the outskirts of Washington. There the principles and structural lines of the proposed new system were worked out and "the Dumbarton Oaks Proposals" agreed to. They, in effect, became the first draft of the Charter of the United Nations and are outlined in the immediately following document.

Meanwhile, active participation in the creation of a new international order had become the main focal point of Canadian foreign policy. As early as July 19, 1943, Prime Minister Mackenzie King called the attention of the House of Commons to the problem of the responsibility for the exercise of authority in any organization set up for the purpose of fostering world peace. He asked quite pointedly where authority in any such body should be located and how it should be administered.

In his view, it would not be wise to restrict authority to the Great Powers alone; also it would be cumbersome to divide it equally among all of the 30-then members of the United Nations, as the countries allied in the war against Germany and Japan were becoming increasingly known, even more so among the then 60 or so countries around the world.

Some compromise was needed and he suggested that representation in each constituent sector of the UN system should be determined on a *functional* basis that would admit countries, large or small, having the most effective contribution to make to the resolution or handling of a particular problem or question.

At about the time that the "functional principle" proposals were being made, the term "Middle Power" was becoming increasingly heard as best describing Canada's position in world affairs.

The functional principle survived Great Power decisions regarding the authority and functions of the UN Security Council only in part, that is, in the understanding that the smaller countries having played the most effective role in ensuring the allied victory or having the most to contribute to world peace should be most frequently selected as members of the Council.

The functional principle survived better among the new postwar international economic and human rights institutions where there was no veto, decisions being taken by majority vote. The description of Canada as a "Middle Power" reflected the functional principle and is still with us.

Doc. 1.1   **Canadian views on the Dumbarton Oaks Proposals, 1945**

MEMORANDUM OF JANUARY 12, 1945, COMMUNICATED TO THE GOVERNMENTS OF THE UNITED STATES, THE UNITED KINGDOM, THE SOVIET UNION AND CHINA AND THE PROVISIONAL GOVERNMENT OF THE FRENCH REPUBLIC (DEA, *EXTERNAL AFFAIRS* XVII, NO. 2, FEBRUARY, 1965, PP. 58-61).[3]

It was the Canadian view that, before the Dumbarton Oaks proposals were formally submitted as a basis for a general conference, efforts should be made to ensure that the "middle powers" would be effectively associated with the enforcement of peace. As the Canadian authorities saw it, difficulties in connection with the position of the more important secondary states centred round: (a) the selection of nonpermanent members of the Security Council; and (b) the authority of the Council to call upon member states not represented on it to join in the imposition of sanctions. In telegrams despatched on January 12, 1945, the Canadian Ambassadors in Washington, Moscow, and Paris and the Canadian Chargé d'Affaires in Chungking were instructed to present a memorandum of the Canadian Government's views to the foreign ministers of the countries to which they were accredited. The text of the memorandum and an extract from the telegrams are reproduced below.

It might be noted in passing that Articles 23 and 44 of the United Nations Charter contain provisions to meet some of the arguments that were advanced by Canada in this memorandum and later at the San Francisco Conference. Thus Article 23, Paragraph 1, of the Charter directs that, in the election of non-permanent members of the Security Council, due regard should be "specially paid, in the first instance

---

[3]**Editor's note:** *External Affairs* was a monthly DEA review of events superseded some time ago by other departmental publications.

to the contribution of members of the United Nations to the maintenance of international peace and security and to the other purposes
of the organization." This was the outcome of a Canadian suggestion
that, since the principle that power was to be combined with responsibility was reflected in the permanent membership of the great powers on the Council, this should also be taken into account in electing the non-permanent members, so that among the six there should
be several states that could make a substantial contribution to the
purposes of the organization. Under this functional approach, it was
clearly intended that equitable geographical representation was to be
a secondary consideration.

Article 44 of the Charter was the result of a Canadian amendment
intended to give effect to the axiom "No taxation without representation" in the most important case in which a state's interest could be
involved, that is, the contribution of its armed forces to enforcement
action. In effect, it provides that, when the Security Council has decided
to use force, each state that has been asked to contribute a contingent
shall have a voice, and a vote, in decisions concerning the employment
of its own military forces.

1) The Canadian Government has welcomed the proposals for the establishment of a general international organization published by
the Governments of the United States, the United Kingdom, the Soviet Union, and China. Certain parts of the proposals, however, create special difficulties for Canada and probably for other states as
well. The difficulties relate to the means whereby the co-operation
of these states in fulfilling the obligations placed upon the Security
Council can best be assured, and the authority of the Security Council thereby increased. Because of the high importance of enlisting
the greatest possible measure of support, the Canadian Government believes that the proposals should be expanded or otherwise
amended to reduce these difficulties, and is of the opinion that
the desired changes can most effectively be introduced before the
proposals are formally submitted as the basis for an international
conference.

2) The proposals recognize the primary responsibilities of the great
powers for the maintenance of peace by according them permanent membership in the Security Council. It is also generally understood that, when the proposals are completed, the individual
concurrence of the great powers will be required in certain important classes of decisions. There is, however, no corresponding
recognition in the proposals that the responsibilities which other
members of the United Nations are asked to assume differ greatly,
despite the fact that their power and their capacity to use it for the
maintenance of peace range from almost zero upwards to a point
not very far behind the great powers.

3) Under the proposals, a country which would be called upon to

make a substantial contribution to world security has no better assurance of election to the Security Council than the smallest and weakest state. Furthermore, such a country, when not holding an elected seat on the Security Council, would be required to obligate itself to accept and carry out the decisions of the Council — decisions which might entail drastic action on its part under the provisions of Paragraphs 3, 4, 5 and 6 of Chapter VIII B. Such action might even be required by the Council without any consultation with the government of the country in question. In contrast, a great power is ensured of participating fully in all the deliberations of the Security Council and is likely also to be assured of exercising a right of individual veto on many of its decisions.

4) It is open to question whether a country such as Canada could undertake to accept such an obligation or could, if the obligation were to be initially accepted, ensure effective collaboration in the indefinite future. Canada certainly makes no claim to be regarded as a great power. The Canadian record in two great wars, however, has revealed both readiness to join in concerted action against aggression and the possession of substantial military and industrial capacity. There are a number of other states the potential contribution of which to the maintenance of future security is of the same order of magnitude. The support of these states is important to the maintenance of peace, and the active collaboration of some at least of them would probably be required for the execution of major decisions of the Security Council under Chapter VIII B of the proposals.

5) The question, therefore, arises whether it is possible, within the framework of the general scheme, to devise means of associating more effectively with the work of the Security Council states of the order of international importance of Canada. This might be achieved by making some changes in the powers conferred on the Council, and by ensuring that such states were chosen to fill elected seats on the Council more frequently (or possibly for longer periods) than states with less to contribute to the maintenance of security.

6) It is suggested that decisions of the Security Council under Chapter VIII B should be made binding, in the first instance, only on states which are members of the Council. States not represented on the Council should be required to take positive action only when the decision has been endorsed by a two-thirds majority of the Assembly (when it would become binding on all members), or when the country or countries concerned have by special invitation participated on the same footing as elected members in the Council's proceedings, or when they have individually agreed with the Council to join in a particular task of enforcement. The adoption of these suggestions would make it far easier for states other than

1 — The United Nations

the great powers to enter into agreements making available to the organization substantial military forces, facilities, and assistance, and would thus increase the effective power at the disposal of the Council. Their adoption would also help to secure the requisite public support in countries not permanently represented on the Council.

7) By the acceptance of these suggestions, a special responsibility would be placed upon all members of the Security Council which would not be imposed on other members of the organization. Thus the changes proposed in the authority of the Council must be considered in conjunction with the suggestion for increasing the effectiveness of the elected section, since they would increase the need for ensuring that the elected section of the Council was made up of states capable of contributing to the discharge of the Council's obligations. A serious effort should, therefore, be made to devise a system of election which would provide that due regard must be paid to the international significance of the countries chosen. If Chapter VI A of the proposals was to be submitted in its present form to a general conference of the United Nations, there would be small chance of securing its amplification in this respect, and it is, therefore, urged that the question should be faced now.

8) In devising methods of achieving this end, it will be generally agreed that it is important to discourage election to the Council being sought for reasons of prestige, and also to avoid the development of electoral understandings, such as those which controlled the election to the Council of the League of Nations. While it is difficult to put forward a satisfactory formula, it is believed that, given the initiative and support of the great powers, the problem can be solved.

EXTRACT FROM THE TEXT OF TELEGRAMS, JANUARY 12, 1945, FROM THE SSEA, OTTAWA, TO THE HIGH COMMISSIONER, LONDON, THE AMBASSADORS IN WASHINGTON, MOSCOW, AND PARIS AND THE CHARGÉ D'AFFAIRES, CHUNGKING.

1) The Canadian Government is deeply convinced of the necessity of establishing an effective general security organization in which it would wish to play its due part. The suggestions in the memorandum are put forward in the belief that their adoption would both strengthen the organization and facilitate completion at a United Nations conference of a Charter based on the Dumbarton Oaks proposals. The expansion in other respects of the Dumbarton Oaks proposals can, in our view, be considered satisfactorily at the proposed general conference.

2) Our reasons for feeling that these changes should be made now are indicated in the memorandum. You should point out, in addition, that, in recent large conferences, groups of states have exercised a disproportionate influence on decisions by adopting a common

line of action. For example, at the Chicago Aviation Conference, the Latin-American states (which would cast nearly half the votes at a conference of the United Nations) were able to secure the election of an agreed slate of countries to the interim aviation body. We feel that similar tactics might be employed at a general international conference to resist amendments designed to protect the position of countries of roughly the order of international importance of Canada.

3) The memorandum deliberately avoids proposing specific amendments, because there are alternative means of meeting most of the points. With regard to the suggestion in Paragraphs 7 and 8 that some standard of eligibility should be adopted to regulate election to the Council, we realize that there is no single satisfactory method of achieving this. In the proposals, the difficulties of defining what constitutes a great power have been avoided by naming the powers with permanent Council membership. The difficulties of defining a so-called "middle power" are still greater. It might be necessary to fall back on some special method of nomination to restrict the choice of the Assembly. Another possibility would be the introduction of weighted voting at Council elections, each state being entitled to cast a number of votes related to its financial or military contribution. Certain general disqualifications could in any event be included, such as rules debarring states which have not made satisfactory military agreements and states in default on their financial obligations to the organization.

4) You should specially emphasize the importance which we attach to Paragraph 6 of the memorandum. The suggestions made therein (or other changes with equivalent effect) seem to us essential if wide membership of the organizations is to be attained.

Doc. 1.2   **Report to Parliament on the San Francisco Conference**

STATEMENT, JUSTICE MINISTER L.S. ST. LAURENT, HOUSE OF COMMONS DEBATES, OCTOBER 16, 1945, PP. 1195-1202.

There was co-operation also not only within our delegation, but with other delegations as well, in respect of the work done at San Francisco. There was, first of all, the closest consultation among members of the British commonwealth. There were frequent commonwealth meetings at which frank discussions took place, but I think the San Francisco conference has proved for once and all the absurdity of the notion that all the countries of the British commonwealth will always speak and vote as a single block ...

The main body of the charter consists of those chapters which outline the international machinery which is to give effect to the purposes and principles of the united nations. This machinery has, I think, been strengthened and improved in many ways as a result of the work of the conference. For example, the scope of the powers of the general assembly have been considerably extended. The place of the assembly and the pattern of organization are a matter of particular concern to the middle and smaller states. The Canadian delegation considered that the powers of the assembly should be as wide as possible and that its scope as a forum of public opinion should not be limited. On the other hand, it was important that full responsibility for the settling of disputes should be put squarely on the shoulders of the security council. This involved one important limitation on the powers of the general assembly. The assembly should not, on its own initiative, be able to make recommendations on a matter relating to the maintenance of international peace and security while it is being dealt with actively and effectively by the security council. As a result of the liberalization of the Dumbarton Oaks proposals, the general assembly now possess the broadest powers of discussion and the right to initiate studies and make recommendations for the purpose of promoting international co-operation.

The Canadian delegation felt that if the assembly were to play its full part as an instrument for focusing public opinion, its sessions must be public. Although the conference left it to the general assembly to fix its own rules of procedure on this point, the Canadian suggestion was adopted that the rules of procedure should provide that "save in exceptional cases, the sessions of the general assembly shall be open to the public and press of the world." ...

The discussion over the powers and organization of the security council raised what proved to be the central question of the conference — how to maintain the unity of the great powers and at the same time create an organization which should be acceptable to the middle and smaller nations. This was the issue underlying the series of debates which took place over the veto powers of the permanent members of the security council. I do not think it would serve any useful purpose here to review that controversy, but without going into detail I shall say a few words about the position which the Canadian delegation took in this matter.

It will be recalled that under the Yalta voting formula, each permanent member of the security council has the power of veto over all questions of substance coming before the councils, with the exception that, with respect to the peaceful settlement of disputes, the party or parties to the dispute must abstain from voting. This veto power accorded to the United States, the United Kingdom, the Soviet Union, China, and France extends over all those activities of the organization which depend upon decisions taken in the security council. It thus affects the entire character of the organization, and I think it is proper to point out that it does constitute a serious exception to the principle of the equal sovereignty of states regardless of their size.

This veto power was attacked with great vigour and persistence by the representatives of many of the middle and smaller countries at San Francisco. While it was generally accepted that there must be unanimity of the great powers in applying peace enforcement action, there was opposition to many other aspects of the veto power, and particularly to its extension to covering the field of the peaceful settlement of disputes. It seemed to many delegations to be unwise that a permanent member, when not a party to a dispute, should be in position to veto the application of the peaceful settlement procedures of the charter in that dispute. It was over this particular aspect of the veto power that the debate really developed.

After a long drawn out discussion the sponsoring powers produced a joint statement in reply to a questionnaire which had been addressed to them as to the application of the Yalta voting formula. The joint statement, although it cleared up some obscurities, left many delegations unsatisfied as it envisaged the application of the rule of the unanimity of the great powers to the peaceful settlement provisions under the charter. The Canadian attitude throughout this controversy was based upon two principal considerations. It was felt in the first place that that veto power as applied to the processes of peaceful settlement was undesirable. We feared too that the incorporation of such a principle would seriously weaken the security council itself. The Canadian delegation recognized that this was in essence a political question as to what was possible of achievement in the way of compromise between the great powers themselves and between the great powers and the other united nations. It was apparent that the joint interpretation of the Yalta formula represented the greatest possible measure of agreement which could be obtained among the great powers themselves at this time on this subject.

The Canadian delegation, therefore, considered that while we could not accept the interpretation of the voting procedure as satisfactory, it was not too high a price to pay for a world organization which held so much promise in other respects. So that, on the final vote in the conference, the Canadian delegation did not oppose the adoption of the Yalta voting formula as defined in the answers made by the sponsoring powers to the questionnaire. We were influenced in this decision by the statement made by the representatives of the great powers that their special voting position would be used with a sense of responsibility and consideration for the interests of smaller states and, therefore, that the veto would be employed sparingly.

In connection with the organization of the security council, an amendment was introduced at the instance of the Canadian delegation, relating to the system of electing non-permanent members of the security council. Members of the house may recall from the Prime Minister's previous statements that the Canadian government felt that the provisions of the Dumbarton Oaks proposals were unsatisfactory in that they contained no qualification for eligibility of election to the council. The principle that power is to be combined with responsibility is recognized in the permanent membership of the great powers on the council. The application of that principle should, in our view, be carried a step further and among the six states elected to the council there should be several which can make a really substantial contribution to the purposes of the organization. The Canadian delegation, therefore, pressed for the adoption of some qualification for election to the council which should recognize this functional point of view. Our attitude was supported by a number of other delegations, but it was principally due to the co-operation of the United Kingdom delegation that an amendment was introduced by the sponsoring powers which now finds its place in article 23 of the charter.

The relevant paragraph of article 23, while it does not lay down detailed rules for the election of non-permanent members, directs that in the election of such members to the security council due regard should be "specially paid, in the first instance to the contribution of members of the united nations to the maintenance of international peace and security and to the other purposes of the organization, and also to equitable geographical distribution." It was explained by the representatives of the sponsoring powers who introduced this amendment that the phrase "in the first instance" applied to the first criterion for the election of non-permanent members; that is "to the contribution of members of the united nations to the maintenance of international peace and security and to the other purposes of the organization," whereas "equitable geographical distribution" was a secondary consideration.[4]

It is the responsibility of the security council to maintain peace, but this does not mean that the council will function only when an emergency has arisen. Any difficult situation which threatens to develop into a disturbance of the peace may be discussed in the council, and plans and recommendations may be made. It is, I think, satisfactory that the charter dealing with peaceful settlement of disputes has been enlarged and improved, because it is before violence has broken out that the organization can do its most useful work in preventing aggression.

The peace enforcement provisions of the Dumbarton Oaks proposals have already been discussed in this house, and they were not altered in many essential points at San Francisco. I should, however, mention one change which resulted from the initiative of the Canadian delegation. It was our view that there should be included in the charter some effective provision under which armed forces pledged in its military agreement by a state not a member of the security council be called out by the council only after that state had effectively taken part in the decision. Accordingly the Canadian delegation put forward

---

[4]In 1965 the Security Council was enlarged to 15 members, 5 permanent and 10 elected; it was agreed further that of the elected seats 5 should be filled by states from Africa and Asia; 2 by Latin American states; 2 by Western European and other states; 1 by Eastern European States. Functional representation in the Security Council has thus been superseded by geographical representation.

an amendment, the substance of which has now been incorporated in article 44 of the charter, which article reads as follows:
When the security council has decided to use force it shall,

before calling upon a member not represented on it to provide armed forces in fulfilment of the obligations assumed under article 43 —

That is the article referring to agreements to be entered into between states and the security council to provide stated quotas of armed forces:

— invite that member, if the member so desires, to participate in the decisions of the security council concerning the employment of contingents of that member's armed forces ...

The peace enforcement powers of the security council are concerned with the negative aspects of keeping the peace. But I think all hon. members will agree that peace is not merely the absence of war. It is a positive condition in which nations can co-operate for the common good. This side of the work of the new organization is of particular importance to Canada. In the field of economic and social progress, Canada has, I believe, an important contribution to make. The Canadian delegation therefore were particularly concerned with the provisions of the charter which deal with the economic and social council.

This body, which had been allotted a subsidiary place in the Dumbarton Oaks proposals, has now been made a principal organ of the united nations. Moreover its scope, which had originally been limited to economic and related social problems, has now been much widened ...

One of the most important conditions for the success of the united nations organization is that it should be served by a genuinely international civil service whose members are responsible, not to their governments or to the governments of which they are nationals, but to the organization itself. This was the viewpoint maintained by the Canadian delegation throughout the discussion in the conference committees at San Francisco which dealt with questions relating to the secretariat of the organization and the office of the secretary-general. I might say that this is the view which prevailed.

I have attempted to touch upon some of the most important developments arising out of the San Francisco conference. The charter which emerged from the conference should be capable of growth and adaptation to changing conditions. Its constitution should not be too rigid. It follows, in the view of the Canadian representatives, that the process of securing constitutional amendments should not be too difficult. We do not, look upon it as perfect in its present form. Moreover, no charter drawn up in 1945 can be complete or final. The states and peoples of the world are, in setting up the united nations organization, experimenting in many new fields of international co-operation. For some years they will be continuing to experiment in the unusual conditions of the transition period from the great war to peace. It is therefore particularly important that the charter should be capable of change by formal constitutional amendment when the world has returned to a more normal state. Unfortunately, the efforts of many of the states represented at San Francisco did not succeed in securing what I would consider a satisfactory, flexible amendment procedure under the charter. Under that charter each of the five great powers possesses the right to veto the coming into force of any amendment. It is to be hoped they will not employ this veto power in such a way as to give the charter a rigid character ...

In looking back on the achievement of the San Francisco conference, I think it may be said that foundations were laid for a system of international co-operation in the interests of order, security, and progress. We hope on these foundations to build world peace and security, but the work of the conference cannot be isolated from the urgent and difficult problems of the post-war period. Only if these problems are wisely solved will the united nations organization have an opportunity to develop its potentialities. In particular, the conditions under which the new organization will function will depend on the nature of the peace settlement in Europe and Asia. I use the term "peace settlement" in its widest sense to include not only the treatment to be accorded the defeated enemy but the relations between the victorious allies.

The Functional Principle

Doc. 1.3

STATEMENT BY ACTING SSEA ST. LAURENT, AT THE GENERAL ASSEMBLY, JANUARY 18, 1946 (DEA, *CONFERENCE SERIES*, 1946, NO. 1, *REPORT ON THE FIRST SESSION OF THE GENERAL ASSEMBLY OF THE UNITED NATIONS*). (EXTRACTS)

The Charter of the United Nations enshrines two principles which are explicitly stated in Article 23 in connection with the election of non-permanent members to the Security Council. It is stated that due regard should specially be paid in these elections in the first instance to the contribution of Members of the United Nations to the maintenance of international peace and security and to the other purpose of the Organization, and also to equitable geographical distribution.

Our Government has always attached great importance to the first of these criteria: to what has been called the functional principle. It is not really an abstract principle at all, but a commonsense prerequisite for the success of the Organization. We believe that special responsibilities within the framework of the Organization should be entrusted to those nations which have the means and the will to make the greatest contribution to the solution of the special problem in hand, and that is not because of any selfish interest in the application of the principle involved. It is because we wish to see the greatest possible measure of achievement, believing, as we do, that the interests of our country can best be served by that which best serves the whole community of nations.

Fortunately there is no contradiction between this principle and that of equitable geographical distribution. There are enough nations, widely dispersed throughout the world, which have contributions to make to the different sides of the work of the Organization. There is plenty of work and plenty of responsibility for all of us.

May I express the hope that membership in the various organs and agencies of the United Nations will always be regarded as no mere prize or token of prestige, but as an honourable and arduous responsibility to the world community. In the same line of thought the Canadian delegation desires to associate itself unreservedly with what was said yesterday by the Secretary of State for Foreign Affairs of the United Kingdom. We also feel that it is essential to the success of the United Nations that it should have in its Secretariat a strong international civil service.

At the beginning of this, a new venture in international cooperation with an Organization which will increasingly become the world community in action, we should recognize that the achievement of our aims may ere long require some amendment of the Charter. Changes may be needed if we are to give effect in a changing world to the purposes and principles of the United Nations. Let us, therefore, keep our minds open on this subject.

We cannot foresee the nature of all the tasks that may confront us in the future. They may well be on a scale which will necessitate some voluntary abatement of the narrower conceptions of national sovereignty. Sovereignty must not mean liberty to defeat the purposes of international peace and security, to which we are all so solemnly dedicated.

1.1. The United Nations Towards the End of the Century

The United Nations is an organization of sovereign states, having no powers of enforcement of its own. It mirrors the world, reflecting the world's ideals and its interests, its virtues and its faults. In an all too human world one should not expect the United Nations to be superhuman, nor for that matter even wise.

The United Nations of 1955 still reflected the conditions and values that had led to its creation a decade earlier. However, many fundamental changes in world affairs have since occurred: the rise of China, decolonization in Africa and Asia, the emergence of the Third World, the dissolution of the Soviet Union.

In political and security terms, the United Nations has found it increasingly difficult to live up to its principles, partly because the organization has remained basically unchanged since the 1940s and partly also because of the growing complexity of some of the problems it has had to cope with, particularly in Africa

(Rwanda, Somalia) and the Balkans. An over-heavy bureaucratic structure, coupled with financial difficulties resulting from delays in the payment dues by some of the larger contributors, has not of course made its task any easier. In addition, the realities of power on which it was built have changed a good deal. The great powers of 1945 or even 1965 are not necessarily, with the exception of the United States, the most significant ones today. Another factor is the growing confrontation between the industrialized states of the world and the developing nations.

Yet, for all its frustrations and weaknesses, the United Nations is still an essential safety-valve. There is no alternative forum today where the nations of the world can make their views known on such a wide range of issues and strive for understanding. To paraphrase Voltaire: "Si l'ONU n'existait pas il faudrait l'inventer."

2. The Economic and Social Council (ECOSOC)

This is the organ responsible under the General Assembly for the conduct of the UN's economic and social functions. Unlike the Security Council, it has no permanent members. Also, there is no veto. ECOSOC works mainly through commissions, committees, and other standing or temporary bodies that deal with such subjects as population questions, statistics, narcotics, trade in commodities. It comprises a number of regional economic commissions, e.g., Africa, Asia, Latin America and it also has ties with a number of other bodies such as the UN Children's Fund.

ECOSOC is empowered to enter into agreements with intergovernmental bodies — the specialized agencies — such as the World Bank, the Food and Agriculture Organization, the World Health Organization, etc., that came into being with the United Nations. It also has agreements with some that were founded well before the UN, for instance, the Universal Postal Union, the International Labour Office.

As indicated in the following document, Canada took an early lead in developing the UN's economic and social responsibilities and has continued to play an active role in ECOSOC and the specialized agencies.[5]

---

[5] Space limitations preclude coverage of Canada's role in the various ECOSOC programmes or in those of the specialized agencies other than the larger ones such as the World Bank, the International Monetary Fund, GATT, dealt with in Chapter 5 below.

Doc. 1.4   **Canadian Amendments on the Economic and Social Part of the United Nations Charter**

DEA, *CONFERENCE SERIES*, 1945, NO. 2, *REPORT ON THE UNITED NATIONS CONFERENCE ON INTERNATIONAL ORGANIZATION*, PP. 42-44.

Among the amendments submitted by the Canadian delegation to the Conference was a complete revision of the important chapter in the Dumbarton Oaks Proposals on international economic and social co-operation. One of the many purposes of the proposed revision was to increase the authority and position of the Economic and Social Council without, however, attempting to extend its functions beyond the scope of studies, reports and recommendations. Another purpose was to clarify the character of the relationship to be established between the Organization and the various specialized intergovernmental agencies and by do doing to strengthen the position of the Economic and Social Council as the body charged with coordinating the activities of the agencies. The Canadian proposals were also an effort to clarify the language of the Dumbarton Oaks draft and to arrange its provisions in a more logical order.

Increased authority for the Council

The following five proposals put forward by the Canadian delegation to strengthen the position of the Economic and Social Council were adopted.

1) One of the purposes of the Organization should be to attain higher standards of living and economic and social progress and development. (Article 55.)
2) The Members of the Organization should undertake to co-operate fully with the Organization and with each other in order to achieve the economic and social purposes of the Organization. (Article 56.)
3) The Economic and Social Council should be authorized not only to make recommendations on matters falling within its competence, but also to make or initiate studies and reports on such matters. The Council should be authorized to address its recommendations to the General Assembly, to the Members of the Organization, and to specialized intergovernmental agencies. Recommendations must be addressed to all Members or to those Members concerned with the particular subject matter of the recommendation. (Article 62.) It was not the intent of the committee that they should be addressed to any one single state.
4) In order to lessen the danger that the recommendations of the General Assembly on economic, social and related matters should remain ineffective, the Council should be authorized to receive reports from the Members of the Organization on the steps they had taken to give effect to the recommendations of the General Assembly and to communicate its observations on these reports to the

1 — The United Nations

General Assembly (Article 64.)

5) The Council should be given explicit authority to perform services at the request of Members of the Organization and of related intergovernmental agencies, subject to the approval of the General Assembly (Article 66.)

Composition of the Council

Under the original Dumbarton Oaks Proposals, the functions of the Economic and Social Council were limited to economic and related social problems. In the light of these Proposals, the Canadian delegation suggested that the General Assembly, in electing the eighteen members of the Economic and Social Council, should "have due regard to the necessity of arranging for the adequate representation of states of major economic importance." Early in the San Francisco Conference, however, the scope of the activities of the Council was extended beyond the strictly economic and social fields to include cultural and educational co-operation, public health, and the promotion of respect for, and observance of, human rights and fundamental freedoms. This weakened the argument for the Canadian proposal, and after it had been discussed in committee the Canadian delegation withdrew it. The discussion, however, demonstrated a general belief that if the Council was to discharge its duties effectively, it would in fact be necessary to have the states of major economic importance continuously represented on it. This belief was reflected in the provision that retiring members of the Council should be eligible for immediate re-election. (Article 61.)

Relationship between the Organization and the Specialized Intergovernment Agencies

The following five proposals put forward by the Canadian delegation for the purpose of clarifying the relationship between the United Nations and the specialized intergovernmental agencies were adopted:

1) Only those specialized agencies which had "wide international responsibilities" should necessarily be brought into relationship with the United Nations. It was not thought possible to define precisely the meaning of the phrase "wide international responsibilities," but it was clear that international agencies established by bilateral agreement need not be brought into official relationship with the Organization. (Article 57.)

2) One of the duties of the Organization should be to initiate negotiations among the stages concerned for the creation of any specialized agency required for the accomplishment of the economic and social purposes of the Organization. The purpose of this Canadian proposal was to develop a practice under which the initiative for the creation of any new specialized agency will come from the Economic and Social Council. This Council will be receiving reports

from the existing agencies and, from its examination of these reports, it will be in a strong position to determine whether any new work which comes up can best be carried on by itself, by an existing agency, or by the creation of a new agency. The proposal is designed to prevent unnecessary multiplication of specialized agencies. (Article 59.)

3) The Economic and Social Council should be empowered to co-ordinate the activities of the various intergovernmental agencies brought into relationship with the Organization through consultation with them and also through recommendations to them and to the General Assembly and the Members of the Organization. (Article 63.)

4) The Economic and Social Council should be empowered to obtain reports from the specialized agencies on the steps they have taken to give effect to its own recommendations and to those of the General Assembly and to communicate its observations on these reports to the General Assembly. (Article 64.)

5) In addition to the representation on the Economic and Social Council of the specialized agencies brought into relationship with the Organization which was provided for in the Dumbarton Oaks Proposals, the Economic and Social Council should make arrangements for its own representatives to participate in the deliberations of these agencies. (Article 70.)

3. Regional Conflicts

3.1. The Middle East

The birth of Israel on May 14-15, 1948, was a difficult one. It had been preceded by armed conflict between the Jewish Agency and Jewish settlers on the one hand and Britain on the other, under whose Mandate from the League of Nations Palestine had been administered since the end of the first World War.

Israel's declaration of independence was followed almost immediately by war as neighbouring Arab countries moved in with their armies. They were thrown back overwhelmingly, their defeat being accompanied by an exodus of hundreds of thousands of Palestinians. As refugees with no homeland, they became dependent on the generosity of UN members since neither Israel nor the Arab countries where they had sought refuge would accept responsibility for their maintenance.

Recognition of Israel as an independent state came about almost immediately. The first country to recognize was the United States; others followed. Armistices among the belligerents were agreed upon in April 1949. Also that month, Israel was admitted to

1 — The United Nations

the United Nations supported by the United States and the Soviet Union, and Canada.

Conflict broke out again between Israel and its neighbours in 1956 that led to the creation of the United Nations Emergency Force (UNEF), a largely Canadian-inspired initiative for which PM Pearson received the Nobel Prize. A short, but particularly devastating war — the so-called Six-Day War — occurred in June 1967. Arab losses were striking: Egypt lost the Sinai Peninsula, Syria the Golan Heights. The West Bank was occupied. A further war occurred in 1973.

An uneasy stalemate followed the 1973 war, until a considerable breakthrough occurred in September 1978 between Israel and Egypt: the Camp David Accords. These were achieved under the direct auspices of President Jimmy Carter of the United States, whereby Israel agreed to return the Sinai Peninsula to Egypt.

Another breakthrough occurred with the signing of an agreement in Washington, D.C., on September 13, 1993, by the Government of Israel and the Palestine Liberation Organization (PLO), whereby each formally recognized the other and Palestinian self-rule in the Gaza Strip and West Bank town of Jericho was sanctioned.

Canada was present at the ceremony, in recognition of our continuing Canadian commitment to the pursuit of peace in the Middle East since 1948; and also because of active participation in the peace process that helped to lead to the agreement, as chair of the Working Group on Refugees in the Middle East.

Nevertheless problems remain, particularly between Israel and Syria resulting from Israeli occupation of the Golan Heights, and in Lebanon resulting from Syrian sponsorship of the Iranian-inspired *hezbollah*. One of the consequences of this situation was Israel's decision to invade Lebanon. Its troops reached Beirut after considerable fighting. When it withdrew from the area around Beirut, its armed forces remained in occupation of a buffer zone in southern Lebanon as a protective measure.[6] An Arab economic boycott of Israel was launched as a counter-measure to the Israeli invasion of Lebanon, with consequent difficulties for Canadian companies, made more complex by the Progressive-Conservative Party's announcement during the election campaign of 1979 that, if elected, it would be prepared to move the Canadian Embassy from Tel Aviv to Jerusalem. It changed its position once in power

---

[6]This zone was evacuated in early 2000.

and no successor government has since revived the idea.

Thus violence and uneasiness have continued to characterize the area and, indeed, particularly in the 1980s, became more intense especially in the Gaza Strip, as manifested by the *intifada*. The situation was made more critical as a result of Iraqi missile attacks against Israel during the Gulf War and the PLO's decision to side with Iraq at the time.

A change of government in Israel in 1992, whereby a Labour coalition under Yitzhak Rabin replaced the Likud government of Yitzhak Shamir set the stage the beginnings of a settlement between Israel and the PLO. After a period of stalemate when the Likud PM Benjamin Netanyahu was in charge, negotiations resumed with the advent to power of the current Labour PM Ehud Barak.

The protagonists proclaim their need, their desire for peace and stability, their yearning for an end to current tensions and uneasiness. Yet peace remains elusive. As a Chinese sage might have put it: they are in the same bed, but are having different dreams.

The Middle East generally remains a problem area despite the recent progress between Israel and the PLO. There is still considerable opposition from extremists, both within Israel and among Palestinians, to the arrangements for a settlement being suggested by the two governments. Conditions in the whole region are uneasy; instability is widespread. The Islamic fundamentalist movement has been gathering strength in the Muslim world; rivalries among the Arab states continue. The future of an eventual Palestinian state; the problem of Iraq; the fate of the Kurds; the evolution of the situation in Afghanistan; relations between Israel, Jordan, Syria, on the one hand, and their respective relations with the PLO, on the other, complicated by extremists on all sides, will bear close watching by the international community for some time to come. Indeed, outside observers may perhaps be forgiven if they are sometimes left with the suspicion that some countries in the area find these unsettled conditions useful for their own foreign policy purposes. In this context a paraphrase of St. Augustine's famous remark about chastity comes to mind. Peace, oh Lord, but not quite yet.[7]

---

[7]Regrettably, it is not possible to document all regional conflicts since mid-century. Some early ones, such as Kashmir — going back to 1947 when India and Pakistan became independent — are still with us although Canadian involvement in this dispute has been relatively modest over the years. Others in Asia and Africa are still extant, while those in Central America (mainly during the 1980s) have been resolved. Suffice it to say here that Canada has taken part in peacekeeping operations connected with just about all of them.

1 — The United Nations

Canada votes for partition

Doc. 1.5

STATEMENT BY J.L. ILSLEY IN THE GENERAL ASSEMBLY, NOVEMBER 26, 1947 (DEA, *CANADA AND THE UNITED NATIONS 1947*, PP. 196–200).

We are voting for the Partition Plan, because it is in our judgment the best of four unattractive and difficult alternatives.

These alternatives are: To do nothing, to set up a Unitary Arab State in accordance with the plan of Sub-Committee II, to set up a Federal State in accordance with the minority recommendations of the United Nations Special Commission on Palestine, and partition.

Let us take these one by one. First, the objections to doing nothing are obvious. For the United Nations to do nothing in this situation would be an abdication, a shirking of its responsibilities in a situation which is pregnant with peril to peace. It would invite not only confusion but widespread violence, involving not only the people of Palestine, but people elsewhere. It would, not improbably, result in blood-shed and a kind of irregular and murderous warfare which might spread far. We dismissed this first alternative as not worthy of the United Nations, highly dangerous in its probable consequences, indeed as virtually unthinkable.

The second alternative is to set up a Unitary Arab State along the lines recommended by Sub-Committee II of the Ad Hoc Committee, or at least to let such a Unitary Arab State emerge at the time of the termination of the mandate. This course would have been the normal and natural one to pursue had it not been for the Balfour Declaration, the League of Nations Mandate, the encouragement given to the immigration of Jews into Palestine over a quarter of a century, the establishment of a well rooted community of nearly 700,000 Jews in Palestine who have invested there, as we are told, $600,000,000, and the devotion on the part of Jews all over the world to the idea of a Jewish national home in a country which once at least was a Jewish land. But these factors cannot be ignored, they make the Palestine problem *sui generis* and unique. They constitute a fatal flaw in the otherwise unanswerable Arab case. It is because of these factors that the project for a Unitary State has been repeatedly dismissed by a multiplicity of commissions on the Palestine problem, of which the United Nations Special Commission on Palestine was the latest, and decisively rejected by the Ad Hoc Committee. There is not a chance that this alternative can find acceptance by any but a small minority of the nations of the world. As a solution it is beyond the realm of the practical.

Similarly, the third alternative, a Federal State, while more defensible than the one I have just discussed, has made in this Organization very little appeal. Espoused by Yugoslavia, which has argued the case with care, patience and conviction, the minority report of the United Nations Special Commission on Palestine has made no headway, received little support from other nations and was not presented for consideration by a section of the Ad Hoc Committee large enough

31

even to justify the setting up of a Sub-Committee to explore its possibilities. Embodying as it does the essential features of a federal scheme, the Yugoslav Plan, as I shall call it, has certain elements of attractiveness to Canadians. As I indicated in my opening speech on the Palestine question before the Ad Hoc Committee, the Canadian Delegation wished that a Federal Plan could be worked out along these or similar lines. They are the lines along which our own national development has proceeded, with reasonable satisfaction to both racial elements in our population. But Palestine is not Canada, and the Yugoslav Plan has received no support whatever either from the Jewish Agency or the Arab Higher Committee. A plan which appeals to neither Jews nor Arabs and which opens up vast vistas of difficulty in adjustment and administration is not a plan upon which this Assembly would be justified in concentrating further attention.

This leaves the fourth plan, the Plan of Partition, which we have decided to support as the least objectionable of the four. We support this plan with heavy hearts and many misgivings. No responsible delegation could do otherwise, after listening to the threats of reprisals and all the talk of fire and sword which we have heard from both sides to this controversy, in the Ad Hoc Committee, and to-day. But it would be folly to assume that there would be any less likelihood of disorder if any of the other alternatives were adopted. Indeed, in our judgment, this likelihood in the case of every one of them would not be less but greater. The fact that after twenty-five years of international action in relation to Palestine, culminating with months of consideration by the General Assembly of the United Nations, we should find ourselves in this atmosphere of acrimonious recrimination is a melancholy one. The air is heavy with gloomy forebodings, represented by one side or the other as savage threats or responsible predictions.

But something must be done with this problem and we are satisfied that, full of difficulties as the Partition solution is, any other solution would be worse. There is, of course, the hope that once definitive action is taken there will be a change of heart on the part of the responsible leaders of the two opposing camps. This is the more likely from the fact that of all the solutions proposed, Partition alone has received the support of the two greatest world powers. We must take it as certain that well meant and fervent exhortations to conciliation, the kind of exhortation that we have heard during the last two months are getting nowhere. These appeals and entreaties may make more progress after a decision by this organization on the Partition solution is arrived at. This is the ray of hope in the situation.

It is not for Canada to advise other nations on the course they should take in this vote, and we doubt whether such advice would be either welcome or effective. But we find it difficult to understand the large numbers of abstentions which we assume will take place when we come to the vote. In the case of some nations reasons have been given. In other cases the explanation probably is that nations like our own, far removed from Palestine, which had no part in the events leading up to this denouement, which made no promise to the Arabs and no promises to the Jews, least of all to both, which played no politics with the situation, and which have nothing but the kindliest feelings toward both Arabs and Jews, find it difficult to see why there should be thrown upon their shoulders a profoundly disturbing responsibility for grave and far-reaching decisions.

The Canadian Delegation appreciates these sentiments on the part of many nations. Indeed to some extent we share them. But we do not feel that they would justify us in abstaining from this vote. We have, as the Assembly knows, taken our full share of responsibility in this matter throughout the entire session. We have worked unremittingly in an attempt to obtain a solution which would be practical and workable, and we feel that our obligations, not only to this organization, but to our own people, are such that we could not justify an abstention and should vote for the resolution. This we propose to do.

3.2. Status of the Palestinians

[Canadian policy]   Doc. 1.6

STATEMENT BY SSEA ALLAN J. MACEACHEN, TO THE UNITED NATIONS GENERAL AS-
SEMBLY, NEW YORK, NOVEMBER 20, 1974. (EXTRACTS)

We consider it essential to any lasting and comprehensive settlement that there be respect for the sovereignty, the territorial integrity and the political independence of Israel and of every other state in the Middle East. We remain opposed to any attempt to challenge the right of Israel or the right of any other state in the region to live in peace within secure and recognized boundaries free from threat and acts of force.

The important issue we are now examining, concerning the status of the Palestinians and their role in efforts to achieve a negotiated peace, has figured prominently in this tragic history. From the outset, Canada has recognized that the Palestinians represent a major interested element in the Middle East situation. Security Council Resolution 242, firmly subscribed to by Canada since its adoption in 1967, called for a just settlement of the Palestine refugee problem. Canada has given and continues to give substantial financial support to the United Nations Relief and Works Agency. Recent developments, including this debate, testify to the growing acknowledgement that cognizance must be taken of the need for the Palestinian people to be represented and heard in negotiations involving their destiny. Canada is fully in accord with the view that any enduring peaceful settlement of the Arab-Israeli dispute must take account of the legitimate concerns of the Palestinians.

We have noted with satisfaction that there have been, within a relatively short space of time, territorial adjustments on two fronts in the form of the existing disengagement agreements. We may also be witnessing a fundamental change of appreciation of existing realities on the part of both sides to the dispute. On the one hand, Arab governments appear more disposed to recognize Israel's right to exist. Israel, for its part, has reaffirmed its intention to pursue the search for peace with its Arab neighbours, and to this end has indicated greater recognition of the fact that Palestinian concerns will have to be taken into account in some way if real peace is to be achieved.

This said, ... it will be clear that the question is how legitimate Palestinian concerns are to be brought to bear in efforts to reach a just and durable settlement. Canada has firmly resisted giving advice on what form Palestinian representation should take in future negotiations. The claim of the Palestine Liberation Organization to represent the Palestinians is thus one that, in our view, is not for Canada to decide. It is a question that remains to be resolved by the parties directly involved in the course of their continuing efforts to work towards an agreed peace, and Israel, in our view, is an essential party in deciding the question.

The manner in which legitimate Palestinian concerns are to be represented in the course of the search for a peace settlement is a matter for agreement by the parties involved. The same principle clearly applies to the declared aspiration of the Palestine Liberation Organization to establish an independent national authority in the region. If the emergence of any Palestinian entity were to be envisaged at some stage, it would be essential that this should be the result of agreement among the parties directly involved, which, of course, include Israel. In this respect, the establishment, evolution and existence of any such entity should in no way prejudice the continued existence of the state of Israel.

Doc. 1.7 **Israeli invasion of Lebanon**

STATEMENT BY THE CANADIAN DELEGATE, MICHAEL KERGIN, TO THE SEVENTH EMERGENCY SPECIAL SESSION OF THE UN GENERAL ASSEMBLY, NEW YORK, JUNE 26, 1982. (EXTRACTS)

Canada views the present hostilities in Lebanon with profound sadness. We should not minimize the complexities of the situation; we recognize that Lebanon is an integral part of a region which itself is in the grip of a long-standing conflict. We are not confident that Lebanon can emerge completely from its present anguish unless wider issues in the Arab/Israeli dispute and the problems of the Palestinians are addressed and resolved.

Canada has spoken out on the recent events in Lebanon. On June 9, the Canadian Prime Minister, in a public message to the Prime Minister of Israel, said the following:

With Israeli air-raids in Lebanon and rocket attacks on Northern Israel already in progress, my letter to you on June 5 counselled restraint to avoid the dangers that further military action would bring. In that same letter I said that we deplored and condemned as heinous crimes acts of terrorism against targets in Israel and elsewhere; but I also said that it was important to avoid actions which fuel rather than dampen the flames of violence and hatred in the Middle East.

I am dismayed by the subsequent escalation of the conflict represented by the massive movement of Israeli forces into Lebanon. Great human suffering is being caused; and the rapid northward expansion of Israeli operations is posing an increasing risk of a wider war. We, in Canada, understand your natural concern for Israeli lives in the Galilee, and believe that acts of violence against Israel and its citizens, as well as against all others in the area, must cease. But we cannot accept the proposition that the present military activities are justified or that they will provide the long-term security which you seek for the Israel people. I appeal to you to respond favourably to the unanimous Security Council resolution by agreeing to a cease-fire and withdrawing immediately and unconditionally from Lebanese territory so that the difficult but necessary task of working for reconciliation in the area can again begin.

In the present critical and rapidly evolving situation in the Middle East, my delegation calls on all parties to exercise maximum restraint in their actions to prevent further deterioration or widening of this conflict.

Official contacts with the PLO — Canadian policy   Doc. 1.8

STATEMENT BY SSEA JOE CLARK, OTTAWA, MARCH 30, 1989. (EXTRACTS)

We have come to certain conclusions in this matter, in accordance with the objectives of Canadian governments over the years. The fundamental principles have long been:

Support for the security, well-being, and rights of Israel as a legitimate, independent state in the Middle East;

Support for a just, lasting, and comprehensive peace settlement based on Israeli withdrawal from occupied territories as enunciated in Security Council Resolution 242 of 1967;

Recognition that for there to be a just peace, the legitimate rights of the Palestinians must be realized, including their right to play a full part in determining their future;

Insistence that for the PLO to play a role in Middle East peace negotiations, it must accept Israel's right to exist within secure and recognized boundaries.

Over the past year and a half, developments in the Middle East have altered Israel's assumptions about the nature of the peace process. The *intifada* in the Occupied Territories has demonstrated that Palestinian nationalism is a reality that must be taken into account. King Hussein's recent withdrawal from Jordan's former responsibilities for the West Bank acknowledged this fact and served notice that Jordan would no longer speak for the Palestinians.

In recent months, constructive and helpful statements by the Palestinian National Council and by Chairman Arafat have addressed some of the basic Canadian concerns about the PLO. I welcomed these developments at the time.

After careful consideration, we have concluded that the changes in PLO positions largely addressed the reservations that Canada has expressed. We have therefore decided to lift as of today our existing restrictions on contacts with representatives of the PLO. This action will allow us to continue to encourage constructive actions by the PLO. I want to take this occasion to reiterate that Canada does not recognize the Palestinian state proclaimed last November. However, the proclamation of a state does cast a different light on the question of Palestinian self-determination. Canada has long accepted the right and need for Palestinians to play a full part in negotiations to determine their future. We have been concerned that the phrase "self-determination" was being used as a code-word for an independent state and that Canadian endorsement of the principle would be interpreted as Canadian advocacy of an independent state. That interpretation is no longer possible, because an independent Palestinian state has been declared, and not recognized by Canada. That allows Canada to endorse the principle that the Palestinians have the right to self-determination in accordance with the International Human Rights Covenants. That right must be exercised through peace negotiations in which the Palestinians play a full part. These negotiations may lead to an independent state, or to a federation with an existing state, or to some other result.

The Canadian Ambassador to the United Nations will meet with a representative of the PLO mission to the United Nations. Other contacts will take place elsewhere as appropriate, as a part of the ongoing pursuit of Canadian foreign policy objectives.

Doc. 1.9   **The Gulf War: The effect of sanctions on Iraq**

STATEMENT BY SSEA, JOE CLARK, BEFORE THE HOUSE OF COMMONS STANDING COMMITTEE ON EXTERNAL AFFAIRS AND INTERNATIONAL TRADE (SCEAIT), OTTAWA, DECEMBER 10, 1990. (EXTRACTS)

Sanctions are one part of a concerted world policy, working through the United Nations, to cause Iraq to withdraw peacefully from Kuwait. Other measures include the presence in the Gulf of military forces from 29 countries. They also include Security Council Resolution 678, adopted a week ago today, which combines the authorization of force with what Mr. Gorbachev calls "a pause of goodwill" to allow time and incentive for a peaceful solution.

In addition, several countries, including Canada, are pursuing initiatives to resolve this crisis peacefully and to prepare for the challenges of the post-crisis period.

Different elements of this concerted policy support one another. For example, one important reason sanctions work against Iraq is because the naval blockade allows enforcement. As of December 3, Canadian ships alone had intercepted 1,085 vessels in the Gulf and boarded nine to help to maintain the naval embargo. Sanctions are of course notoriously hard to have respected and, so far, the Iraq embargo has been one of the most successful the world has known. But all our evidence is that it has been more successful on the outside than on the inside. Iraq has diverted the effects of sanctions away from its military capacity and its political leaders. There is no evidence that sanctions are persuading Iraq to comply with the Security Council resolutions and withdraw from Kuwait.

The question is now whether the combination of sanctions, plus the authorization of force, can lead together to a peaceful solution. We believe that this combination offers the best prospect for a peaceful withdrawal from Kuwait.

To save time I will circulate. but not read, information available to Canada, and which we believe to be reliable, respecting the effect of sanctions on particular sectors of the Iraqi economy and society.

What has been the result of the collective decision to impose economic sanctions on Iraq?

Sanctions are, unquestionably, having an impact on economic conditions and living standards within Iraq. But there is no evidence that they have caused the Government of Iraq to have a change of heart regarding Kuwait. There is no reason to believe that sanctions alone are going to bring the Iraqi economy to its knees or be sufficient in and of themselves to force Saddam Hussein to withdraw from Kuwait. All the available evidence suggests that it would be a considerable time before sanctions had a truly decisive effect on Iraq's economy and military machine.

Iraq's trade links have been severed. Its funds abroad have been frozen. Iraqi and stolen Kuwaiti vessels and aircraft have been denied port and airport facilities. The only authorized exceptions to the sanctions are for the import of medical supplies and, in humanitarian circumstances, for foodstuffs delivered through appropriate humanitarian agencies, as well as the transport of released hostages.

All Iraqi government assets are frozen. Financial transfers are prohibited. Trade with Iraq and occupied Kuwait is banned and all permits to export controlled goods to Iraq and Kuwait remain suspended. Canadian exporters have suffered considerable losses, particularly grain exporters, since Iraq was Canada's fourth largest market for grain.

An air embargo is in place for Iraqi aircraft. Exceptions have been made for humanitarian reasons on several occasions, for example, re-fuelling of Iraqi aircraft carrying freed hostages.

Effective enforcement measures are being taken by Canadian enforcement agencies, including the RCMP and Revenue Canada Customs and Excise. Close international cooperation is being maintained. To date, no violations have been reported in Canada and no prosecutions are pending.

A committee of the Security Council, co-chaired by Finland and Canada, monitors implementation of the sanctions.

The question that has been repeatedly asked is: "Why don't we simply wait until sanctions force Saddam Hussein to withdraw?"

That question involves two assumptions: first, that sanctions will ultimately work; and second, that time is neutral, and that nothing else will happen while we wait.

Time is not neutral, and not cost-free.

Every day the sacking of Kuwait continues. Time is not neutral for the people of Iraq. Saddam Hussein is not noted for his compassion towards his own people. The economic impact of uncertainty, and high oil prices, is costly everywhere, including Eastern and Central Europe where it threatens economic reform, but its impact is most cruel on the developing world. Finally, this is the most volatile and heavily-armed region in the world. An accident could trigger a tragedy.

Sanctions, in sum, are necessary but not sufficient to meet our declared objective: the withdrawal of Iraq from Kuwait and the restoration of its sovereignty and legitimate government.

Now is the time for resolve. Collective action stopped Iraqi aggression at the Saudi border. The Government intends to hold to the full range of policies which we have helped to fashion in the Security Council. A comprehensive approach based on all the UN resolutions, including Resolution 678, represents the best hope of a peaceful outcome to this crisis.

4. Peacekeeping

In some fields the United Nations has had more success than in others. Success has usually occurred where narrow local interests have been concerned rather than those of the Great Powers. Peacekeeping is one of these fields.

Established to maintain world peace and to promote international security, the United Nations has been rather more successful at peacekeeping than peacemaking. Armed conflicts have been distressingly numerous over the past five decades and the United Nations has managed to contain only those local conflicts involving lesser powers mainly. Nevertheless, the United Nations' role should not be belittled for all that, since some local conflicts, in the Eastern Mediterranean and the Middle East, for instance, could easily have escalated into major wars.

Logically, peacekeeping should lead to peacemaking, but this has rarely been the case. Separated by United Nations peacekeepers, local antagonists have usually found it easier to put off peacemaking, and conflicts have tended to perpetuate themselves: witness for instance, Kashmir, Cyprus, the Middle East.

Canada has participated in every peacekeeping operation since 1948, under the United Nations' umbrella, and in non-UN settings, such as Indochina. Canada's peacekeeping activities between 1955 and 1965 carried our influence in world affairs to a peak. Nevertheless, this has been a thankless, costly, and frustrating task. Satisfaction at the thought of being the world's most experienced peacekeeper is perhaps somewhat numbed now.

Creation of UNEF   Doc. 1.10

STATEMENT MADE ON NOVEMBER 2 AT AN EMERGENCY SPECIAL SESSION OF THE UNITED NATIONS GENERAL ASSEMBLY BY THE CHAIRMAN OF THE CANADIAN DELE-GATION, L.B. PEARSON.[8]

I rise not to take part in this debate, because the debate is over. The vote has been taken. But I do wish to explain the abstention of my delegation on that vote.

It is never easy to explain an abstention, and in this case it is particularly difficult because we are in favour of some parts of this resolution, and also because this resolution deals with such a complicated question.

Because we are in favour of some parts of the resolution, we could not vote against it, especially as, in our opinion, it is a moderate proposal couched in reasonable and objective terms, without unfair or unbalanced condemnation; and also, by referring to violations by both sides to the armistice agreements, it puts, I think, recent action by the United Kingdom and France — and rightly — against the background of those repeated violations and provocations.

We support the effort being made to bring the fighting to an end. We support it, among other reasons, because we regret that force was used in the circumstances that face us at this time. As my delegation sees it, however, this resolution which the General Assembly has thus adopted in its present form — and there was very little chance to alter that form — is inadequate to achieve the purpose which we have in

---

[8]This statement was made in explanation of Canada's vote on a resolution, adopted by the Assembly, calling on all parties involved in hostilities to agree to an immediate cease-fire and to halt the movement of military forces and arms into the area.

mind at this Assembly. These purposes are defined in that resolution of the United Nations under which we are meeting — resolution 377(V), uniting for peace — and peace is far more than ceasing to fire, although it certainly must include that essential factor. This is the first time that action has been taken under the "Uniting for Peace" resolution, and I confess to a feeling of sadness, indeed even distress, at not being able to support the position taken by two countries whose ties with my country are and will remain close and intimate; two countries which have contributed so much to man's progress and freedom under law; and two countries which are Canada's mother countries.

I regret the use of military force in the circumstances which we have been discussing, but I regret also that there was not more time, before a vote had to be taken, for consideration of the best way to bring about that kind of cease-fire which would wave enduring and beneficial results. I think that we were entitled to that time, for this is not only a tragic moment for the countries and peoples immediately affected, but it is an equally difficult time for the United Nations itself. I know, of course, that the situation is of special and, indeed, poignant urgency, a human urgency, and that action could not be postponed by dragging out a discussion, as has been done so often in this Assembly. I do feel, however, that had that time, which has always, to my knowledge, in the past been permitted for adequate examination of even the most critical and urgent resolution, been available on this occasion, the result might have been a better resolution. Such a short delay would not, I think, have done harm, but, in the long run, would have helped those in the area who need help most at this time.

Why do I say this? In the first place, our resolution, though it has been adopted, is only a recommendation, and its moral effects would have been greater if it could have received a more unanimous vote in this Assembly — which might have been possible if there had been somewhat more delay.

Secondly, this recommendation which we have adopted cannot be effective without the compliance of those to whom it is addressed and who have to carry it out. I had ventured to hope that, by a short delay and in informal talks, we might have made some headway, or at least have tried to make some headway, in securing a favourable response, before the vote was taken, from those governments and delegations which will be responsible for carrying it out.

I consider that there is one great omission from this resolution, which has already been pointed out by previous speakers — more particularly by the representative of New Zealand, who has preceded me. This resolution does provide for a cease-fire, and I admit that that is of first importance and urgency. But, alongside a cease-fire and a withdrawal of troops, it does not provide for any steps to be taken by the United Nations for a peace settlement, without which a cease-fire will be only of temporary value at best. Surely, we should have used this opportunity to link a cease-fire to the absolute necessity of a political settlement in Palestine and for Suez, and perhaps we might also have been able to recommend a procedure by which this absolutely essential process might begin.

Today we are facing a feeling of almost despairing crisis for the United Nations and for peace. Surely that feeling might have been harnessed to action or at least to a formal resolve to act at long last and to do something effective about the underlying causes of this crisis which has brought us to the very edge of a tragedy even greater than that which has already taken place. We should then, I think have recognized the necessity for political settlement in this resolution and done something about it. And I do not think that, if we had done that, it would have postponed action very long on the other clauses of the resolution. Without such a settlement, which we might have pushed forward under the incentive of fear, our resolution, as I see it, may not make for an enduring and real peace. We need action, then, not only to end the fighting but to make the peace.

I believe that there is another omission from this resolution, to which attention has also already been directed. The armed forces of Israel and of Egypt are to withdraw, or if you like, to return to the armistice lines, where presumably, if this is done, they will once again face each other in fear and hatred. What then? What then, six months from now? Are we to go through all this again? Are we to return to the *status quo*? Such a return would not be to a position of security or even a tolerable position, but would be a return to terror, bloodshed, strife, incidents, charges and counter-charges, and ultimately another explosion which the United Nations armistice commission would be powerless to prevent and possibly even to investigate

I therefore would have liked to see a provision in this resolution — and this has been mentioned by previous speakers — authorising the Secretary-General to begin to make arrangements with member governments for a United Nations force large enough to keep these borders at peace while a political settlement is being worked out. I regret exceedingly that time has not been given to follow up this idea, which was mentioned also by the representative of the United Kingdom in his first speech, and I hope that even now, when action on the resolution has been completed, it may not be too late to give consideration to this matter. My own government would be glad to recommend Canadian participation in such a United Nations force, a truly international peace and police force.

We have a duty here. We also — or, should I say, we had — an opportunity. Our resolution may deal with one aspect of our duty — an urgent, a terribly urgent, aspect. But, as I see it, it does nothing to seize that opportunity which, if it had been seized, might have brought some real peace and a decent existence, or hope for such, to the people of that part of the world. There was no time on this occasion for us to seize this opportunity in this resolution. My delegation therefore felt because of the inadequacy of the resolution in this respect, that we had no alternative in the circumstances but to abstain in the voting.

I hope that our inability to deal with those essential matters at this time will very soon be removed and that we can come to grips with the basic core of this problem.[9]

Doc. 1.11 **Functions of UNEF**

STATEMENT BY SSEA L.B. PEARSON, AT THE UNITED NATIONS GENERAL ASSEMBLY, NOVEMBER 23, 1956. (EXTRACTS)

What are the functions of this United Nations Emergency Force? Those functions and the task — and it is a very difficult task indeed which confronts the Force — have been laid down by resolutions of the General Assembly and they are found also in the Secretary-General's second and final report, which has been approved by the Assembly. The basic resolution for these purposes is that which we adopted on November 4-5 (A/RES/394) which states that the function of this Force is "to secure and supervise the cessation of hostilities in accordance with all" — and I emphasize the word "all" — "the terms of the resolution of the General Assembly of November 2" (A/RES/390). In that latter resolution, as representatives will remember, provision is made for a cease-fire, for a prompt withdrawal of forces, and also — and this is not the time to forget this provision — "that all member states refrain from introducing military goods in the area of hostilities and in general refrain from any acts which would delay or prevent the implementation of the present resolution". And in Para 4 of that resolution we have this provision, namely, that upon a cease-fire, steps are to be taken to re-open the Suez Canal and restore secure freedom of navigation.

5. Atomic Energy

Doc. 1.12 **[The Canadian position]**

STATEMENT BY THE CANADIAN REPRESENTATIVE ON THE ATOMIC ENERGY COMMISSION, GENERAL A.G.L. MCNAUGHTON, AT THE 157TH PLENARY MEETING OF THE GENERAL ASSEMBLY, NOVEMBER 4, 1948. (DEA, S AND S 48/57). EXTRACTS.

In the course of the long debate on atomic energy which has taken place in this Assembly, the issues have been made quite clear. I wish now to re-state in the form of a series of brief propositions the position which the Canadian Government holds in regard to atomic energy, and because of which the Canadian delegation will give its full support to this resolution on adoption of report of Atomic Energy Commission.

In the first place, the Canadian Government believes that it is pos-

---

[9]On November 7, PM St. Laurent announced in Ottawa that the Canadian Government had agreed to offer a Canadian contingent of battalion strength to the international United Nations force for the Middle East. UN action was taken under the 1950 "Uniting for Peace" resolution that gave the General Assembly certain functions and duties in case of a Security Council deadlock.

sible to establish a practicable system for the control of atomic energy which will protect the nations of the world from the dangers of atomic war and which will give freedom to use atomic energy for peaceful purposes. This belief is demonstrated by the time and attention which the Canadian delegation has devoted to the work of the Atomic Energy Commission and it is demonstrated also by the anxiety of the Canadian Government that the work of the Commission should continue and that the difficulties standing in the way of agreement between nations should be removed. Canada possesses, as is well known, extensive resources of the raw materials from which atomic energy may be derived, and Canadian scientists and engineers have acquired special skills and knowledge in the field. These conditions made possible for Canada a considerable national development of atomic energy. We believe nevertheless that full benefits can come only through the organization of this development on an international rather than on a national basis.

My second proposition is the following: atomic warfare cannot be prohibited nor the international development of atomic energy ensured except on a basis which provides proper security for all nations. The principles through which these two objectives may be realized have been set forth in the majority reports of the Atomic Energy Commission. These principles have been arrived at by a long and arduous process of study and discussion in which representatives of seventeen nations have been engaged. Fourteen nations have agreed on the majority reports and only three have dissented. The Canadian Government, which was represented in the discussions in which these principles were evolved, adheres to them firmly, and confidently recommends their acceptance to other members of the United Nations as the "necessary basis" from which progress can be made towards the solution of the complicated problems of the prevention of atomic warfare and the freeing of the world's resources of atomic energy for peaceful purposes.

In the third place, the Canadian Government believes that the stage has been reached in the work of the Atomic Energy Commission where, before further significant progress can be made, clear direction must be given to the Commission by the Assembly. It was from this General Assembly in its first session that it derived its original mandate. The resolution which is now before the General Assembly gives confirmation to the conclusions which have already been accepted by a majority of the members of the Commission. On the strength of this resolution it will be possible for the members of the Commission to return to their task and to proceed to such further studies as are practicable in the confidence that they will have the support which comes from the acceptance, by a majority of the nations of the world, of the basic conclusions which they have already reached ...

My final proposition is this. The problem of atomic energy is so complicated and the issues are so fateful that the world must not be led into the belief that any simple solution is adequate. This is our serious and honest objection to the Soviet proposal, which we consider to represent an oversimplification of the grave problems at issue. The processes for the preparation of the materials which release atomic energy are long and complicated and costly. The process by which these materials are assembled in an atomic bomb is quick and relatively simple; it is the same material that serves for peaceful uses in the arts and sciences or for destruction, and as a consequence every step of the process from the time the ores are first separated from the ground must be controlled. The world will be free from the danger of atomic warfare only if the whole process from beginning to end is placed within the framework of an adequate system of control and development. It is because of the absence of this effective control that we are convinced that the proposal which the Soviet delegation has made is quite inadequate to give the assurance of security which the nations of the world require.

Our position, which has been stated in detail by the Canadian delegation in the Political Committee of this Assembly and elsewhere, is held in the serious belief that it gives not only the best but the only hope of relieving humanity from fear of atomic warfare, and of giving freedom for the development of atomic energy for peaceful purposes. We shall vote for this resolution not with any sense that we have reached an end in the process of negotiation on the subject of the control of atomic energy, but for the purpose of marking a first stage which we hope will constitute the necessary basis for further progress.[10]

6. Human Rights

Since the adoption of the Universal Declaration of Human Rights (largely drafted by Dr. John Humphrey, a Canadian), Canada has worked consistently to advance respect for human rights throughout the world. All Canadian governments since have applied the Declaration's principles to their policies and programmes. Since 1984, criteria such as good governance and the promotion of the rights of women and children have also been considered as human-rights facets of Canadian aid and development programmes abroad.[11]

Canada does of course face some complexities under this heading. Owing to our constitutional structure, the federal gov-

---

[10]On July 21, 1949, C.D. Howe, Minister of Reconstruction and Supply (later Trade and Commerce) announced in a press release on behalf of the Government that Canada had chosen to explore only the *peaceful* uses of atomic energy.

[11]See Chapter 6 under North-South Issues and Chapter 9 regarding aid and the rights of women in *La Francophonie.*

ernment does not have full powers to enforce international human rights commitments if they affect provincial jurisdiction. Happily, however, when problems have arisen, it has been possible to reach understandings with the provinces concordant with the principles of the Declaration.[12]

The Universal Declaration of Human Rights   Doc. 1.13

STATEMENT ON THE UNIVERSAL DECLARATION OF HUMAN RIGHTS BY THE CHAIR-MAN OF THE CANADIAN DELEGATION, L.B. PEARSON, IN THE GENERAL ASSEMBLY, DECEMBER 10, 1948 (DEA, *CANADA AND THE UNITED NATIONS 1948*, PP. 247-249). EXTRACTS.

Before a vote is taken on the Draft Declaration on Human Rights in the form which it has now taken, I wish to make clear the attitude which the Canadian government adopts, generally, towards it.

In the first place, we regard this document as one inspired by the highest ideals; as one which contains a statement of a number of noble principles and aspirations of very great significance which the peoples of the world will endeavour to fulfil, though they will make these efforts variously, each nation in its own way and according to its own traditions and political methods. In an imperfect world, it is clearly impossible to secure a perfect application of all these principles immediately. The Charter itself commits the members of the United Nations to principles which are not yet applied uniformly throughout the world. The difficulties in the way of a full and universal application of the principles of the Declaration of Human Rights will be even more complex. We must, however, move towards that great goal.

The Draft Declaration, because it is a statement of general principles, is unfortunately, though no doubt unavoidably, often worded in vague and imprecise language. We do not believe in Canada that legislation should be placed on our statute books unless that legislation can indicate in precise terms the obligations which are demanded of our citizens, and unless those obligations can be interpreted clearly and definitely in the courts. Obviously many of the clauses of this Draft Declaration lack the precision required in the definition of positive obligations and the establishment of enforceable rights. For example, Article 22 which gives the right to public employment to people irrespective of political creed might, unless it is taken in conjunction with Article 31, be interpreted as implying an obligation to employ persons in public service even if it was their stated and open desire and intention to destroy all the free institutions which this Declaration of

---

[12]The International Covenant of Economic, Social, and Cultural Rights, as well as the International Covenant on Civil and Political Rights and its Optional Protocol, are examples of shared human rights jurisdictions. These international legal instruments reaffirm principles contained in the Declaration and establish new procedures to promote compliance with its provisions. After consultations with the provinces, Canada acceded to these Covenants in May 1976.

Rights is intended to preserve and extend. Without those free institutions, which can only flourish in a liberal democratic society, there can be no human rights.

It is our view that some of the difficulties and ambiguities in this Declaration might have been removed had this document been reviewed by a body of international jurists, such as the International Law Commission, before final action was taken by the General Assembly; and we regret that the general desire to expedite this important matter has made such a reference impossible. If the Soviet Delegation had had this in mind in their amendment, we would have been able to support it. But in their speeches, Mr. Vishinsky and Mr. Manuilsky showed that, for them, a reconsideration of this Declaration would merely mean a further attempt to include in it ideas which, in our view, are far removed from human rights: as far removed as a town meeting from a slave labour parade. We do not accept — and never will accept — the doctrine that the rights of man include only those which are sanctioned and sanctified by communist doctrine; that all other rights are to be outlawed as "fascist," a word which once had a clear, if dread meaning in the dictionary of despotism, but which now has become blurred by its abuse to cover any person or any idea of which communism does not approve.

So far as the position of Canada in regard to the maintenance and extension of human rights is concerned, we shall, in the future, as we have in the past, protect the freedom of the individual in our country where freedom is not only a matter of resolutions but also of day-to-day practice from one end of the country to the other.

The freedoms to which I refer have developed in Canada within the framework of a system of law derived both from statutes, and from the judgments of the courts. We have depended for the protection of the individual upon the development of this system rather than upon general declarations. Because this method is in accord with our tradition, we shall continue to depend on it and to expand it as the need may arise. While we now subscribe to a general statement of principles such as that contained in this Declaration, in doing so we should not wish to suggest that we intend to depart from the procedures by which we have built up our own code under our own federal constitution for the protection of human rights.

In this regard, there is a special circumstance which applies to Canada. When some of the articles of the Draft Convention were adopted in committee, the Canadian Delegation abstained, explaining that the subject under consideration was in some of its important aspects within the field of provincial jurisdiction in Canada. I wish to make it clear that, in regard to any rights which are defined in this document, the federal government of Canada does not intend to invade other rights which are also important to the people of Canada, and by this I mean the rights of the provinces under our federal constitution. We believe that the rights set forth in this Declaration are already well protected in Canada. We shall continue to develop and maintain these rights and freedoms, but we shall do so within the framework of our constitution which assigns jurisdiction in regard to a number of important questions to the legislatures of our provinces.

Because of these various reservations on details in the Draft Declaration, the Canadian Delegation abstained when the Declaration as a whole was put to the vote in committee. The Canadian Delegation, however, approves and supports the general principles contained in the Declaration and would not wish to do anything which might appear to discourage the effort, which it embodies, to define the rights of men and women. Canadians believe in these rights and practice them in their communities. In order that there may be no misinterpretation of our position on this subject therefore, the Canadian Delegation, having made its position clear in the committee, will, in accordance with the understanding I have expressed, now vote in favour of the resolution, in the hope that it will mark a milestone in humanity's upward march.

2

Security and Peace: NATO

AN IRON CURTAIN, in Winston Churchill's striking phrase, descended upon Soviet-occupied Eastern Europe shortly after the Second World War and Western countries began to consider urgently how best to protect their political institutions and values. Indeed their very independence. The Communist takeover of Czechoslovakia in early 1948 provided the catalyst.

The Brussels Pact between Britain, France, and the Benelux countries in 1948 led directly to the North Atlantic Treaty Organization (NATO), in the creation of which Canada played a prominent role, particularly as regards Article 2. That Article urged the parties to eliminate conflict in their international economic policies and to encourage economic collaboration between any or all of them. It became known as the Canadian Article. It was not an easy sell; the idea was considered to be somewhat on the fringes of the Treaty's main purpose. Nevertheless it was accepted unanimously.

The text of the Treaty was agreed to in the House of Commons at the end of March 1949 with only two dissenting votes. It was signed by Canada and the other member countries in Washington on April 4, 1949.

Its main purpose is conveyed in Article 5 which states succinctly that an "armed attack against one or more of them in Europe or North America shall be considered an attack against them all". A former Minister of National Defence put it a good deal more pungently: "Rape is more difficult when there are 15 in the bed".

From the perspective of the year 2000, it is clear that NATO served its original purpose extremely well. Under the umbrella that it provided, the European Union came into being. Europe and North America have prospered. Communism has receded around the world and the Soviet Union has disappeared. This was not all NATO's doing of course, but without NATO it would have been much more difficult to achieve.

1. NATO

[From the Brussels Pact to the North Atlantic Treaty]

Doc. 2.1

STATEMENT BY PM ST. LAURENT, HOUSE OF COMMONS, MARCH 28, 1949. (EXTRACTS)

The fear of subversive communism allied to Soviet might is in fact the mainspring of the development leading up to this North Atlantic security pact. Hon. members know what those developments were. On January 22, 1948, Mr. Bevin (Britain's Foreign Secretary) declared that Soviet hostility to the European recovery program and Soviet obstructionism over the German settlement had convinced the United Kingdom government that the time had come to go ahead with plans for closer political and economic unity of willing western European states. Hastened in their negotiations by the communist seizure of power in Czechoslovakia in February and Soviet pressure for a treaty with Finland, the United Kingdom, France, and the Benelux countries signed the treaty of Brussels on March 17, 1948.

Under this treaty, these signatory governments undertook that if any one of them should be the object of armed attack in Europe, the others would, in accordance with provisions in article 51 of the charter of the United Nations, afford the party so attacked all military and other aid and assistance in their power.

On July 6, the representatives of Belgium, Canada, France, Luxembourg, The Netherlands, the United Kingdom, and the United States met in Washington for the first phase of the series of non-committal and exploratory talks on security problems of common interest. These talks have now culminated in the draft text tabled in the house on March 18.

This treaty is to be far more than an old-fashioned military alliance. It is based on the common belief of the north Atlantic nations in the values and virtues of our Christian civilization. It is based on our common determination to strengthen our free institutions and to promote conditions of stability and well-being. It is based on the belief that we have in our collective manpower, in our collective natural resources, in our collective industrial potential and industrial know-how, that which would make us a very formidable enemy for any possible aggressor to attack.

North Atlantic Treaty

Doc. 2.2

TEXT OF TREATY SIGNED AT WASHINGTON ON APRIL 4, 1949 (CTS 1949/7).

Preamble

The Parties to this Treaty reaffirm their faith in the purposes and principles of the Charter of the United Nations and their desire to live in peace with all peoples and all governments.

They are determined to safeguard the freedom, common heritage, and civilization of their peoples, founded on the principles of democracy, individual liberty, and the rule of law.

They seek to promote stability and well-being in the North Atlantic area.

They are resolved to unite their efforts for collective defence and for the preservation of peace and security.

They therefore agree to this North Atlantic Treaty:

Article 1

The Parties undertake, as set forth in the Charter of the United Nations, to settle any international disputes in which they may be involved by peaceful means in such a manner that international peace and security, and justice, are not endangered, and to refrain in their international relations from the threat or use of force in any manner inconsistent with the purposes of the United Nations.

Article 2

The Parties will contribute toward the further development of peaceful and friendly international relations by strengthening their free institutions, by bringing about a better understanding of the principles upon which these institutions are founded, and by promoting conditions of stability and well-being. They will seek to eliminate conflict in their international economic policies and will encourage economic collaboration between any or all of them.

Article 3

In order more effectively to achieve the objectives of this Treaty, the Parties, separately and jointly, by means of continuous and effective self-help and mutual aid, will maintain and develop their individual and collective capacity to resist armed attack.

Article 4

The Parties will consult together whenever, in the opinion of any of them, the territorial integrity, political independence, or security of any of the Parties is threatened.

Article 5

The Parties agree that an armed attack against one or more of them in Europe or North America shall be considered an attack against them all; and consequently they agree that, if such an armed attack occurs, each of them, in exercise of the right of individual or collective self-defence recognized by Article 51 of the Charter of the United Nations, will assist the Party or Parties so attacked by taking forthwith, individually and in concert with the other Parties, such action as it deems necessary, including the use of armed force, to restore and maintain the security of the North Atlantic area.

Any such armed attack and all measures taken as a result thereof shall immediately be reported to the Security Council. Such measures shall be terminated when the Security Council has taken the measures necessary to restore and maintain international peace and security.

Article 6

For the purpose of Article 5 an armed attack on one or more of the Parties is deemed to include an armed attack on the territory of any of the Parties in Europe or North America, on the Algerian departments of France, on the occupation forces of any Party in Europe, on the islands under the jurisdiction of any Party in the North Atlantic area north of the Tropic of Cancer or on the vessels or aircraft in this area of any of the Parties.

Article 7

This Treaty does not affect, and shall not be interpreted as affecting, in any way the rights and obligations under the Charter of the Parties which are members of the United Nations, or the primary responsibility of the Security Council for the maintenance of international peace and security.

Article 8

Each Party declares that none of the international engagements now in force between it and any other of the Parties or any third state is in conflict with the provisions of this Treaty, and undertakes not to enter into any international engagement in conflict with this Treaty.

Article 9

The Parties hereby establish a council, on which each of them shall be represented, to consider matters concerning the implementation of this Treaty. The council shall be so organized as to be able to meet promptly at any time. The council shall set up such subsidiary bodies as may be necessary; in particular it shall establish immediately a defence committee which shall recommend measures for the implementation of Articles 3 and 5.

Article 10

The Parties may, by unanimous agreement, invite any other European state in a position to further the principles of this Treaty and to contribute to the security of the North Atlantic area to accede to this Treaty. Any state so invited may become a Party to the Treaty by depositing its instrument of accession with the Government of the United States of America. The Government of the United States of America will inform each of the Parties of the deposit of each such instrument of accession.

Article 11

This Treaty shall be ratified and its provisions carried out by the Parties in accordance with their respective constitutional processes. The instruments of ratification shall be deposited as soon as possible with the Government of the United States of America, which will notify all the other signatories of each deposit. The Treaty shall enter into force between the states which have ratified it as soon as the ratification of the majority of the signatories, including the ratifications of Belgium, Canada, France, Luxembourg, the Netherlands, the United Kingdom, and the United States, have been deposited and shall come into effect with respect to other states on the date of the deposit of their ratifications.

Article 12

After the Treaty has been in force for ten years, or at any time thereafter, the Parties shall, if any of them so requests, consult together for the purpose of reviewing the Treaty, having regard for the factors then affecting peace and security in the North Atlantic area, including the development of universal as well as regional arrangements under the Charter of the United Nations for the maintenance of international peace and security.

Article 13

After the Treaty has been in force for twenty years, any Party may cease to be a party one year after its notice of denunciation has been given to the Government of the United States of America, which will inform the Governments of the other Parties of the deposit of each notice of denunciation.

Article 14

This Treaty, of which the English and French texts are equally authentic, shall be deposited in the archives of the Government of the United States of America. Duly certified copies thereof will be transmitted by that Government to the Governments of the other signatories.

In witness whereof, the undersigned plenipotentiaries have signed this Treaty. Done at Washington, the 4th day of April, 1949.[13]

2. Defence

For purposes of chronological sequence and convenience of reference, major Canadian foreign and defence policy issues in the 1950s, such as Korea and Indochina, are dealt with here rather than in Chapter 4 on the Far East.

---

[13]Greece and Turkey acceded in 1951 and West Germany in 1954.

2 — Security and Peace: NATO

2.1. The Korean War

At the end of the Second World War, Korea was occupied jointly by the United States and the Soviet Union, with the 38th Parallel as the agreed dividing line between them: Soviet forces occupying the area north of the parallel and the Americans the south.

On June 25, 1950, large-scale North Korean forces suddenly invaded the South. The United States requested an emergency meeting of the Security Council the same day. The Soviet Union was boycotting the UN at the time because Communist China had not been admitted to membership. It was thus unable to veto Security Council action which decided to counter the invasion.[14]

Several Western countries provided forces under the UN umbrella in order to resist the aggression. Canadian participation was extensive. Some 27,000 from the armed forces took part during the three years that the war lasted.

Initially, North Korea was able to move into the South with considerable success. However, as UN forces gathered strength, they eventually pushed the North Koreans well back beyond the 38th Parallel. At this point, China intervened and a period of violent hostilities resulted.

Eventually a stalemate ensued and hostilities ended in July 1953 when an Armistice was negotiated. It was based on the final territorial position of the opponents. As a result, the Korean Peninsula again found itself divided largely along the 38th Parallel, but this time with adjustments that reflected the territorial gains achieved by UN forces somewhat to the north of the demarcation line. A demilitarized zone separating the armies was also established, with North Korean forces patrolling one side of the line and U.S. and South Korean forces the other. The territorial situation between North and South Korea has remained unchanged since 1953.

Relations between North and South Korea over the decades have been characterized by uneasiness, to say the least, and at times by outright hostility. Meanwhile, South Korea has become a vigorous, prosperous, free-enterprise economy, while North Korea has languished under a diehard Communist régime. Recently, tentative steps towards a *rapprochement* between the two have been taken.

A political conference was held in Geneva during the summer

---

[14]The General Assembly's "Uniting for Peace" Resolution of October 1950 strengthened its powers to recommend action in dealing with aggression. Canada voted in favour. See also House of Commons Debates, June 28, 1950.

of 1954 to deal with Korea and also Indochina. As a participant in the Korean War, Canada was invited to attend conference sessions on Korea, but not on Indochina.

2.2. Indochina

No progress was made on Korea at Geneva, but considerable progress occurred as regards Indochina, where war had broken out in 1945 as Japan left the peninsula and France sought to resume control over its former colonies there. France had suffered serious reverses in 1953 at the hands of the Vietminh, as the forces of North Vietnam were called. The French were seeking a settlement that would allow them to end the hostilities and withdraw from the peninsula. With that purpose in mind, it had already recognized the independence of the three Indochinese states: Cambodia, Laos, and Vietnam. The French readily agreed to a cease-fire throughout the peninsula, subject to the establishment of peace supervisory arrangements in each one.

It was this provision of the Geneva Conference which produced an outcome for Canada that was totally unexpected and one that would involve us in Indochinese affairs for nearly 20 years: an invitation to take part in the International Commissions being set up to supervise the ceasefire in Cambodia, Laos, and Vietnam, as well as the political arrangements eventually to emerge there. The Cabinet was of two minds about accepting the invitation, but eventually decided to do so in the hope of helping to foster peace in the area.

Regrettably, the Indochina Commissions were severely hamstrung in their mandate from the very beginning. They had no powers of enforcement; they were *supervisory* bodies. They could note infractions; even make recommendations to the Co-Chairmen of the Geneva Conference but, as Commission decisions had to be unanimous, very little action of substance resulted over the years. (An exception in the early years was the large-scale population transfers in Vietnam). Minority reports could be submitted to the Co-Chairmen of the Geneva Conference, but they were merely filed away.

For convenience the Geneva Conference invitation from Co-chairmen Eden and Molotov and Canada's acceptance thereof are given below. Also documented is Canada's participation in a second Indochina Commission set up in South Vietnam under the Paris Agreement of 1973.[15]

---

[15]For an account of how DEA handled the invitation, see *Special Trust and*

2 — Security and Peace: NATO

Indochina — Membership on the International Commissions

Doc. 2.3

INVITATION FROM THE GENEVA CONFERENCE, JULY 21, 1954 (DEA, *EXTERNAL AF-FAIRS*, AUGUST, 1954, PP. 257-60).

We have the honour to address you as co-chairman of the Geneva Conference on Indochina which concluded its work on July 20th 1954. The Conference took note of agreements ending hostilities in Vietnam, Laos, and Cambodia, and organizing international control, and the supervision of the execution of the provisions of these agreements. In particular it was agreed that an international commission should be set up in each of the three countries for control and supervision of the application of the provisions of the agreement on the cessation of hostilities in Indochina. It was further proposed that these commissions should be composed of an equal number of representatives of Canada, India and Poland, presided over by the representative of India.

On behalf of the Conference, we accordingly have the honour to invite the Canadian-Indian Government in consultation with the Governments of Canada-India-Poland to designate representatives to form the International Supervisory Commissions for Vietnam, Laos and Cambodia as envisaged in the agreements on the cessation of hostilities, and on supervision in those three countries.

It is hoped that the three International Supervisory Commissions can be established on the spot as soon as possible from the date on which the cease-fire comes into force.

The text of the final declaration adopted by the Conference, and of all other agreements and declarations concerning the cessation of hostilities, and the organization of supervision in the three countries of Indochina will be transmitted to you as soon as possible.

We have the honour to request an early reply which we shall at once transmit to the members of the Conference.

Signed: Anthony Eden
      V. Molotov

REPLY TO INVITATION, JULY 27, 1954 (*IBID.*).

I have the honour to acknowledge your message of July which you and Mr. Molotov sent in your capacity as co-chairmen of the Geneva Conference on Indochina, containing the invitation to the Canadian Government to designate, in consultation with the Governments of India and Poland, representatives to form the International Supervisory Commissions for Vietnam, Laos and Cambodia as envisaged in the agreements on the cessation of hostilities, and on supervision in those three countries.

Conscious of the grave responsibilities which the task will impose, but in the hope that it can contribute to the establishment of

---

Confidence, Carleton University Press, 1996, Chapter 3, by the current editor (DEA Indochina Desk Officer at the time). See also DEA Press Release of July 27, 1954.

peace and security in Indochina, the Canadian Government accepts this invitation. The Canadian Government has been in touch with the Government of India concerning preliminary arrangements and intends to send representatives to New Delhi in the immediate future to consult with Indian and Polish officials on the setting up of the International Supervisory Commissions provided for in the agreements drawn up by the Geneva Conference.

The Canadian Government would be grateful if you would transmit the text of this reply to the members of the Geneva Conference on Indochina, whose continuing interest and support will be required if the Commissions are effectively to carry out their functions and if the agreements on the cessation of hostilities are to be successfully implemented.

Doc. 2.4   **Canada withdraws from Indochina: 1973**

STATEMENT IN THE HOUSE OF COMMONS BY SSEA MITCHELL SHARP, MAY 31, 1973.

Speaking in the House on March 27, I said that the Government had decided to extend Canadian participation in the ICCS[16] until May 31 and that before that date the Government would decide whether to remain or to withdraw.

At that time I said that we would withdraw our contingent by June 30 unless there had been a substantial improvement in the situation or some signs of an imminent political agreement between the two South Vietnamese parties.

The decision is a serious one and the Government so regards it. Canada has a reputation, I believe, for responsibility in international affairs. We have served in more peace-keeping and peace-observer roles than any other country and we remain ready to serve wherever we can be effective. We have also, in the course of this varied and extensive experience, including 19 years in Indochina, learned something about the conditions that are necessary to success in peace-keeping and peace-observer activities.

The House will recall the efforts that the Government made to establish conditions which would help to improve the prospects for the successful functioning of the International Commission of Control and Supervision provided for in the Paris agreement on Vietnam. I shall not repeat them now. The record of Canada's approach to the question of participation in the ICCS up to the end of March 1973 is to be found in a White Paper that I shall table at the conclusion of this statement.

Stated briefly, what we sought to ensure was that the new International Commission would be an impartial, fact-finding body, supported by the parties to the peace agreement, with sufficient freedom of access to enable it to ascertain the facts about any alleged breach

---

[16]**Editor's note:** ICCS stands for International Commission for Control and Supervision.

of the agreement and reporting quickly not only to the parties to the agreement but also to the international community as a whole. While we did not achieve all our purposes, I think it is fair to say that we helped to effect some improvements, at least in form.

What we could not ensure, and what the ICCS could not ensure, was peace in Vietnam. That depends on the parties to the peace agreement and not on the ICCS. Nor can Canada alone ensure that the ICCS fulfils its function of peace observing and reporting as provided for in the peace agreement. That too depends on the parties to the agreement and on the other member delegations of the Commission.

Notwithstanding our hesitations and doubts, we accepted membership for a trial period of 60 days. At the end of that first 60 days our hesitations and doubts had been reinforced but we were urged by many countries to show patience. So we agreed to another two-month period, which is now coming to an end.

By and large, there has been no significant change in the situation that would alter the view we formed at the end of the first 60 days, notwithstanding the strenuous efforts of the Canadian contingent to support the functioning of the International Commission.

Let me repeat that our attitude results from Canadian experience in the old ICSC[17] and the Canadian conception of the functioning of a peace-observer body. We are not criticizing the peace agreement. We welcomed that agreement, we regard it as a good agreement that provides as sound and honourable a basis for peace as was negotiable. If the parties will set themselves to applying it, as we hope they may yet do, it can bring lasting peace to Vietnam. We hope that the efforts of Dr. Kissinger and Mr. Le Due Tho to achieve a stricter observance of the agreement will be crowned with success.

We have come to the conclusion, however, that the Canadian conception of the functioning of the International Commission has not been accepted and that it would be in the interest of all concerned if we were to withdraw. Nor do we believe that Canadian withdrawal would have any significant effect upon the prospects for peace in Vietnam. That depends upon the parties to the peace agreement and not upon the ICCS. It is only if the parties are co-operating in a strict observance of the agreement and are willing to use the ICCS as a means of reinforcing the agreement that the Commission can perform its function with any hope of success.

Throughout our tenure on the ICCS, we have sought above all else to be objective. We have represented none of the contending parties. We have been as insistent in calling for and participating in investigations of alleged violations by the United States and the Republic of Vietnam as we have with regard to alleged violations by the Democratic

---

[17]**Editor's note:** ICSC was the International Commission for Supervision and Control, more commonly known as the International Supervisory Commission, or simply 'The Commission'.

Republic of Vietnam and the other South Vietnamese Party. If the RVN or U.S.A. has been at fault, we have said so. If the other parties were to blame for cease-fire violations, we also have said so. I assure the House that we have no need to listen mutely now or later to any charges that we have acted partially; we can be proud of our objectivity in the Commission and of our attempts to see this impartiality as an integral part of Commission activities.

I also said, in my statement to the House on March 27, that Canada would be prepared to return to Vietnam to participate in the international supervision of an election clearly held under the terms of the Paris agreement and therefore with the concurrence and participation of the two South Vietnamese parties. It went without saying that our participation would not be necessary if a replacement were found for Canada on the ICCS. I am not convinced that there is much chance that an election will take place as provided for in the agreement but, if it should (and we should want to examine it carefully to make sure it was this kind of election), and if no replacement had been found for Canada, we should consider sympathetically a request to return temporarily to the ICCS for this purpose, in the light of the circumstances then prevailing and our assessment of the chances for effective supervision.

The peace agreement itself anticipates the replacement of the named members of the ICCS — Canada, Hungary, Indonesia and Poland — or any of them. I have also said that we should be prepared to remain on the Commission until June 30 so that a replacement could be found. We have since learned that the discussions which took place recently between Dr. Kissinger and Mr. Le Due Tho will be resumed in June. We want to give those discussions every chance of success and we would certainly wish to do nothing that would complicate them in introducing what might seem to be too short a deadline for agreeing on a replacement for Canada on the Commission.

In recognition of that possible difficulty, we are prepared, if the parties to the agreement so wish, to stay for a period beyond June 30 but not later than July 31. Canada's decision to withdraw is firm and definite, but the additional flexibility should give the parties adequate time to find a replacement for the Canadian delegation. Should a successor be named and be ready to take its place before July 31, we should, of course, be prepared to hand over our responsibilities at any mutually convenient earlier time. We shall, of course, continue to function as we have been doing during the remaining period of our stay on the Commission.

3. Defence Reviews

The first defence review to seriously question some aspects of earlier ones, all based on unvarying support for NATO, was made by PM Trudeau shortly after being elected leader of the Liberal Party in 1968.

His approach to defence has had lasting results; in the defence facets of their budgets, both the Mulroney and Chrétien governments have maintained much the same defence downsizing and cost-cutting policies as those he announced in 1968.[18]

[The Trudeau Defence Review: 1968-1969]   Doc. 2.5

STATEMENT TO THE PRESS BY PM TRUDEAU, APRIL 3, 1969. (EXTRACTS)

We shall take a fresh look at the fundamentals of Canadian foreign policy. ... Also we shall take a hard look, in consultation with our allies, at our military role in NATO and determine whether our present military commitment is still appropriate to the present situation in Europe. ...

In summary, Canada will continue to be a member of NATO and to cooperate with the United States in NORAD and in other ways in defence arrangements. We shall maintain appropriate defence forces which will be designed to undertake the following roles:

(a) the surveillance of our own territory and coastlines, i.e., the protection of our sovereignty;

(b) the defence of North America in cooperation with the United States;

(c) the fulfilment of such NATO commitments as may be agreed upon; and

(d) the performance of such international peacekeeping roles as we may, from time to time, assume.

The kinds of forces and armaments most suitable for these roles is now being assessed in greater detail for discussion with our allies.

White Paper on Defence 1971   Doc. 2.6

DEFENCE IN THE 1970S: BOOKLET ISSUED BY DEFENCE MINISTER D. MACDONALD, OTTAWA, AUGUST 1971. (EXTRACTS)

The results of the assessment forecast in the defence review were announced in the White Paper issued in August 1971.

The reduction in the strength of Canadian Forces assigned to Allied Command Europe ... has now been effected. The land element

---

[18]The foreign policy reviews carried out by various governments since 1945 all reflect the principles outlined in SSEA St. Laurent's 1947 Gray Lecture. Space does not allow presentation of these reviews (covered in some detail in A.E.B. I, pp. 162-166 and 179-193; A.E.B. II, pp. 329-357; and A.E.B. III, pp. 156-160, respectively). It has therefore been decided to concentrate on the defence reviews, since trends and conclusions in defence reviews stem from and reflect foreign policy objectives, with the added attraction that they are usually in point form and generally shorter.

has been co-located with the air element in Southern Germany, with headquarters at Lahr, giving our forces in Europe a distinctive Canadian identity. Their combined strength is approximately 5,000 instead of the 10,000 formerly stationed in Europe. The Government has no plans for further reductions.

Doc. 2.7   **Defence and the 1989 Budget[19]**

BUDGET IN BRIEF: BOOKLET ISSUED BY THE DEPARTMENT OF FINANCE, OTTAWA, APRIL 27, 1989. ALSO AVAILABLE FROM DND OTTAWA. (EXTRACTS)

National Defence

Previously planned spending increases will be restrained to save a total of $2,7 billion over the next five years. The basic parameters of the White Paper remain government defence policy, but that policy will need to be implemented more slowly. As a result of these decisions, the government will close or reduce in size 14 military bases and stations across the country. The government is not proceeding with acquisition of nuclear-propelled submarines.

Doc. 2.8   **1994 Defence White Paper**

SUMMARY AND ANALYSIS

The White Paper on Defence issued in 1994 by the Chrétien government shortly after its accession to office, maintained much the same basic international and domestic approaches to defence policy as its predecessors, that is:

(a) internationally: NATO, NORAD, peace-keeping, humanitarian operations, to which were added global land-mine action, fisheries patrols, among others; and

(b) domestically: search and defence operations, coastal, northern, and aerospace surveillance, counter-terrorism and national emergency response.[20]

Editor's notes: It is interesting to note here that, in its companion foreign policy White Paper *Canada in the World*, the Chrétien government places the "promotion of prosperity and employment" prominently in first place among its "three key foreign policy objectives", followed by the "protection of our security within a sta-

---

[19]The provisions carried in the booklet supersede those in the 1987 White Paper on Defence *Challenge and Commitment*. See A.E.B. III, pp. 41-43, for details.

[20]The *1994 White Paper on Defence* is available from DND, Ottawa, through its website, given at the end of this book, in "Suggested Reading", or from the Canada Communications Group — Publishing, Public Works and Government Services Canada, Ottawa.

ble global framework", and the "projection of Canadian values and culture."[21]

In keeping with its emphasis on the economy, particularly its policy of eliminating annual deficits, the Chrétien government intensified budget cuts at DND with consequent reductions in service and civilian strength, as well as equipment. By 1999, for instance, the Regular Forces had been reduced from 88,000 in 1989 to about 60,000 in 1999, and the Primary Reserves to approximately 12,000. Between 1989 and 2,000, civilian personnel in DND dropped from roughly 36,000 to 20,000.

At the same time, the government also began increasingly to implement a contracting-out system (in DND jargon: alternative service delivery) that uses civilian companies to provide support to the military in various sectors, notably transport and maintenance. This of course carries with it the possibility of contract disputes, misinterpretations, or disruptions.

Incidentally, DFAIT was also affected by this policy of budgetary restraint with resulting post closings, salary freezes, and other economy measures.

3.1. Canada and the Balkans

Many critics, both Canadian and foreign (particularly in the NATO context), have complained that our Armed Forces now seriously lack the manpower and equipment, as well as the maintenance facilities, to fulfil the international commitments the government has taken on. Much of this criticism was aimed at Canada's role in the Balkans and also in East Timor.

Canada and Kosovo   Doc. 2.9

ADDRESS BY FM AXWORTHY TO A JOINT MEETING OF THE HOUSE OF COMMONS STANDING COMMITTEE ON FOREIGN AFFAIRS AND INTERNATIONAL TRADE AND THE HOUSE OF COMMONS STANDING COMMITTEE ON NATIONAL DEFENCE AND VETERANS AFFAIRS. DFAIT STATEMENT NO. 99/26, MARCH 31, 1999. (EXTRACTS)

Many Canadians are aware that Kosovo is important. For 10 years now, we have witnessed in the Balkans actions and attitudes that we had thought and hoped belonged to another era.

Since 1991, when the dissolution of Yugoslavia began to accelerate, the régime of President Slobodan Milosevic has waged wars against Slovenia, Croatia, and Bosnia. In Bosnia, we intervened militarily to stop a campaign of ethnic cleansing accompanied by massive summary executions, rape, and the destruction of entire communities, in violation

---

[21] *Canada in the World* is available from DFAIT Information Systems through the website, telephone, and/or fax numbers given under *Suggested Reading*.

of all norms of civilized behaviour.

In Kosovo, the Yugoslav régime has engaged in a campaign of brutal repression ever since it unilaterally stripped the province of its autonomy and abolished its local institutions in 1989 and 1990.

Our preference has always been for a diplomatic solution to the problem. The diplomatic track has been given every chance to succeed. Only when these efforts had been exhausted did the Allies resort to military action.

The NATO operation is entering its eighth day. Let me remind you that its objective is to make the Yugoslav government end the savage repression of its own people. The longer Milosevic resists, the more the Yugoslavia infrastructure of repression will be progressively destroyed. Unfortunately, this takes more time than a few days.

Meanwhile we have seen increasing reports of a growing humanitarian disaster in Kosovo. Yugoslav forces are reported to be carrying out a campaign of terror and expelling large numbers of Kosovars. It is estimated that over 200,000 persons have found refuge in neighbouring countries and regions. This massive flow of refugees is the most dramatic we have seen since the Second World War. Together with our Allies, we are dealing with this humanitarian disaster. The total number of displaced persons and refugees has now reached 560,000. This is a clear sign that it is Milosevic's reign of terror, and not NATO action, that is the cause of the crisis.

NATO is concentrating its efforts on the Yugoslav machine of repression, and Canada is offering six additional CF-18s for that purpose. The aim is to destroy as quickly as possible Yugoslavia's capability to repress the people of Kosovo.

In addition, we are increasing our assistance to humanitarian organizations providing help to refugees from Kosovo. Yesterday, we announced that Canada will contribute $10 million in humanitarian aid to be distributed by the UN High Commissioner for Refugees and the International Committee of the Red Cross. In addition, Canada has been a major contributor to and supporter of the International Criminal Tribunal for the former Yugoslavia.

Finally, I would like to praise the work of the Canadians who have been playing an extremely important role in the Balkans in recent years. Canadians performed admirably in Bosnia on peacekeeping missions in which they assisted with humanitarian relief, rebuilding democratic institutions, and bringing peace to the region.[22]

---

[22]The problems connected with activities in Rwanda and Somalia also drew considerable fire, but they were of a quite different nature.

4.   Arms Control and Disarmament

Disarmament has been a constant theme of negotiation and study since the establishment of the United Nations. It has been debated at every session of the General Assembly since the beginning. The ideal is noble; its realization elusive.

In Dr. MacKay's words describing the situation between 1945 and 1955:

> Debate on disarmament continued in the new Disarmament Commission and annually in the General Assembly but with little practical result. Both sides continued to "talk for the record" rather than with any real hope of advancing the cause of disarmament. Slowly discussions turned towards practical, if limited, expedients to reduce the danger, as for example, prohibition of nuclear tests.[23]

Canada has been involved in all aspects of United Nations disarmament negotiations since the beginning. All Canadian Prime Ministers and Foreign Ministers have taken a personal interest in the subject, but none more so than Howard Green, who was SSEA between 1959 and 1963. It became virtually a crusade with him. Some mocked his efforts as being quixotic. Yet, in retrospect, at the end of the century, it is clear that his views on disarmament were prophetic.

Canada is located between the two major nuclear powers, and so her concern about surprise nuclear attack and the effects of nuclear explosions is understandable. The Diefenbaker government took two striking initiatives in this field. It offered to open Canadian Arctic areas for inspection and to make available the facilities of Canadian laboratories for the analysis of radiation samples in order to study the biological and other effects of radiation resulting from nuclear testing. The Soviet Union did not take the offer up.

Recognition began to grow in the early 1960s that, however desirable the goal of general and complete disarmament might be, it was not likely to be achieved. Attention began to be focused, therefore, on specific ways and means of limiting some elements of armament development. The Cuban missile crisis, in October 1962, was a chastening experience and helped to foster progress.

The pattern of piecemeal progress by sectors established with the Partial Nuclear Test Ban Treaty in 1963 continued to prevail. The important Nuclear Non-Proliferation Treaty (NPT) came

---

[23]See R.A.M., p. 111.

into being in 1968. A number of Canadian ideas were reflected in that Treaty as it finally emerged.

The NPT was opened for signature in July 1968. By September of that year, some eighty states had signed it, including Canada. Today the total is much greater. Only a handful of countries, including some known as "rogue" states such as North Korea, still remain outside the system.

Doc. 2.10 **Nuclear Non-Proliferation Treaty: The Canadian position**

FROM *EXTERNAL AFFAIRS*, OCTOBER 1968, PP. 425-426. CTS 1970/7 PROVIDES THE COMPLETE TEXT OF THE TREATY.[24]

As one of the four Western members of the ENDC, Canada has from the start been actively involved in the formulation of the NPT. It has strongly supported the principle of and has attached high priority to the treaty. It believes that the treaty will be an important factor in maintaining stability in areas of tension, in creating an atmosphere conducive to nuclear-arms control and generally enhancing international stability.

Basic Formula

Canada considers that it will effectively prevent proliferation without prejudicing the right to legitimate collective defence arrangements.

Safeguards Article

Canada believes that effective safeguards are essential to the effectiveness and durability of the treaty. It would have preferred that safeguards be applied equitably to all parties, but it realizes that the Soviet position has made this impossible. However, with the U.S. and British undertakings to accept safeguards voluntarily on their peaceful nuclear activities, it acknowledges that all parties to the treaty but one will be effectively subject to safeguards on their peaceful nuclear programmes.

Peaceful Uses of Nuclear Energy

Canada does not believe that the NPT will inhibit the development of the nuclear programmes of signatories for legitimate peaceful purposes or interfere with international trade in nuclear material and equipment. On the contrary, it believes that the treaty will tend to enhance such development and trade. It has strongly supported the provision that will prohibit non-nuclear states from conducting nuclear explosions for peaceful purposes, since it maintains that military and civil nuclear explosive technologies are indistinguishable and that

---

[24]**Editor's note:** In September 1971, during the Conference of the Committee on Disarmament, Canada called for a halt to all testing.

the development of the latter would inevitably accord a non-nuclear state a nuclear-weapon capability. It has, however, been insistent that, in return for surrendering their nuclear-explosion option, non-nuclear states should be guaranteed access to peaceful nuclear-explosive services from the nuclear powers under appropriate international procedures and on a bilateral basis or through an international body. While this principle is contained in Article V, Canada thinks it should be further elaborated in a separate agreement.

Nuclear-Arms Control

Canada believes the nuclear parties have made an important commitment to achieve further progress rapidly towards effective measures of nuclear-arms control. Canada supports the right of groups of states to establish nuclear-free zones.

Procedural Questions

Canada considers that the procedural provisions will enable the treaty to be implemented smoothly and will, at the same time, give it sufficient flexibility for adaptation to changing circumstances.

In sum, Canada considers the treaty to be a major contribution to international peace and security and to represent the optimum reconciliation of many divergent national objectives, interests and concerns in respect of the threat of the further proliferation of nuclear weapons. It hopes that, in the near future, there will be a sufficient number of ratifications to enable the treaty to come into force.

Editor's notes: Canada could only be on the sidelines of an issue involving primarily the two superpowers and was not of course a party to their negotiations, as embodied in SALT I and II, START I and II, the INF.[25]

These were the crucial talks and, until the two superpowers could reach an understanding, there was not really much that third parties could do about the nuclear-arms race except to exhort and plead. They could certainly not play a decisive role. Even the UN found itself rather marginal and unproductive on the issue, despite the great amount of attention it paid to the subject. It convened three Special Sessions on Disarmament (UNSSOD), none of which was particularly successful.

The real breakthrough came with the arrival of Mikhail Gorbachev on the scene in Moscow. His policies of *glasnost* and *pere-*

---

[25]SALT (Strategic Arms Limitation Talks); START (Strategic Arms Reduction Talks); INF (Intermediate-Range Nuclear Force Treaty). A.E.B. III, p. 56, gives an outline of the results of these developments. Russia recently ratified START II and the Comprehensive Test Ban Treaty. Arms talks between Russia and the United States are still going on.

stroika opened up the U.S.S.R. They also set it on a course which he may not have fully foreseen or intended, culminating eventually in the liberation of Eastern Europe and the breakup of the Soviet Union. As well, they made possible the great reductions in the armaments of the two superpowers, beginning with the INF Treaty in 1987, a convention barring chemical weapons and, eventually the START Treaties. For this, and for many other things, the world is in his debt.

Canadian preoccupations and concerns about the nuclear-arms crisis were both genuine and pressing. They were shared, in equal measure, if not always in equal intensity, by all governments in power in Ottawa during the period covered by this book. Their frequent exhortations and reminders, prodding and pushing, acquired the characteristics of a crusade.

The following three documents show the continuity in Canada's basic approach to disarmament since the 1950s.

Doc. 2.11   **[Disarmament]**

GENERAL STATEMENT TO THE HOUSE OF COMMONS BY PM DIEFENBAKER, FEBRUARY 11, 1960. (EXTRACTS)

What we believe in is that there should be an agreed Western position to serve as a point of departure in the negotiations with the U.S.S.R. in the 10-Power talks which start next month in Geneva, and this is what we are aiming at: to make a contribution by the submission of proposals and comments which will assist in bringing about a plan for international disarmament which will be realistic, negotiable, and at the same time not imperil national security.

These are views expressed in summary which I think represent the thinking of Canadians as a whole on this matter. First, Canada's policy should be directed to the achievement of maximum disarmament and the reduction of armed forces which can be verified and controlled without endangering the security of the nation against aggression.

Second, whatever is done cannot be achieved overnight and will require to be done by steps or stages. To that end I suggest that immediate consideration and priority might be given to the control of missiles designed to deliver nuclear weapons of mass destruction and also to bring about an agreement whereby the location of missile sites should be designated.

Third, I believe the time has come that the nations should agree that the manufacture and use of biological and chemical weapons should be banned.

Fourth, we come to the problem which transcends all these problems, namely that of outer space. If we are to preserve the future of mankind I believe that outer space should now, before further advances are made in its exploration, be declared banned to other than peaceful purposes and that the mounting of armaments on satellites should be outlawed. These are several suggestions that I think represent initial steps, for if there is any desire on the part of the nations to bring about disarmament those principles could be accepted and I think should be accepted.

Now then you say, what about the production of fissile material for weapons? I think that was one of the questions asked. I would think that a major course leading to disarmament would be a declaration that the production of fissile material for weapons should be ended and that existing stocks should be transferred to peaceful uses as soon as a practical plan can be agreed upon. You say, what about the interim? You proceed by stages. What will you do in the meantime? How do you preserve the security of your state?

Indeed on more than one occasion Canada has agreed unreservedly to her northern areas and Arctic regions being made available for inspection in order to ensure that surprise attacks will not take place.

These views have been communicated to Mr. Khrushchev on two occasions. The first was on January 18, 1958 when I wrote him and said this:

> I give assurance that in the context of a disarmament agreement the Canadian Government would be willing to open all or part of Canada to aerial and ground inspection on a basis of reciprocity. It seems to me that this is the type of proposal which should prove attractive to both our countries since we are neighbours across the Arctic. I have in mind in particular the kind of proposal Canada joined in sponsoring last August involving a system of inspection in the Arctic regions. We were willing then and are willing now to take such action in order to provide assurance against the fear of surprise attack.

This was turned down by Mr. Khrushchev in a subsequent letter or at least he did not deal with the matter because he said we would have to have it as part of a world agreement. On May 9, 1958, I wrote to him in part as follows:

> If you are really anxious about developments in the Arctic and if you wish to eliminate the possibility of surprise attack across the polar regions, I find it hard to understand why you should cast aside a proposal designed to increase mutual security in that area. Let me repeat here, Mr. Chairman, that we stand by our offer to make available for international inspection or control any part of our territory, in exchange for a comparable concession on your part. I would hope that you would accept some arrangement along these lines not only as an indication of our good faith but as part of a first, experimental step in building a system of international safeguards against surprise attack. When there is, by

your own admission, a danger of nuclear war breaking out by accident or miscalculation, it is difficult for Canadians to comprehend your refusal to engage even in technical discussions intended to explore the feasibility of an international system of control.[26]

That was Canada's stand.

Doc. 2.12 | **Disarmament: The problem of organizing the world community**

SPEECH BY PM TRUDEAU, TO THE UN SPECIAL SESSION ON DISARMAMENT, NEW YORK, MAY 26, 1978. (EXTRACTS)

Canada takes its place in a world discussion on disarmament as an industrial country, geographically placed between two heavily-armed superpowers, with an obvious stake in the prevention of war in a nuclear age.

We are a member of a regional defensive alliance that includes three of the five nuclear-weapon states. We are, nonetheless, a country that has renounced the production of nuclear weapons or acquisition of such weapons under our control.

We have withdrawn from any nuclear role by Canada's armed forces in Europe and are now in the process of replacing with conventionally-armed aircraft the nuclear-capable planes assigned to our forces in North America. We were thus not only the first country in the world with the capacity to produce nuclear weapons that chose not to do so; we are also the first nuclear-armed country to have chosen to divest itself of nuclear weapons.

We have not, for more than a decade, permitted Canadian uranium to be used for military purposes by any country. We are a country that maintains strict controls over exports of military equipment and does not export any to areas of tension or actual conflict. We are, on the other hand, a major source of nuclear material, equipment, and technology for peaceful purposes.

It has been an assumption of our policy that countries like Canada can do something to slow down the arms race. But, obviously, we can do a great deal more if we act together.

Doc. 2.13 | **In pursuit of peace**

SPEECH BY PM MULRONEY TO THE CONSULTATIVE GROUP ON DISARMAMENT AND ARMS CONTROL, OTTAWA, OCTOBER 31, 1985. (EXTRACTS)

Shortly after assuming office, I said that Canada would work relentlessly to reduce tensions, to alleviate conflict, and to create conditions

---

[26]Disarmament is of course a complex and serious subject, but certain simplifications are possible. At the height of Cold War concerns about nuclear weapons, Chairman Kruschchev is said to have remarked that "quantity has a quality all its own"!

for a general and lasting peace.

Within the field of arms control and disarmament, our government has six specific objectives:

1) Negotiated radical reductions in nuclear enforcement and the enhancement of strategic stability;
2) Maintenance and strengthening of the nuclear non-proliferation régime;
3) Negotiation of a global chemical weapons ban;
4) Support for a comprehensive test ban treaty;
5) Prevention of an arms race in outer space;
6) The building of confidence sufficient to facilitate the reduction of military forces in Europe and elsewhere.

Another initiative involving Canada is worthy of note at this point: the banning of chemical weapons.

[Chemical weapons]   Doc. 2.14

STATEMENT BY SSEA JOE CLARK, AT THE PARIS CONFERENCE ON CHEMICAL WEAPONS, JANUARY 8, 1989.

In April 1915, Canadian soldiers in Flanders were among the first to suffer the terror, pain, and death inflicted by chemical weapons. Of those who recovered from exposure to poison gas, many suffered on for their remaining years. As a result, at least three generations of Canadians — parents, children, and grand-children — became acutely aware of the cruel and horrible effects of the use of such weapons. It is a tragic part of Canada's national memory.

Canada's goal is to have all nations ban all chemical weapons: to get rid of them everywhere and forever. We seek a comprehensive ban that prohibits not only the use but the production and stockpiling of chemical weapons. That will not happen overnight and will require a reliable means of verification.

Specifically, we can condemn the use of chemical weapons and commit ourselves not to use them.

We can reaffirm the Geneva Protocol of 1925 and call on other states to adhere to it.

We can strengthen the capacity of the Secretary General of the United Nations to investigate allegations of chemical weapons use.

As a party to the 1925 Geneva Protocol, Canada has accepted fully its obligations on chemical weapons use. Our policy is clear. Canada does not at any time intend to initiate the use of chemical weapons. Canada does not intend to develop, produce, acquire, or stockpile such weapons, unless these weapons are used against the military forces or the civil population of Canada and its allies.

What does this mean?

First, it means that Canada is applying its obligations under the Geneva Protocol to parties and non-parties alike.

Second, we have adopted a firm policy of non-production to help to achieve a comprehensive ban on chemical weapons.

Third, Canada has already advised other nations of the destruction of the bulk of useable chemical warfare agents which its had stockpiled during the Second World War.[27]

4.1. Conference on Security and Cooperation in Europe (CSCE)

The CSCE discussions began in 1973. At the time, the U.S.S.R. sought to confine the discussions to security and economic issues. The West insisted on including human rights. The upshot was the Helsinki Final Act, signed in 1975, whereby the 35 participating countries recognized Europe's post-1945 boundaries and in addition made solemn, although not legally-binding, promises on: security and human rights, known as "Basket I"; economic cooperation, "Basket II"; and human contacts, "Basket III".

The 35 states included the NATO and Warsaw Pact states, the balance being a group of 12 non-aligned European countries. Early CSCE meetings were not particularly productive. The Soviet invasion of Afghanistan proved a major setback. However, none of the parties sought to kill the process.

Things began to improve in 1986 with the first East-West agreement, at Stockholm, to cover conventional military forces throughout Europe, providing rules, for instance, on the notification of large-scale troop movements and the right to observe them, as well as on verification procedures, that is, ways of checking that each side is in fact respecting the rules. By the time of the Vienna meetings (1986–1989), the atmosphere had started to clear a good deal. Vienna produced a mandate for Conventional Stability Talks on reducing non-nuclear forces, as well as more precise pledges of respect for human rights than those found in the Helsinki Final Act, with appropriate verification measures also included.

By then, also, the CFE Negotiation was getting under way and the current relationship between East and West had set in.

Human rights and, in particular, family contacts involving visits or reunification, have been the prime focus of Canada's approach to CSCE deliberations since the beginning.

---

[27]In this speech, PM Mulroney also refers to his government's decision not to participate on a government-to-government basis in the U.S. Strategic Defense Initiative (SDI), dealt with in the following chapter.

2 — Security and Peace: NATO

The improved view from Vienna: 1989

SPEECH BY SSEA JOE CLARK, ON CONCLUSION OF THE CSCE MEETING IN VIENNA, JANUARY 19, 1989. (EXTRACTS)

When this conference began in 1986, I said in my opening statement that our task would not be easy. The problems seemed intractable. Our world has changed since we began this negotiation and has generally changed for the better. For the first time in history, there is an agreement to abolish a whole class of nuclear weapons. Some regional conflicts have ben resolved or are in the process of resolution in the Middle East, Africa, and Asia. Mr. Gorbachev has offered unilateral force reductions in Eastern Europe. Our political environment has become more positive, more hopeful.

From the beginning of this meeting, Canada raised the fundamental issue of compliance with CSCE commitments. Canada has played an active role in all three CSCE Baskets.

When the Vienna meeting opened, we had just succeeded in the Stockholm Conference in establishing a set of Confidence and Security Building Measures that carried considerable political and military significance, but what we did not know then was how these measures would work out in practice. Since 1986, we have seen gratifying progress. Canada wholeheartedly supports the establishment of negotiations on such measures to build upon the work of the Stockholm Conference.

Other specific elements of this Concluding Document are very important to Canada. We have achieved firm commitments that will improve the conditions under which business people and entrepreneurs can perform their central role in economic cooperation. We have sharpened the commitment to promote contacts between business people and potential buyers and end users, and to publish useful, detailed, and up-to-date economic information and statistics.

Canada is particularly pleased with the agreement to promote direct contacts between scientists and institutions and to respect the human rights of scientists.

We are encouraged that the importance of environmental protection has been recognized.

We think that the progress on tourism is important. Eliminating minimum exchange requirements makes tourism more attractive, and easing contacts between tourists and the local population (including permitting them to stay in private homes) will offer greater human contact and understanding.

In the section on principles, we have adopted a firm statement on terrorism and have made a breakthrough in acceptance of the principle of third-party involvement in the peaceful settlement of disputes.

In the field of human rights, long a focal point of Canadian policy at CSCE meetings, some of the accomplishments of special interest to Canada are:

The commitment to respect the rights of all citizens to associate together and participate actively in the protection and promotion of human rights, without discrimination against those who exercise these rights;

The undertaking to ensure freedom of religion and to allow communities to have places of worship, to participate in public

The commitment to protect the human rights of national minorities;

We have committed ourselves to ensuring that no one is subject to arbitrary arrest, detention, and exile, as well as to improving the treatment of prisoners;

We have undertaken to respect the right of people to move within and between countries;

A range of measures to remove obstacles to family reunification and travel has been agreed to;

We have undertaken to respect the privacy and integrity of postal and telephone communications and to allow people to listen to radio from outside the country and to receive, publish, and disseminate information more freely.

There are many, many, more provisions on human rights and humanitarian cooperation in the Vienna Concluding Document.

Canada considers all of them important. Together, they are a great achievement. In most cases, they are clear and unequivocal. We recognize that there is still room for improvement, but what is in this Document will — if fully implemented by all participating States — lead to great changes in the lives of millions of people.

4.2. Mutual and Balanced Force Reductions (MBFR)

The MBFR talks in Vienna went on, rather unproductively on the whole, for many years. Canada took part in the negotiations from the outset in 1973.

The Cold War background marking the start of the MBFR talks was beginning to change by the mid-1980s. The CSCE negotiations also were becoming involved in some aspects of the issue. In particular, the results of the CSCE conference in Stockholm in 1986 established important confidence-building measures that did much to open the way for a new approach to conventional arms discussions in Europe. A consensus was forming that a new forum would be preferable. It took the name of the Negotiation on Conventional Armed Forces in Europe (CFE).

The CFE talks began in Vienna on March 9, 1989. They were divided into two parts: one dealing with Confidence and Security Building Measures; and the other with a Negotiation on Conventional Armed Forces in Europe. The CFE Negotiation is not a CSCE conference as such, but it is taking place within the CSCE framework. Canada is a charter member of the CFE.

Signed on November 10, 1990, the CFE provisions did not enter into force in their entirety until July 17, 1992. Briefly, the CFE restricts the NATO alliance and states that belonged to the now-defunct Warsaw Pact (or their successors) to equal holdings of Treaty-limited equipment. It also requires exchanges of information to record where this equipment is located and to whom it belongs. The CFE also requires the destruction of Treaty-limited equipment that exceeds national entitlements, although limited quantities of some equipment can be converted to non-military uses. Extensive on-site inspection provisions permit signatories to monitor whether other parties are fulfilling their obligations.

Following entry into force in mid-1992, states began an intensive programme of verifying the initial exchanges of military information. By 1993 good progress was being reported, although participants had discovered that CFE arms procedures and associated verification activities were proving to be more costly than anticipated.

Within the CSCE and CFE context, Canada promoted negotiations to establish an *Open Skies* régime, from which an Open Skies Treaty emerged as the result of a conference held in Budapest in April–May 1990 and subsequent meetings. An Open Skies Consultative Commission has come into being. It deals primarily with the technical issues involved in the Treaty. Canada is actively engaged in the work of the Commission and chaired its first sessions in 1992.

The end of the MBFR talks   Doc. 2.16

COMMUNIQUÉ ISSUED BY SSEA JOE CLARK, FEBRUARY 7, 1989.

The SSEA today took note of the final plenary meeting, in Vienna, of the Negotiations on the Mutual Reduction of Forces and Armaments and Associated Measures in Central Europe. The decision to conclude these negotiations was taken by the participating states in the light of the agreement to open the new Negotiations on the Conventional Armed Forces in Europe (CFE), in March of this year. Canada, as a participant in the MBFR Talks, will play a full role in the new negotiation.

The MBFR negotiations, which began in 1973, have provided a valuable multilateral forum for the discussion of proposals aimed at strengthening security in Europe, although there has been insufficient common ground to the conclusion of a treaty. However, the experience gained in this pioneering attempt to arrive at conventional arms control measures will serve us well in the new negotiation.[28]

4.3. Land Mines

Land mines have not been the subject of traditional disarmament negotiations. Nevertheless, they are particularly destructive devices maiming and/or killing hundreds of people each year. Canada has played a leading role in seeking to eliminate them, reflecting FM Axworthy's policy of human security aimed at protecting individuals as much as possible from violence around the world.

In a press release issued on October 5, 1996, FM Axworthy announced that a major strategy conference would be convened in Ottawa in December 1997 bringing together foreign ministers and experts on the subject.

The Conference resulted in a Convention, signed in Ottawa by 122 countries, including Canada, that prohibits the use, stockpiling, production, and transfer of anti-personnel mines. Signatory countries also undertook to destroy existing stockpiles within four years and to clear minefields within 10 years. The Ottawa Convention, as it is known, became international law on March 1, 1999.

5. Canada's Uranium Policy

Canada's uranium exports had, until 1974 when India exploded a nuclear device, been governed by the guidelines announced in the House of Commons by PM Pearson on June 3, 1965. They stipulated that exports would be for peaceful purposes only, subject to verification and control. The Indian explosion led to a considerable tightening of previous policy as announced by PM Trudeau and by SSEA MacEachen on June 17, 1975, and May 18, 1976, respectively.[29]

---

[28]These measures were notable achievements. However, they came into effect at a point when, because of the dissolution of the Warsaw Pact and of the Soviet Union itself, they were overtaken by events and became largely irrelevant.

[29]Canada and India signed an agreement in New Delhi on April 28, 1956, whereby — under the Colombo Plan — Canada would provide an NRX Atomic Research and Experimental Reactor to India with the proviso (Article 2) that the Government of India would ensure that the reactor and any products resulting from its use would be employed for peaceful purposes only. See A.E.B. I, pp. 274-279 for details. Since the 1974 explosion, Canada/India relations in this sector have been at a virtual standstill and recent Indian nuclear testing has further complicated matters.

2 — Security and Peace: NATO

[Uranium exports]

Doc. 2.17

TEXT OF THE PRESS RELEASE ISSUED BY THE PM'S OFFICE, OTTAWA, JUNE 3, 1965. (EXTRACTS)

As the House is aware, the Government has been reviewing its policy with respect to the export of uranium.

World requirements for uranium for peaceful purposes will increase very greatly in the years to come. Canada holds a substantial portion of the known uranium reserves of the world and in the future may well be the largest single supplier for the rest of the world. It is vital that the Canadian industry be in the best possible position to take advantage of expanding markets for the peaceful uses of this commodity.

As one part of its policy to promote the use of Canadian uranium for peaceful purposes the Government has decided that export permits will be granted, or commitments to issue export permits will be given, with respect to sales of uranium covered by contracts entered into from now on only if the uranium is to be used for peaceful purposes. Before such sales to any destination are authorized, the Government will require an agreement with the Government of the importing country to ensure, with appropriate verification and control, that the uranium is to be used for peaceful purposes only.

Canada has been a member of the International Atomic Energy Agency since its inception and successive governments have vigorously supported the principle of safeguards on uranium sales. This policy is a fundamental part of Canada's general policy to work internationally to avoid the proliferation of nuclear weapons.

As to the commercial aspects of the policy, two general principles will apply, designed to facilitate exports and to ensure that the requirements of both export and domestic consumers are met in an orderly way.

First, the Government recognizes that countries constructing or planning to construct nuclear reactors will wish to make long-term arrangements for fuel supply. Accordingly, the Government will be prepared to authorize forward commitments by Canadian producers to supply reactors which are already in operation, under construction or committed for construction in other countries for the average anticipated life of each reactor, generally calculated for amortization purposes to be 30 years.

Second, and in addition, the Government will be prepared to authorize the export for periods of up to 5 years of reasonable quantities of uranium for the accumulation of stocks in the importing country.

Within the terms of the policy I have outlined, the Canadian Government will actively encourage and assist the Canadian uranium industry in seeking export markets. The commercial aspects of the policy will, of course, be reviewed from time to time in the light of changing conditions.

75

Finally, in order to avoid any reduction in the current level of employment and production in the industry in Canada, the Government will purchase uranium for stockpiling to the extent that current sales prove insufficient to achieve this objective during the next 5 years. These purchases will be made at a price of $4.90 per pound of Uranium Oxide. Purchases will be made only from companies which have previously produced uranium, and will be limited in the case of each company willing to sell at $4.90 to the amount necessary to maintain an appropriate minimum level of employment and production for that company.

As soon as the details of the stockpiling program, including arrangements for eventual disposal, have been discussed with the uranium industry and decided upon, they will be announced to the House and Parliament will be asked to approve the necessary expenditure for the current fiscal year.

5.1. Human security and disarmament

FM Axworthy's most noticed contributions to Canadian foreign policy since becoming minister have been his concepts of human security and soft power in international relations.

As he put it on April 17, 1997:

> the basic premise behind *human security* is that human rights and fundamental freedoms, the rule of law, good governance, and social equity are as important to global peace as are arms control and disarmament. In other words, that security should be measured in terms of the ultimate outcome for individuals and for peoples, rather than in terms of the numbers of arms control agreements signed.[30]

Like his distant predecessor, Howard Green, whose quest for disarmament was laughed at — even mocked — at the time, let us hope that he too, like Green, becomes a prophet.

---

[30]See DFAIT News Release No. 97/21, April 17, 1997.

3

Relations with the United States

CANADIAN RELATIONS WITH THE UNITED STATES are now and have always been — even well before Confederation — a key component of Canada's external relations.[31]

Before the Second World War they were much less structured, pervasive, and intricate than now. Canada was a small player on the world scene then, politically, economically, financially, and commercially. We had achieved Dominion status within the British Commonwealth only in the 1930s and were understandably preoccupied by the Depression that hit Canada hard during the same period. Our international trade was modest and so too was industrial production. Our dollar was a relatively minor currency. The war changed all that, and generally for the better.

Since mid-century, relations have grown to the point of affecting almost every aspect of Canadian life today: from matters of broad policy such as free trade, investments, defence, the environment, energy, air and water pollution; to matters directly touching on the personal every-day life of most of us. To mention but a few: automobiles, meat, fish, lumber, beer and wine, cigarettes and tobacco, even such relatively recent developments as annual school breaks in Florida!

It is not possible in a book of this size to deal with all aspects of Canada's relations with the United States, but all major policy trends and events are included.

1. Defence Questions

Joint arrangements governing defence relations between the two countries go back to August 1940, when President Roosevelt and PM Mackenzie King met at Ogdensburg, N.Y., and agreed that a

---

[31]For an excellent account of Canada's relations with the United States throughout the 19th century down to the creation of DEA by the Laurier Government in 1909, see Chapter I of *Canada's Department of External Affairs* by John F. Hilliker (The Institute of Public Affairs of Canada and McGill-Queens University Press, 1990).

Permanent Joint Board on Defence should be set up immediately between Canada and the United States to consider questions related to the defence of the northern half of the Western Hemisphere. It was renewed in 1947 and continues to underlie defence relations between the two countries today.

1.1. Permanent Joint Board on Defence

Doc. 3.1   STATEMENT BY THE GOVERNMENTS OF CANADA AND THE UNITED STATES OF AMERICA REGARDING DEFENCE COOPERATION BETWEEN THE TWO COUNTRIES AND STATEMENT BY PM MACKENZIE KING (HOUSE OF COMMONS, FEBRUARY 12, 1947; CTS 1947/3.)

I wish to make a statement which is also being made today by the Government of the United States regarding the results of discussions which have taken place in the Permanent Joint Board on Defence on the extent to which war-time co-operation between the armed forces of the two countries should be maintained in this postwar period. In the interest of efficiency and economy, each Government has decided that its national defence establishment shall, to the extent authorized by law, continue to collaborate for peace-time joint security purposes. The collaboration will necessarily be limited and will be based on the following principles:

1) Interchange of selected individuals so as to increase the familiarity of each country's defence establishment with that of the other country.

2) General co-operation and exchange of observers in connection with exercises and with the development and tests of material of common interest.

3) Encouragement of common designs and standards in arms, equipment, organization, methods of training and new developments. As certain United Kingdom standards have long been in use in Canada, no radical change is contemplated or practicable and the application of this principle will be gradual.

4) Mutual and reciprocal availability of military, naval and air facilities in each country; this principle to be applied as may be agreed in specific instances. Reciprocally each country will continue to provide, with a minimum of formality, for the transit through its territory and its territorial waters of military aircraft and public vessels of the other country.

5) As an underlying principle all co-operative arrangements will be without impairment of the control of either country over all activities in its territory.

While in this, as in many other matters of mutual concern, there is an identity of view and interest between the two countries, the decision of each has been taken independently in continuation of the practice developed since the establishment of the permanent joint board on defence in 1940. No treaty, executive agreement, or contractual obligation has been entered into. Each country will determine the extent of its practical collaboration in respect of each and all of the foregoing principles. Either country may at any time discontinue collaboration on any or all of them. Neither country will take any action inconsistent with the charter of the united nations. The charter remains the cornerstone of the foreign policy of each.

An important element in the decision of each government to authorize continued collaboration was the conviction on the part of each that in this way their obligations under the charter of the united nations for the maintenance of international peace and security could be fulfilled more effectively. Both governments believe that this decision is a contribution to the stability of the world and to the establishment through the united nations of an effective system of world wide security. With this in mind each government has sent a copy of this statement to the secretary general of the united nations for circulation to all its members.

In August, 1940, when the creation of the board was jointly announced by the late President Roosevelt and myself as Prime Minister of Canada, it was stated that the board "shall commence immediate studies relating to sea, land and air problems including personnel and material. It will consider in the broad sense the defence of the north half of the Western hemisphere." In discharging this continuing responsibility the board's work led to the building up of a pattern of close defence co-operation. The principles announced today are in continuance of this co-operation. It has been the task of the governments to assure that the close security relationship between Canada and the United States in North America will in no way impair but on the contrary will strengthen the co-operation of each country within the broader framework of the United Nations.

1.2. NORAD

Discussions for setting up a system of integrated operational control of the air defence forces of Canada and the United States began in 1957 as the Cold War heightened. The North American Air Defence Command Agreement (NORAD) that emerged from the talks was formalized in an Exchange of Notes between the two Governments, documented immediately hereunder.[32]

---

[32]NORAD was renewed in 1981, 1986, 1991 and 1996. On the occasion of the renewal of NORAD on March 11, 1981, the name "North American Aerospace Defence Command" (NORAD) was adopted as better reflecting the defence situation facing the two countries today. Incidentally, the 1986 agreement dropped a clause which specified that Canada's NORAD role excluded participation in an anti-ballistic missile arrangement.

Doc. 3.2   **[NORAD Treaty]**

TEXT OF NOTES EXCHANGED BY THE GOVERNMENTS OF CANADA AND THE UNITED STATES. (FROM) CANADIAN EMBASSY WASHINGTON, D.C.

No. 263   May 12, 1958.

Sir,

I have the honour to refer to discussions which have taken place between the Canadian and the United States authorities concerning the necessity for integration of operational control of Canadian and United States Air Defence and, in particular, to the study and recommendations of the Canada-United States Military Study Group. These studies led to the joint announcement of August 1, 1957, by the Minister of National Defence of Canada and the Secretary of Defense of the United States, indicating that our two Governments had agreed to the setting up of a system of integrated operational control of the air defence in the Continental United States, Canada and Alaska under an integrated command responsible to the Chiefs of Staff of both countries. Pursuant to the announcement of August 1, 1957, an integrated headquarters known as the North American Air Defence Command (NORAD) has been established on an interim basis at Colorado Springs, Colorado.

For some years prior to the establishment of NORAD, it had been recognized that the air defence of Canada and the United States must be considered as a single problem. However, arrangements which existed between Canada and the United States provided only for the coordination of separate Canadian and United States air defence plans, but did not provide for the authoritative control of all air defence weapons which must be employed against an attacker.

The advent of nuclear weapons, the great improvements in the means of effecting their delivery, and the requirements of the air defence control systems demand rapid decisions to keep pace with the speed and tempo of technological developments. To counter the threat and to achieve maximum effectiveness of the air defence system, defensive operations must commence as early as possible and enemy forces must be kept constantly engaged. Arrangements for the coordination of national plans requiring consultation between national commanders before implementation had become inadequate in the face of a possible sudden attack, with little or no warning. It was essential, therefore, to have in existence in peacetime an organization, including the weapons, facilities and command structure, which could operate at the outset of hostilities in accordance with a single air defence plan approved in advance by national authorities.

Studies made by representatives of our two Governments led to the conclusion that the problem of the air defence of our two countries could best be met by delegating to an integrated headquarters, the task of exercising operational control over combat units of the national forces made available for the air defence of the two countries.

3 — Relations with the United States

Furthermore, the principle of an integrated headquarters exercising operational control over assigned forces has been well established in various parts of the North Atlantic Treaty area. The Canada-United States region is an integral part of the NATO area. In support of the strategic objectives established in NATO for the Canada-United States region and in accordance with the provisions of the North Atlantic Treaty, our two Governments have, by establishing the North American Air Defence Command, recognized the desirability of integrating headquarters exercising operational control over assigned air defence forces. The agreed integration is intended to assist the two Governments to develop and maintain their individual and collective capacity to resist air attack on their territories in North America in mutual self-defence.

The two Governments consider that the establishment of integrated air defence arrangements of the nature described increases the importance of the fullest possible consultation between the two Governments on all matters affecting the joint defence of North America, and that defence co-operation between them can be worked out on a mutually satisfactory basis only if such consultation is regularly and consistently undertaken.

In view of the foregoing considerations and on the basis of the experience gained in the operation on an interim basis of the North American Air Defence Command, my Government proposes that the following principles should govern the future organization and operations of the North American Air Defence Command.

1) The Commander-in-Chief NORAD (CINCNORAD) will be responsible to the Chiefs of Staff Committee of Canada and the Joint Chiefs of Staff of the United States, who in turn are responsible to their respective Governments. He will operate within a concept of air defence approved by the appropriate authorities of our two Governments, who will bear in mind their objectives in the defence of the Canada-United States region of the NATO area.

2) The North American Air Defence Command will include such combat units and individuals as are specifically allocated to it by the two Governments. The jurisdiction of the Commander-in-Chief, NORAD, over those units and individuals is limited to operational control as hereinafter defined.

3) "Operational Control" is the power to direct, co-ordinate, and control the operational activities of forces assigned, attached or otherwise made available. No permanent changes of station would be made without approval of the higher national authority concerned. Temporary reinforcement from one area to another, including the crossing of the international boundary, to meet operational requirements will be within the authority of commanders having operational control. The basic command organization for the air defence forces of the two countries, including administration, dis-

81

cipline, internal organization and unit training, shall be exercised by national commanders responsible to their national authorities.

4) The appointment of CINCNORAD and his Deputy must be approved by the Canadian and United States Governments. They will not be from the same country, and CINCNORAD staff shall be an integrated joint staff composed of officers of both countries. During the absence of CINCNORAD, command will pass to the Deputy Commander.

5) The North Atlantic Treaty Organization will continue to be kept informed through the Canada-United States Regional Planning Group of arrangements for the air defence of North America.

6) The plans and procedures to be followed by NORAD in wartime shall be formulated and approved in peacetime by appropriate national authorities and shall be capable of rapid implementation in an emergency. Any plans or procedures recommended by NORAD which bear on the responsibilities of civilian departments or agencies of the two Governments shall be referred for decision by the appropriate military authorities to those agencies and departments and may be the subject of intergovernmental co-ordination.

7) Terms of reference for CINCNORAD and his Deputy will be consistent with the foregoing principles. Changes in these terms of reference may be made by agreement between the Canadian Chiefs of Staff Committee and the United States Joint Chiefs of Staff, with approval of higher authority as appropriate, provided that these changes are in consonance with the principles set out in this Note.

8) The question of the financing of expenditures connected with the operation of the integrated headquarters of the North American Air Defence Command will be settled by mutual agreement between appropriate agencies of the two Governments.

9) The North American Air Defence Command shall be maintained in operation for a period of ten years or such shorter period as shall be agreed by both countries in the light of their mutual defence interest, and their objectives under the terms of the North Atlantic Treaty. The terms of this Agreement may be reviewed upon request of either country at any time.

10) The Agreement between parties to the North Atlantic Treaty regarding the status of their forces signed in London on June 19, 1951, shall apply.

11) The release to the public of information by CINCNORAD on matters of interest to Canada and the United States of America will in all cases be the subject of prior consultation and agreement between appropriate agencies of the two Governments.

If the United States Government concurs in the principles set out above, I propose that this Note and your reply should constitute an Agreement between our two Governments effective from the date of your reply. (Reply of agreement not printed)

3 — Relations with the United States

Accept, Sir, the renewed assurances of my highest consideration.

"N.A. Robertson"
Ambassador of Canada

The Honourable John Foster Dulles,
Secretary of State of the United States,

Washington, D C

Editor's notes: The Trudeau government's narrower and more nationalistic outlook towards the United States did have some repercussions on defence relations with the United States. For instance, it tended to renew the NORAD Agreement for shorter periods of time than the usual five years. It also maintained its opposition to participation in the United States Anti-Ballistic Missile System. But it did enter into an agreement with the U.S. to allow the testing of cruise missiles in Canada: a policy continued by the Mulroney government.

An offer by the Reagan administration to take part in its Strategic Defence Initiative (SDI), an anti-ballistic missile shield more commonly known as Star Wars, was not taken up by the Mulroney government. The Strategic Defence Initiative, as originally planned, succumbed to tight budgets and high technological costs in the United States, but especially to the reduced military tensions of the Gorbachev era, although research in this sector continued. The United States has recently been concentrating on a modified version of the proposal called the National Missile Defence project that takes into account recent technological advances. Russia, along with a number of U.S. allies, including Canada, have been sceptical about it on the ground that it might start a new nuclear arms race. Discussions and research continue.

1.3. Cruise Missiles

[Canada's position on testing]   Doc. 3.3

OPEN LETTER FROM PM TRUDEAU, TO ALL CANADIANS, MAY 9, 1983. (EXTRACTS)

In recent months I have received a great number of letters and petitions protesting against the possible testing of Cruise Missiles in Canadian territory. In recent years, the Soviet Union has deployed hundreds of new SS-20 missiles, each equipped with three nuclear warheads, capable of reaching all the great cities of Western Europe.

That the Soviet people have not protested against this action of their leaders surprises no one. What is surprising, however, is that those in the West who are opposed to nuclear weapons have remained relatively silent about the installation of the SS-20s. In contrast, they are now taking to the streets to oppose the possible deployment of American *Pershing II* and Cruise Missiles to protect Europe against the Soviet nuclear threat.

What is particularly surprising in Canada is to see protesters opposing the possible testing of Cruise Missiles in Canadian territory, but not opposing the fact that similar missiles are already being tested in the Soviet Union, as was confirmed in December by General-Secretary Andropov.

Because people in the free world feel powerless to influence the leaders of the USSR, there is a great temptation to direct the whole force of their anguish and their protests against the only decision-makers who are sensitive to public opinion, namely the leaders of the democratic countries.

Because the strategy of suffocation I proposed at UNSSOD I, in the name of Canada, was rejected by the Soviet Union as evidenced by the continued deployment of the SS-20s, there was no question of its acceptance by the NATO countries alone. That is why we allied ourselves with the "two-track" strategy of our NATO allies. Those two tracks are to seek to negotiate the removal of the SS-20s and, at the same time, to prepare for the deployment of new American missiles in Europe so as to pressure the Soviet Union towards serious negotiations.

I hope that my explanation of our policy will have established that, were we able to collaborate in testing the guidance system of the Cruise Missiles, it would be because of our solidarity with the other Western democracies, in a world which had turned a deaf ear to our suggested strategy of suffocation. Having supported the two-track strategy, Canada should bear its fair share of the burden which that policy imposes on the NATO alliance.[33]

1.4. Star Wars

Doc. 3.4   **[Canadian position]**

SUMMARY OF REMARKS BY PM MULRONEY, DURING A PRESS CONFERENCE, SEPTEMBER 7, 1985.

On March 26, the United States invited Canada and other friendly countries to participate directly in research under the Strategic Defence Initiative (SDI). After careful and detailed consideration, the government has concluded that Canada's own policies and priorities do not warrant a government-to-government effort in support of SDI research. Although Canada does not intend to participate on a government-to-

---

[33]An agreement between Canada and the U.S. for testing Cruise Missiles in Canadian territory was signed on February 10, 1983. DFAIT communiqué of July 15, 1983, provides details about the agreement and testing stipulations. A useful booklet, *Cruise Missiles: Background, Technology, and Verification*, was published (undated, but probably 1989) by and is available from DFAIT.

government basis in the SDI research programme, private companies and institutions interested in the programme will continue to be free to do so.

As stated in the House of Commons on January 21, by the SSEA, this government believes that SDI research by the United States is both consistent with the ABM Treaty and prudent in light of significant advances in Soviet research and deployment of the world's only existing ballistic missile defence system.

I conveyed the government's decision to the President of the United States today and informed him of this. I had discussed it, as you might imagine, with my caucus and my cabinet. And that is our position with regard to this particular item.

Editor's note: Since 1993, when the Chrétien government was elected, defence relations with the United States and defence policy generally have remained largely unchanged.

2. Economic Matters

2.1. Joint economic arrangements with the United States

One of the first joint post-war steps taken by the two countries was initiated by the United States. It suggested that the successful economic and industrial war-production arrangements concluded by President Roosevelt and PM Mackenzie King on April 20, 1941, known as the Hyde Park Declaration, should be prolonged into the post-war period with special reference to the reconversion of industry.

This was done by an Exchange of Notes between the two governments on May 7 and May 15, 1945.[34]

The United States also proposed the establishment of a Joint Industrial Mobilization Committee between the two countries, along the lines of the joint committees developed during war. Canada readily agreed.

[The Joint Industrial Mobilization Committee]   Doc. 3.5

EXCHANGE OF NOTES, APRIL 12, 1949 (CTS 1949/8).

The United States Ambassador to Canada to the Secretary of State for External Affairs

United States Embassy

Ottawa, April 12, 1949.

---

[34]See R.A.M., pp. 52-59, for the text of the Notes (given in an Appendix on pp. 58-59) reaffirming the Hyde Park Declaration.

Excellency,

I have the honour to inform Your Excellency that the common interests of Canada and the United States in defence, their proximity, and the complementary characteristics of their resources clearly indicate the advantages of coordinating their plans for industrial mobilization, in order that the most effective use may be made of the productive facilities of the two countries.

The functions of the Department of Trade and Commerce and the Industrial Defence Board in Canada and those of the National Security Resources Board and the Munitions Board in the United States suggest that, for the present, it would be appropriate to use these agencies to assist the two Governments in coordinating their industrial mobilization plans.

Therefore, my Government wishes to propose that the two Governments agree:

(a) that a Joint Industrial Mobilization Committee be now constituted consisting, on the United States side, of the Chairman of the National Security Resources Board and the Chairman of the Munitions Board and, on the Canadian side, of the Chairman of the Industrial Defence Board and a senior official of the Department of Trade and Commerce;

(b) that the Joint Committee:

    (i) exchange information with a view to the coordination of the plans of the United States and Canada for industrial mobilization;

    (ii) consider what recommendations in the field of industrial mobilization planning in areas of common concern should be made to each Government;

    (iii) be empowered to organize joint sub-committees from time to time to facilitate the discharge of its functions;

    (iv) be responsible for co-operation with the Permanent Joint Board on Defence on matters of industrial mobilization.

If your Government is agreeable to the above proposals, it is understood that this note, together with your note in reply agreeing thereto, shall constitute an agreement between our two Governments which shall enter in force on the date of your reply and shall remain in force indefinitely subject to termination by either Government at any time on giving six months' notice.

Please accept, Excellency, the renewed assurances of my highest consideration. (Reply of agreement not printed.)
Laurence A. Steinhardt

3 — Relations with the United States

[Principles for Economic Cooperation]

EXCHANGE OF NOTES, OCTOBER 26, 1950 (CTS 1950/15).

The Secretary of State of the United States of America to the Canadian Ambassador in the United States of America
Department of State
Washington, D.C. October 26, 1950
Excellency:

I have the honour to refer to recent discussions between representatives of our two Governments for the general purpose of reaching an agreement to the end that the economic efforts of the two countries be coordinated for the common defense and that the production and resources of both countries be used for the best combined results. Their deliberations were based on concepts of economic co-operation which were inherent in the Hyde Park Agreement of 1941 and which are still valid today. They formulated and agreed to the "Statement of Principles for Economic Cooperation" annexed hereto, which is intended to guide, in the light of these basic concepts, the activities of our respective Governments.

If this attached statement is agreeable to your Government, this note and your reply to that effect will constitute an agreement between our two Governments on this subject.

Accept, Excellency, the renewed assurances of my highest consideration. (Reply of agreement not printed.)
Dean Acheson

Statement of Principles for Economic Co-operation

The United States and Canada have achieved a high degree of cooperation in the field of industrial mobilization during and since World War II through the operation of the principles embodied in the Hyde Park Agreement of 1941, through the extension of its concepts in the post-war period and more recently through the work of the Joint Industrial Mobilization Planning Committee. In the interests of mutual security and to assist both governments to discharge their obligations under the United Nations Charter and the North Atlantic Treaty, it is believed that this field of common action should be further extended. It is agreed, therefore, that our two governments shall co-operate in all respects practicable, and to the extent of their respective executive powers, to the end that the economic efforts of the two countries be coordinated for the common defense and that the production and resources of both countries be used for the best combined results.

The following principles are established for the purpose of facilitating these objectives:

1) In order to achieve an optimum production of goods essential for the common defense, the two countries shall develop a coordinated program of requirements, production and procurement.

2) To this end, the two countries shall, as it becomes necessary, institute coordinated controls over the distribution of scarce raw materials and supplies.

3) Such United States and Canadian emergency controls shall be mutually consistent in their objectives, and shall be so designed and administered as to achieve comparable effects in each country. To the extent possible, there shall be consultation to this end prior to the institution of any system of controls in either country which affects the other.

4) In order to facilitate essential production, the technical knowledge and productive skills involved in such production within both countries shall, where feasible, be freely exchanged.

5) Barriers which impede the flow between Canada and the United States of goods essential for the common defense effort should be removed as far as possible.

6) The two governments, through their appropriate agencies, will consult concerning any financial or foreign exchange problems which may arise as a result of the implementation of this agreement.[35]

3. American Investments in Canada

After the War, Canada opened its doors to investments from the United States. These were on a large scale and wide-ranging. They did much to ensure the growth and prosperity of the Canadian economy. Yet, as shall be seen in the following documents, problems arose. These were connected primarily with the exports of American branch plants in Canada, affected by United States legislation, such as the prohibition of U.S. trade with Cuba. Some of these problems are still with us.

Doc. 3.7   STATEMENT BY TRADE AND COMMERCE MINISTER C.D. HOWE, TO THE CANADIAN CLUB OF CHICAGO, OCTOBER 15, 1956. (EXTRACTS)

These remarks are addressed particularly to United States businessmen who have investments in Canada or who contemplate making investments in Canada. At the outset, let me make one thing quite clear: the Canadian Government and, I have reason to believe, the vast majority of the Canadian people have welcomed, and will continue to welcome, investment from the United States. We are not allergic to outside capital.

It is well understood in Canada that to put obstacles in the way of

---

[35]The United States also proposed the creation of a Joint Committee on Trade and Economic Affairs, but it did not prove to be very effective and was subsequently superseded by other arrangements. R.A.M., pp. 88-89, gives the text of this agreement and other details. See also CTS 1953/18.

3 — Relations with the United States

capital imports would involve a cut-back in the Canadian rate of development. This is so partly because our need for capital exceeds our rate of savings, and partly because of the Canadian pattern of investment.

At the present time Canadians, individuals and corporations, are saving a higher proportion of their incomes than Americans. But even so, they are not saving enough to finance the current rate of capital investment, which is quite fantastic. The face of Canada is literally being transformed.

Since Canada is the freest of free countries and there are no obstacles to capital movements, inward or outward, some Canadians have chosen to invest abroad, as well as at home. It may come as a surprise to you to learn that, on a per capita basis, Canadians have invested more in the United States than Americans in Canada. The proportion in favour of Canadians is two to one.

The net result is that about three-quarters of Canada's current capital investment is being financed out of domestic savings, and the balance by imports of capital, mostly from the United States.

As I have said, we welcome this inflow of capital from south of the border. We welcome it the more because it has brought with it managerial enterprise, production and marketing experience, engineering and technical know-how and research, modern equipment, and perhaps most important, skilled American men and women who have helped to build up our own country more rapidly than we could have done ourselves.

Both the United States and Canada have benefited. The United States has found new markets and obtained new sources of raw materials. A goodly proportion of earnings of United States controlled corporations in Canada — something like one-half in recent years — has been reinvested in Canada. The rest has been freely transferred in the form of dividends to American parent companies and shareholders.

Canadians have been able to speed up their own economic development. New resources have been proven up, our northern frontier has been pushed back, and new factories have been opened, providing more opportunities for employment and the improvement of earnings.

If both countries have benefited from this flow of capital northward, is there anything more to be said? I think there is.

I am going to make a number of suggestions to United States businessmen who operate branch plants in Canada or are considering doing so. You may not accept them; you may not agree with them. You may have better methods of achieving the same result. I do wish you to know, however, that these suggestions have one purpose and one purpose only, namely, to underpin the friendly and harmonious economic relations that now exist between Canada and the United States.

Because of our closeness to the United States, our similar institutions and habits and the way we do things, Americans often treat Canada, for business purposes, almost as a part of the United States. In a sense this is a good thing, a tribute to common sense. But it has

89

its dangers if it leads American businessmen to treat branch plants in Canada just as if they were located in the United States.

In my judgment, this is not likely to be the most successful method of conducting a subsidiary business enterprise in Canada. Certainly, it is not the method calculated to make the most friends and influence the most customers in Canada.

I suggest to you a very simple rule. Other things being equal, it is good business for a Canadian subsidiary of a foreign company to become as Canadian as it can, without losing the benefits of association with the parent company. In many countries, of course, there are rigid laws applying to foreign controlled companies, requiring them, for example, to give local inhabitants a share in the enterprise and requiring them to employ a minimum proportion of local labour and so forth.

There are no such laws in Canada. I hope there never will be. I believe that those who are prepared to share with Canadians in the risks of developing our country should be as free as Canadians themselves in deciding how to conduct their enterprise.

Nevertheless, anyone who does business in Canada should reckon with the pride and the legitimate pride of Canadians in their country. In other words, they should reckon with the normal feeling of nationalism which is present in Canada, just as it is in the United States. Canadians do not like to be excluded from an opportunity of participating in the fortunes, good or bad, of large-scale enterprise incorporated in Canada but owned abroad.

They may not buy many shares, but they resent the exclusion. They do not like to see large-scale Canadian enterprises entirely dependent upon foreign parents for their research and top management. They do not like to see the financial results of large-scale Canadian enterprises treated as if they were the exclusive concern of the foreign owners.

I make bold therefore to offer three suggestions for the consideration of United States corporations establishing branch plants in Canada or searching for and developing Canadian natural resources:

1) Provide opportunities for financial participation by Canadians as minority shareholders in the equities of such corporations operating in Canada.
2) Provide greater opportunities for advancement in U.S. controlled corporations for Canadians technically competent to hold executive and professional positions.
3) Provide more and regular information about the operations of such corporations in Canada.

I am pleased to say that an increasing number of American companies are now giving Canadians an opportunity to participate in the equity holdings of Canadian-operated enterprises. This is an encouraging trend. Canadians welcome this development, not just because it is in Canada's national interest, but also because we think it makes

90

good business sense from the point of view of the American parent corporation.

I was told that Canadian taxation discouraged Canadian participation in Canadian subsidiaries. If it did, that particular obstacle has been removed, at least insofar as Canadian law is concerned.

The agreement for the avoidance of double taxation between the United States and Canada provided for certain tax advantages for parent companies controlling 95 per cent or more of the equity of the subsidiary corporation in the other country. Last summer the United States and Canada reached an agreement, subject to ratification by your Congress and our Parliament, whereby the percentage of share ownership, entitling the parent company to a reduced rate of 5 per cent on dividends from its subsidiary operating in the other country, has been reduced from 95 per cent to 51 per cent. This amendment of our taxation agreement with the United States has since become law in Canada. It is still awaiting ratification by the U.S. Congress. Our Government made it quite clear, in proposing this amendment to the Canadian Parliament, that the new tax arrangement was designed to encourage U.S. parent corporations to give Canadian investors opportunities to buy share ownership in their subsidiary companies in Canada. Hence, as far as Canada is concerned, the tax disadvantage that used to exist for a U.S. corporation offering Canadian minority equity holdings in U.S. branch plants has been removed.

Undoubtedly, there are other difficulties, difficulties about exchange of research between parent and partially-owned subsidiaries, difficulties of control of subsidiaries with minority shareholders. That these are very real difficulties, I would be the first to admit. I ask only that they be weighed in the balance against the advantages in terms of goodwill of giving Canadians a sense of identity with the United States-controlled enterprises.

My second suggestion is that Canadians should be given greater opportunities for advancement in subsidiary enterprises controlled by United States parents. I am pleased to report that more and more U.S. corporations operating in Canada are hiring Canadians for responsible positions, when well-qualified people can be found, and that young Canadians are being advanced as rapidly as their ability and experience will warrant. Responsible Canadians are being invited to sit on Boards of Directors. If this trend continues, there will be little for Canadians to complain about.

My third suggestion is that U.S. corporations should report the results of operations of their subsidiaries in Canada. As you are aware, the S.E.C. requires regular reporting by all the large corporations in the United States. We do not have similar regulations in Canada. Nevertheless, the Canadian public is interested in knowing how these large Canadian corporations are getting on in Canada. Since many of our large corporations are U.S.-controlled, the demand for the release of such information at regular intervals, say in the form of annual reports, has been increasing.

One U.S. corporation, with a 100 per cent controlled subsidiary operation in Canada, added a supplement to its last annual report outlining the extent of its operations and its achievements in Canada. This endeavour to let Canadians know how this company is doing with respect to operations in Canada was well received. It could serve as a useful guide to those who feel as I do that it is good business to treat branch plants in Canada as thoroughly Canadian enterprises.

These are my three specific recommendations. I believe they are worth careful consideration. I believe their adoption will be in the interests of United States corporations with subsidiaries in Canada. There may be other ideas equally good which serve the same purpose. Be assured of one thing, that my purpose is to improve business relations between the United States and Canada by giving Canadians a greater interest and a greater stake in the success of United States companies operating branch plants across the border.

Before leaving this subject, there is one other point very close to my heart as Minister of Trade and Commerce which I put before you for consideration. Branch plants are usually established to do business in the area they serve. But I ask you again to bear in mind that a branch plant in Canada is not the same thing as a branch plant in California or Louisiana. A Canadian branch plant is situated in a country that depends for its very existence upon international trade. It is situated in a country which maintains an external trade service which others tell us is second to none and which is ready to serve any Canadian enterprise, whoever owns it.

Too often, I regret to say, our trade representatives abroad turn up export opportunities for a subsidiary company operating in Canada only to find that the United States parent does not permit the export business to be done from the Canadian plant. Mind you, we do not object to doing occasional export promotion for United States corporations, but you will agree that it is rather difficult to justify the expense to the Canadian taxpayer!

Once again I recognize that there are problems. But I do plead for a careful re-examination of export policies affecting Canadian branch plants. Canada as a nation is an efficient producer. Given sufficient volume, Canadian plants can often produce as cheaply as United States plants. Sometimes, too, Canada has an advantage in duty in supplying goods to countries of the British Commonwealth; indeed, many plants have been established in Canada just to take advantage of this preference. I am not suggesting that United States corporations should act contrary to their interest. I am suggesting that they may be overlooking a good bet by not allowing their Canadian plants to take on more export business. By being prepared to accept export business United States-controlled subsidiaries will also act more like good, solid Canadian enterprises.

3 — Relations with the United States

3.1. Effects in Canada of U.S. Anti-Trust Laws

NOTES FOR A SPEECH BY JUSTICE MINISTER E.D. FULTON, TO THE ANTI-TRUST SEC- Doc. 3.8
TION OF THE NEW YORK STATE BAR ASSOCIATION, NEW YORK, JANUARY 28, 1959.
(EXTRACTS)

It gives me great pleasure to be with you this evening and to be given the opportunity to address you on the subject of the extraterritorial application of the United States anti-trust laws.

Perhaps I should soften the effects of anything I may say later by emphasizing also that the anti-trust law of the United States and the anti-combines law of Canada appear to have much in common. Under both systems, for example, the issue in combination cases is the extent to which competition has been interfered with; and practices like price fixing have been declared by the courts to be per se offenses, at least when they affect a substantial part of the market. In such cases, the courts of both our countries have held that they will not entertain any defence to the effect that the prices that have been fixed or the other like restraints that have been imposed are moderate or reasonable.

The real issue, for us, in an anti-trust case launched in the United States, is not the merits or defects of the institutions or arrangements in Canada which the case seeks to alter. It is rather that in important aspects such cases appear to be directed against arrangements entered into by Canadian companies in Canada which are matters of Canadian commerce governed by Canadian laws including the anti-combines legislation and the patent legislation.

Such cases appear to illustrate a tendency, apparent in the field of foreign affairs as well as of anti-trust, for United States authorities to regard foreign subsidiaries of United States parent companies merely as projections of United States trade and commerce and thereby subject to United States policies in priority to the laws, customs and interests of the countries in which such subsidiaries are incorporated and carry on business.

Our specific objections to an action such as this are threefold: That it is concerned not so much with strict compliance with United States laws in the United States as it is concerned with actions in Canada of Canadian companies which actions are in accord with Canadian laws and Canadian commercial policy; that compliance with the decree sought may bring these companies in Canada into conflict with Canadian laws and/or policy; and thirdly that the only way effect could be given to such a decree is if American directors of U.S. companies give instructions to directors of Canadian companies to do something in Canada which is not in accord with Canadian business or commercial policy but is dictated by American policy. Nothing could more clearly illustrate the objectionably extra-territorial effect of the action taken.

The situation, as it strikes us, can be put in this way: that these cases reach into affairs that we regard as relating to our own sovereignty. These cases involve on the part of the United States more interference, and apparent assertion of a right to interfere, in commercial projects in Canada than is fitting or acceptable between two friendly but independent countries.

I understand that some legislation of a "fencing out" nature in response to this sort of thing was passed not long ago by The Netherlands. Perhaps also some such course could be followed in connection with our problem. But it would seem to create almost as many difficulties in other fields as it would cure in the particular field.

To mention only one complication, what for instance of the increasingly lugubrious position of the poor director? Increasingly he would be stretched and shackled, as it were, over the international boundary, with Washington putting lighted splinters under his toenails and Ottawa tearing off his fingernails.

No, the situation is bad enough now, but it might be even worse if each country takes ever more rigid positions, standing fast on its own legislation and insisting it is justified on the basis of strict legalistic interpretation of international law The prospect presents an undignified international spectacle, to say nothing of the discomfort it causes the poor director!

We feel that the proper solution to the problem lies in the full realization by United States authorities of the direct and indirect effects of these cases abroad and in a restraint in seeking from the courts, or applying, measures that interfere directly, substantially and deliberately with matters that are essentially matters of Canadian commerce within Canada. If United States authorities entertain feelings of concern that practices carried on in Canada are unduly restrictive of international trade, it would appear that this concern should be expressed through the usual channels. And I should like to emphasize that we agree that you would be entitled to expect us to act in a similar way.

3.2. The Issue of Foreign Investment

Doc. 3.9   STATEMENT BY MINISTER OF INDUSTRY, TRADE AND COMMERCE J.-L. PÉPIN, TO THE CHAMBER OF COMMERCE, VICTORIA, MAY 8, 1972.

British Columbia, like the rest of Canada, has generally welcomed, as we shall continue to welcome, the addition from the outside of capital, technology, and management to help develop Canadian resources.

Partly because of that "open-door" policy, Canadians have come to enjoy ... and take for granted ... many advantages — including our high standard of living.

Quite naturally, concern over our ability to direct our own economy has risen along with the degree of foreign ownership.

Most Canadians remain ambivalent on the subject, but, according to one recent survey, almost 44 per cent of us view American ownership of Canadian companies as having an adverse effect on our economy. This compares with 41 per cent two years ago, and 34 per cent three years ago.

Strangely enough, while Ontario is normally considered Canada's centre of "economic nationalism", the same survey found that the greatest anxiety actually exists in British Columbia, where 53 per cent of the public said U.S. ownership was a "bad thing" (University of Windsor, International Business Studies research, sample 5,000 Canadians).

The Federal Government shares this concern — hence the thorough examination, hence the announcement of May 2.

Screening, Another Step

Canada has, in the past, adopted a number of measures to maintain and foster Canadian control.

Foreign investment in banks and other key financial institutions, broadcasting facilities, newspapers and magazines is subject to specific laws effectively keeping them under Canadian control.

On the positive side, the present Government has set up the Canada Development Corporation, which will play an active role in developing strong Canadian-controlled businesses. The previous Government had set up the very successful Panarctic (Panarctic Oils Ltd).

The tax reform of last year contained several measures deliberately designed to reach the same objective I refer, for instance, to the 10 per cent limit on investment abroad by Pension Funds, and to small business tax advantages available to Canadians only.

Now another step is taken: the screening of takeovers.

The Policy

Foreign companies seeking to buy out or take over an existing Canadian business above a certain size will be screened.

The purpose will be to examine the proposals; to approve those that, on balance, will bring "significant benefits" to Canada; to negotiate with the proposed acquirer in those cases where he can reasonably expect to make a greater contribution to Canadian development; and to refuse to allow those takeovers that would not bring significant benefits to Canada.

Five factors will be taken into account:

1) the effect of the acquisition on the level and nature of Canadian economic activity and employment;
2) the degree and significance of participation by Canadians;
3) the effect of the acquisition on Canadian productivity, industrial efficiency, technological development, product innovation and product variety;
4) the effect of the acquisition on competition within Canadian industry or industries; and
5) the compatibility of acquisition with Canadian industrial and economic policies.

Some commentators have expressed regret at the generality of these factors. We couldn't help it. Right or wrong, criteria would have had to be too general; if made specific, they could be counterproductive (e.g. money inflow).

Why the Executive Branch?

Some have wondered why screening by the executive branch and not an independent tribunal?

The question to be answered in the screening process is not a legal one at all; it's basically an economic one — with social and political considerations.

Two ways of doing it were left — screening by a board or commission, or by a department. In both cases, the Minister and Government are "responsible", with different degree of autonomy for the instrument. We compromised — there will be an office of takeovers in the department, with a "registrar" leading it.

The office will use the knowledge and judgment of the nine specialized branches of Industry, Trade and Commerce and of other departments, Energy, Mines and Resources, Finance, etc. Had we set up a semi-independent commission, it would have had to create another centre of competence, bringing about costly and unnecessary duplication.

Why Not More Than Takeovers?

Why not extend the screening process to all forms of foreign investment, for example?

It was not judged to be politically practical and economically realistic — *in principle* by some, or *at this time* by others.

There was also the problem of administration. The complexities of screening 150 cases a year for "significant benefits" should be easy to imagine.

And there is no single way to increase the control by Canadians on their economy; just a few weeks ago, for example, my Department announced support for management training and for export marketing which will be used mostly by Canadian-owned firms

How Important Is the Decision to Screen Takeovers?

It has been observed that takeovers represent a fairly small portion of foreign investment, only between S and 20 per cent, annually.

I suggest that the establishment of the principle and of the apparatus for the screening of takeovers is a major development. The "standards" applicable to the screening of takeovers will sooner or later influence all foreign ownership. I call that the "exemplary value" of the new system.

Some have argued that the takeover law means little, because foreign firms can still enter the country directly and run a Canadian company out of business. Yes, but this would be done by direct competition, which means that the new company has out-performed, to the advantage of Canadian consumers, the existing Canadian operation. In most cases, there will be room for both.

The Interim Period

Questions have been raised over a possible flood of foreign takeovers occurring before the policy becomes law.

I hope this will not happen. Foreign investors are now well aware of the Government's intentions. Even in recent months, the Government has been voluntarily informed of many proposed acquisitions; I trust that companies contemplating important takeovers during the interim period will keep the Government advised.

While there will always be a wide range of opinion among Canadians about the actual balance between the benefits and costs of foreign investment, there is certainly no disagreement with the proposition that foreign direct investments should work in our best interests. The main purpose of the screening process will not be to block — though there will be some refusals — but to optimize the Canadian interest.

4. Automotive Products

Commonly known as the Auto Pact, the agreement signed in early January 1965 by PM Pearson and President Lyndon B. Johnson in Johnson City, Texas, was fundamental to the viability and growth of the Canadian automobile industry, then considerably limited in scale owing to the small size of the Canadian market. Under the terms of the Agreement, the industry took off.

The original intent was to integrate the industry into the overall North American market. Under the Agreement, Canada provided import-duty exemptions so as to encourage U.S. automobile companies to expand their production facilities in Canada. In return, these companies had to meet Canadian performance and content requirements. It also established tariffs (6.1%) against imports of automobiles from other countries, essentially Asian and European, and several overseas companies decided to set up branch plants in Canada in order to take advantage of the Agreement. However, its tariff provisions were opposed by some countries on behalf of some of their producers. The imports into Canada in this context were relatively small in terms of the overall market. Nevertheless, the representations of the countries concerned were considered by the World Trade Organization and it recently ruled in their favour. Canada has accepted the ruling and is now considering how best to accommodate it.

It is arguable whether there is still a need for the Agreement today. Its objectives were fully met some time ago. Not only did it boost the Canadian automobile manufacturing industry, particularly in Ontario, but it also created a thriving automotive parts industry. As a result of the Pact, Canada's automotive industry has become highly efficient and profitable, fully-integrated, internationally competitive, and strong.

Doc. 3.10   **The Automobile Pact**

AGREEMENT CONCERNING AUTOMOTIVE PRODUCTS BETWEEN THE GOVERNMENT OF CANADA AND THE GOVERNMENT OF THE UNITED STATES, JANUARY 16, 1965.

The Government of Canada and the Government of the United States of America,

Determined to strengthen the economic relations between their two countries;

Recognizing that this can best be achieved through the stimulation of economic growth and through the expansion of markets available to producers in both countries within the framework of the established policy of both countries of promoting multilateral trade; Recognizing that an expansion of trade can best be achieved through the reduction or elimination of tariff and all other barriers to trade operating to impede or distort the full and efficient development of each country's trade and industrial potential;

Recognizing the important place that the automotive industry occupies in the industrial economy of the two countries and the interests of industry, labour and consumers in sustaining high levels of efficient production and continued growth in the automotive industry;

Agree as follows:

Article I

The Governments of Canada and the United States, pursuant to the above principles, shall seek the early achievement of the following objectives:

(a) The creation of a broader market for automotive products within which the full benefits of specialization and large-scale production can be achieved;

(b) The liberalization of Canadian and United States automotive trade in respect of tariff barriers and other factors tending to impede it, with a view to enabling the industries of both countries to participate on a fair and equitable basis in the expanding total market of the two countries;

(c) The development of conditions in which market forces may operate effectively to attain the most economic pattern of investment, production and trade.

3 — Relations with the United States

It shall be the policy of each Government to avoid actions which would frustrate the achievement of these objectives.

Article II

(a) The Government of Canada, not later than the entry into force of the legislation contemplated in paragraph (b) of this Article, shall accord duty-free treatment to imports of the products of the United States described in Annex A. (Not printed.)[36]

(b) The Government of the United States, during the session of the United States Congress commencing on January 4, 1965, shall seek enactment of legislation authorizing duty-free treatment of imports of the products of Canada described in Annex B. (Not printed.)

In seeking such legislation, the Government of the United States shall also seek authority permitting the implementation of such duty free treatment retroactively to the earliest date administratively possible following the date upon which the Government of Canada has accorded duty-free treatment Promptly after the entry into force of such legislation, the Government of the United States shall accord duty-free treatment to the products of Canada described in Annex B. (Not printed)

Article III

The commitments made by the two Governments in this Agreement shall not preclude action by either Government consistent with its obligations under Part II of the General Agreement on Tariffs and Trade.

Article IV

(a) At any time, at the request of either Government, the two Governments shall consult with respect to any matter relating to this Agreement.

(b) Without limiting the foregoing, the two Governments shall, at the request of either Government, consult with respect to any problems which may arise concerning automotive producers in the United States which do not at present have facilities in Canada for the manufacture of motor vehicles, and with respect to the implications for the operation of this Agreement of new automotive producers becoming established in Canada

(c) No later than January 1, 1968, the two Governments shall jointly undertake a comprehensive review of the progress made towards achieving the objectives set forth in Article I.

During this review the Governments shall consider such further steps as may be necessary or desirable for the full achievement of these objectives.

---

[36]This agreement should be read in conjunction with the report of the Royal Commission on the Automotive Industry, Queen's Printer, 1961 (The "Bladen" Report).

Article V

Access to the Canadian and United States markets provided for under this Agreement may by agreement be accorded on similar terms to other countries.

Article VI

This Agreement shall enter into force provisionally on the date of signature and definitively on the date upon which notes are exchanged between the two Governments giving notice that appropriate action in their respective legislatures has been completed.

Article VII

This Agreement shall be of unlimited duration Each Government shall however have the right to terminate this Agreement twelve months from the date on which that Government gives written notice to the other Government of its intention to terminate the Agreement.

IN WITNESS WHEREOF the representatives of the two Governments have signed this Agreement.
DONE in duplicate at Johnson City, Texas, this 16th day of January 1965, in English and French, the two texts being equally authentic.
EN FOI DE QUOI les représentants des deux Gouvernements ont signé le présent Accord.
FAIT en double exemplaire à Johnson City, Texas, le 16 janvier 1965, en anglais et en français, les deux textes faisant également foi.

For the Government of Canada:
Pour le Gouvernement du Canada:

LESTER B. PEARSON
PAUL MARTIN

For the Government of the United States of America:
Pour le Gouvernement des États-Unis d'Amérique:

LYNDON B. JOHNSON
DEAN RUSK

Editor's notes: Regarding U.S. investments during the Trudeau years, 1968-1984, the Trudeau government was a good deal more nationalistic in its outlook vis-à-vis the United States, not only as regards investments, but also energy. It established a Foreign Investment Review Agency (FIRA) in 1974 to screen such investments. It was aimed primarily at the United States. The Agency did not survive the advent, in 1984, of the Mulroney government, which transformed FIRA into Investment Canada with a mandate aimed primarily at encouraging foreign investment.

3 — Relations with the United States

The Mulroney government also undid much of its predecessor's more nationalistic policies regarding energy, notably the National Energy Policy (NEP) and Petro Canada.[37]

The Chrétien government, elected in 1993, has maintained much the same approach as its predecessor.

4.1. New Climate for Investment

ADDRESS BY PM BRIAN MULRONEY, TO THE MEMBERS OF THE ECONOMIC CLUB, NEW YORK, DECEMBER 10, 1984. (EXTRACTS)

Doc. 3.11

My government has embarked on a new direction, which I want to talk to you about tonight. It is my fundamental belief that the challenge to our two countries is to improve and strengthen the mutual benefits from our roles as friends and partners.

In 1983, there was a national convention of my party, at which I sought the party leadership. During the campaign that preceded the convention, and in my speech to the convention, I pledged to re-establish that special relationship of trust with the United States and with all our allies.

Three months ago, there was a general election, in which I repeatedly stated my intention as head of a new government to restore harmony and cooperation with the United States. The statements that the new government has made were overwhelmingly endorsed by the people of Canada.

Many U.S. citizens are aware of the similarities between our two countries, a common heritage of individual liberty, shared democratic values, vast commercial links, an immense geography spanning a continent with an open and undefended border. Today, the most noteworthy measure of our relations is in our economic ties — in investment, in trade, in technology flows.

Almost one fifth of your exports go to Canada. Canada is the largest trading partner of the United States. The United States is the largest market for Canadian goods, services, and investment. In 1983, total trade between Canada and the United States exceeded $90 billion (U.S.). That amount exceeds by more than $27 billion (U.S.) your trade with Japan. In 1984, Canada-U.S. trade is likely to exceed $110 billion (U.S.). In fact, your trade with Canada exceeded total American trade with Germany, France, and Great Britain by almost $34 billion (U.S.) in 1983.

To put it somewhat differently, Canada is the leading trading partner of the United States, and your second largest trading partner is not Germany or Japan, but Ontario, a province of Canada.

---

[37]In 1991, the Mulroney government sold 30% of its holdings in Petro Canada to the public, in keeping with its policy of privatizing Crown corporations. The Chrétien government has maintained this policy and is currently considering further privatization measures.

The restoration of good and sound relationships between our two countries is clearly a top priority. So how should we manage our bilateral affairs. I have suggested several initiatives, both to President Reagan and to his cabinet colleagues.

The most important one is yearly meetings between the President of the United States and the Prime Minister of Canada: a process already begun. Second, regular meetings of senior ministers to be held alternately in the U.S. and Canada. Third, we favour an accelerated rhythm of bilateral parliamentary and congressional meetings to cover a wide range of topics of interest to our two countries, from steel imports to acid rain. Fourth, our provincial governments can and should meet more frequently with their geographical counterparts in the state governments.

During the years preceding the advent of my government, Canada turned inward and interventionist, at a time when the world economy was becoming more interdependent and open. In 1974, we started down that costly path with the Foreign Investment Review Act and, in 1981, we continued this approach with the New Energy Programme.

At the same time that Canada was turning inward economically, we were also giving other signals that led our friends and allies to question our commitment to the international agenda. Our support for NATO dropped to an embarrassingly low level, to the point that only tiny Luxembourg was contributing less on a *per capita* basis than Canada. So these are the main reasons why my government is so committed to rebuilding Canada's image in the world.

Our new government has embarked on a fundamental change in our economic direction. Our first priority and most immediate challenge is to restore fiscal responsibility in the federal government. Rising deficits have been recorded in each of the last 10 years. Restoring fiscal flexibility will require difficult decisions. And we have begun that process. After only two months in office, we were able to announce expenditure savings and revenue enhancement measures of over $4 billion on an annual $100 billion budget. This is a beginning.

The second part of our strategy for economic renewal is that we intend to redefine the role of government itself. Traditionally, government has had a much more activist role in Canada than in the United States. Today's reality, however, is that government in Canada has become much too big. It inhibits and distorts entrepreneurial activity. Some industries are over-regulated; others are over-protected. Getting the economy back on course means that we must adopt an approach that rewards entrepreneurship and risk-taking, and facilitates adjustment to the changing realities of markets and technologies.

The third part of our strategy is that we must adopt policies that foster higher investment. One immediate contribution is to change the Foreign Assessment Review Agency. My government has just introduced legislation, the specific purpose of which is to close down the old Foreign Investment Review Agency and to put in place a new body called Investment Canada, whose mandate will be to encourage and facilitate investment in Canada.

Investment Canada will be governed by two fundamental operational objectives: first, to facilitate investment in Canada; and second, to limit government intervention in the foreign investment area.

Our message in clear: Canada is open for business.

4.2. Energy

New climate for energy in Canada   Doc. 3.12

ADDRESS BY PM BRIAN MULRONEY, TO THE MEMBERS OF THE ECONOMIC CLUB OF NEW YORK, NEW YORK, DECEMBER 10, 1984. (EXTRACTS)

I would now like to say a few words about the directions we will be taking in the energy sector.

The goals of the NEP are commendable: its methods and its results clearly are not. Simply put, the NEP has failed to meet its three stated objectives: fairness, security of supply, and Canadianization.

Our immediate objective is to build a dynamic and growing energy sector. We want to reassure investors that Canada's energy sector offers outstanding opportunities to do business. We believe in the discipline of the marketplace.

We are undertaking now the consultations necessary to remove controls on oil prices in Canada. The same philosophy is being applied to our energy exports. Since November 1, for example, natural gas has been moving south at market-oriented prices by the buyers and the sellers, not the government.

We want to make changes in the back-in, the Crown interest provision which reserves 25% of all interests in Canada lands for the government. Canada was not built by expropriating retroactively other people's property. This practice is odious and shall not be followed by the new government of Canada.

Finally, in view of the major changes in the energy price outlook, we will be undertaking a comprehensive review of federal energy taxation. Our objective is the ensure that appropriate investment incentives are provided in the taxation system. Canadianization remains an objective. But the system must be fair, and it shall be.

5. The Free Trade Agreement

Initially, the Free Trade Agreement (FTA) was a very controversial subject. It did not have the support of the majority of Canadians during the 1988 elections. Both the Liberals and NDP — whose combined share of the national vote was higher than that of the Conservatives — opposed it. Several provinces, likewise, were sceptical about it. Nevertheless, with a comfortable majority (169 out of 295 seats) in the House of Commons, the Government went ahead with its project, secured parliamentary approval, and put it into effect on January 1, 1989, as scheduled. Although the Liberal Party was opposed to the FTA during the 1989 election campaign and subsequently, the Chrétien government accepted it when it came to power in 1993.

The Mulroney government began its campaign to secure a Free Trade Agreement with the United States not long after the elections of 1984. The rationale or philosophy behind the move was to seek to protect Canada from growing trade protectionist pressures in the United States: In other words, to shelter and protect Canadian trade with the United States and, in that respect, one of the most important provisions of the FTA is its mechanism for the adjudication of disputes.

The FTA's trade results have been extremely positive for both countries and in this respect analyses and comments made on the occasion of its Tenth Anniversary in January 1999 were generally laudatory and favourable. Trade between the two countries has increased dramatically. Most Canadian companies adjusted reasonably well to the new situation and, helped along by a generally weak Canadian dollar, exports rose as they became more competitive. In addition, unemployment decreased towards the end of the 1990s as the economy gained strength.

Yet, the trade boom tells only part of the story. The Canadian economy on the whole has performed less well than that of the United States. The gap in productivity between the two countries, although lessening somewhat, is still considerable. Salary levels and living standards in Canada, compared with those in the United States, are lower.

It is of course impossible to say how much all of this has been due solely to the FTA or whether things would have been equally successful without it. They certainly would have been different. All told, however, the results especially on the trade side — its primary objective — have been good and perhaps two cheers for the FTA, instead of the usual three, sums it up best. However that may be, the FTA is here to stay.

The Free Trade Agreement is an extremely voluminous and complex document that took many months of intense effort to negotiate and complete. It contains more than 2,000 articles. It is hoped that the following summaries will provide guidelines for further research on an extremely complex subject.[38]

---

[38]The handiest summary of NAFTA and, by extension, the FTA is contained in

3 — Relations with the United States

The Free Trade Agreement: Highlights

Doc. 3.13

ADDRESS BY INTERNATIONAL TRADE MINISTER JOHN C. CROSBIE, TO THE NATIONAL CITIZENS' COALITION, TORONTO, OCTOBER 18, 1988. (EXTRACTS)

Let me outline for you ten of the major benefits of the Free Trade Agreement:

1) Increased and more secure access to our major export markets in the U.S., that accounts for almost 80% of Canada's overall exports;

2) All tariffs will be eliminated on trade with the U.S. by 1998 (Article 401), helping Canadian exporters to sell into the U.S. and reducing prices for Canadian consumers;

3) This will mean greater opportunity for further resource processing in Canada: for example, the current tariff of up to 25% on processed fish exports will be eliminated opening up new jobs for value added in places like Newfoundland;

4) The FTA establishes free access for Canadian red meat exports and removes the threat of quotas (Article 704). Australia and New Zealand recently agreed to restrict beef exports to the U.S., faced with the threat of U.S. quotas;

5) It will be much easier for temporary entry for Canadian business people and service personnel (Article 1502); this is especially important for small and medium-sized businesses, including those in the service industries;

6) Canadian businesses gain access to an additional $3 billion in U.S. federal procurement contracts (Article 1304);

7) The FTA greatly limits the threat of quantitative restrictions and the U.S.'s ability to use these to force Canada to adopt "voluntary" export restraints, such as for steel (Article 407);

8) The U.S. will give Canadian energy products secure access to the U.S. market; this is important for oil, gas, electricity and uranium (Articles 902 and 905);

9) Canada will no longer be hit by U.S. global safeguard actions aimed at others (Article 1102);

10) The dispute settlement procedure will protect against politically-inspired misuse of U.S. trade laws, to prevent the repetitions of decisions like that on softwood lumber (Chapter 19).

Chapter 14 of the FTA deals with services. It lists the services that are covered by the obligations in the Agreement. If a service is not on the list, then it is not covered. Neither our publicly-provided health care system, nor other services provided by the government is

---

DFAIT's News Release No. 165 of August 12, 1992. It also published two useful booklets about NAFTA in 1992. They are *NAFTA: At a glance* and *NAFTA: What's it all about?* The trilateral trade figures are from the latter publication and are based on data from Statistics Canada and the U.S. Department of Commerce, as are the figures for 1998.

included. (For that matter, privately-provided health care is not on the list either.)

The services chapter of the FTA does cover commercially-provided health care management services. However, there is no obligation under the FTA for governments in Canada to permit any such commercially-provided management of health care services, for instance, contracting for a private company to manage purchasing for a hospital.

Of course, the FTA is not yet in place, but I am confident that in the electoral contest now underway, Canadians will support the government, in part because of Free Trade.

Doc. 3.14   **The Canada-U.S. Free Trade Agreement: Synopsis**
MONOGRAPH PUBLISHED BY THE INTERNATIONAL TRADE COMMUNICATIONS GROUP, DFAIT, OTTAWA. EFFECTIVE JANUARY 1, 1989. (EXTRACTS)[39]

Part Seven, Chapter 20: Other provisions

During the course of the negotiations, the two governments worked on an overall framework covering the protection of intellectual property rights (trademarks, copyright, patents, industrial design, and trade secrets). The two governments agreed to continue to cooperate and work towards better international intellectual property rules.

From the beginning of the negotiations, Canadians expressed concern that an agreement might erode the government's capacity to encourage and help Canada's cultural industries (film and video, music and sound recording, publishing, cable transmission, and broadcasting) and thus contribute to the development of Canada's unique cultural identity. In order to remove any ambiguity that Canada's unique cultural identity remains untouched by the FTA, the two governments agreed in Article 2005 on a specific provision indicating that nothing in the FTA affects the ability of either Party to pursue cultural policies.

Other provisions, in résumé

New businesses in Canada or the United States will operate under rules for domestic investors.

A panel of two Canadians, two Americans, and a mutually-acceptable fifth person, will adjudicate disputes over unfair subsidies of goods and review antidumping and countervailing duty decisions, based on applicable Canadian or U.S. legislation. The two parties will negotiate definitions of fair subsidies.

The combined effect of the bilateral review of existing law and

---

[39]**Editor's note:** The Synopsis is a comprehensive summary (61 pages) of the FTA. In order to avoid duplication with the immediately preceding document, the following extracts deal with some of the important items in the FTA not covered in Mr. Crosbie's address. (The monograph is available for consultation in the DFAIT library).

3 — Relations with the United States

the development of a new set of rules will be to ensure that, by the time all tariffs are removed and other aspects of the Agreement are phased in, Canadian firms will have not only more open access but also more secure and more predictable access.

The Free Trade Agreement: Timetable (Extracts from: Synopsis)

Effective January 1, 1989.

The FTA and its rules covering such issues as procurement, services and investment, and border measures come into effect after both countries exchange Instruments of Ratification, when the first round of tariff reductions will begin. For those sectors ready to compete now, tariffs will be eliminated; other goods will begin phasing out their tariffs over a 5- or 10-year period. The first tranche will cover about 15% of all goods traded between the two countries including:

computer and related equipment	some pork
some unprocessed fish	fur & fur garments
leather	whiskey
yeast	animal feeds
unwrought aluminum	ferro alloys
vending machines & parts	needles
airbrakes for railway cars	skis
skates	warranty repairs
some paper-making machinery	motorcycles

Both nations will end any direct export subsidies to agricultural products going to the other partner. The embargo on used-vehicles imports (those less than 15 years old) from the U.S. will be lifted in stages. Cars more than 8 years old will be allowed entry to Canada duty-free immediately. The age limit will drop about two years every 12 months, until 1994. The embargo on used aircraft parts will be lifted. Buy-Canadian and Buy-American government procurement policies will be eased. The Canadian markup difference beyond normal commercial considerations on U.S. wines will begin to be phased out. The differential markups on imports of U.S. distilled liquor will be eliminated entirely. The federal government will only review direct U.S. takeovers of Canadian companies worth more than $25 million, up from the current $5 million. For indirect takeovers, review will be set at assets of $100 million, up from $50 million. Improved temporary entry for business people is implemented in both countries. U.S. uranium enrichment restrictions cease.

October 1, 1989

Tariffs on exports to the U.S. of specialty steel products will be lifted in stages.

Canadian Foreign Policy 1945-2000

January 1, 1990

Tariffs will drop another fifth or tenth depending on the schedule.

January 1, 1991

Foreign investment review for direct takeovers rises to $100 million; for indirect takeovers, $500 million. Tariffs will continue to drop; the 35% U.S. duty on Canadian shakes and shingles is scheduled to come off.

January 1, 1992

Tariffs will have been lifted on another 35% of dutiable goods, including:

subway cars	chemicals, including resins but excluding drugs & cosmetics
printed matter	furniture
paper & paper products	hardwood plywood
paints	aftermarket auto parts
explosives	some meats, including lamb
telecommunications	engineering

The embargo on the import of used cars ends, as does the U.S. curb on lottery materials,

January 1, 1994

U.S. customs user fees and duty drawbacks in other countries will end. U.S. foreign trade provisions will change to Canada's benefit. New régimes on countervail and anti-dumping should come into effect.

January 1, 1995

Tariffs take another drop.

January 1, 1996

There will be another tariff cut. This is the final deadline for Canada and the U.S. to agree on new trade-remedy rules. Production-based duty waivers for production in the auto industry will end.

January 1, 1997

Another tariff reduction.

January 1, 1998

Tariffs will have ended on remaining goods:

most agricultural products	steel
textiles & apparel	appliances
softwood plywood	beef
pleasure craft	tires

The snapback provisions on vegetables and fresh fruits will remain for another decade.

6. The North American Free Trade Agreement (NAFTA)

Canada, Mexico, and the United States concluded negotiations regarding NAFTA in August 1992. The Agreement was approved by Parliament at the end of 1992 and by the Congresses of Mexico and the United States at the end of 1993, for implementation as from January 1, 1994.

It is basically a Mexican idea and the then President of Mexico, Salinas de Gortari, lobbied particularly vigorously in its favour. Several countries in Latin America and the Caribbean area have expressed an interest in joining, but so far none has done so.[40]

Like the FTA between Canada and the United States, on which it is modelled and which it closely resembles, NAFTA is an extremely voluminous document. It too contains more than 2,000 articles.

In short, the Agreement when fully implemented will eliminate trade and investment barriers among the three countries. It provides for the eventual disappearance, in *tranches* of five and ten years, of most tariffs on Canadian, Mexican, and United States goods produced by the NAFTA partners and traded among the three countries. While tariffs on some Mexican goods were eliminated on January 1, 1994, others will be phased out in five or ten equal annual stages, as provided in the Agreement. A five-year extension to 15 years of tariff protection for certain sensitive products, mainly agricultural, was approved. In the financial services field Canadian and United States banks, for instance, will be able to gradually expand their operations in Mexico and all restrictions will be eliminated within ten years.

Tariffs on goods traded between Canada and the United States will continue to be eliminated at the rates negotiated under the FTA, but could be eliminated faster under the NAFTA accelerated

---

[40]At the Inter-American Heads of Government Summit Meeting in Miami, in 1994, it was resolved to conclude by 2005 the negotiations for a Free Trade Agreement of the Americas (FTAA), in which barriers to trade and investment would be progressively eliminated. These negotiations are on-going. DFAIT News Release No. 98/21, March 19, 1998, provides a summary of the FTAA's General Principles and Objectives, along with a report on organization and progress of the negotiations. Incidentally, Canada and Chile signed a free trade agreement modelled on NAFTA, on November 18, 1996. See DFAIT No. 211, November 18, 1996, for a summary of its main features.

tariff elimination process.

NAFTA protects the cultural industries of both Canada and Mexico. Canada's Auto Pact with the United States remained intact until recently. Social and health services, as well as the large-scale exportation of water, are exempt from its provisions. Mexico's nationalized petroleum industry is also exempt, on constitutional grounds, although its petro-chemical and related industries are included. In the energy sector, the provisions of the FTA remain unchanged regarding Canada's energy relations with the United States, particularly its stipulation that Canada continue to supply oil and natural gas to the United States in times of emergency or shortages. The Liberal government, elected in the fall of 1993, sought to obtain the same energy protection as Mexico under NAFTA, but was unable to get the United States to agree. Instead, it issued a unilateral declaration that Canada would interpret and apply NAFTA's provisions in a way that maximizes energy security for Canadians. However, it did secure an undertaking from the United States to negotiate clear definitions of fair government subsidies and unfair export pricing or dumping. (Discussions with the United States in this and other sectors are ongoing.) Like the FTA, NAFTA contains provisions for the settlement of disputes.

The Agreement was strongly opposed in Canada and the United States by groups worried about Mexico's laxer environmental and labour practices and procedures, particularly its lower labour costs. With that in mind, as regards the environment, NAFTA allows Canada and the United States to maintain stringent standards, including the right to prohibit imports that fall short of those standards. In addition, as regards labour, in order to protect against actual or threatened injury from increased imports, the Agreement permits the temporary re-imposition of higher pre-NAFTA tariff rates.

The three-way merchandise trade flows involved in the Agreement are impressive. The 1992 statistics of imports and exports to and from Canada, the United States and Mexico are as follows:

	Exports (to)		
	Canada	Mexico	U.S.A.
(From)			
Canada	——	$771 million	$125.5 billion
Mexico	$2.8 billion	——	$42.5 billion
U.S.A.	$96.6 billion	$48.6 billion	——

By the end of the decade, Canadian annual exports to the United States had more than doubled, reaching $271 billion, and exports to Mexico had also nearly doubled to $1.4 billion. Currently, annual two-way trade between Canada and the United States now stands at more than $1 billion of exchanges in goods and services per day.

In Canada, political opinion was split about NAFTA, particularly in Ontario where the provincial government of the time (NDP) opposed it. On the other hand, the Official Opposition (Conservative) was in favour. After the defeat of the NDP government at the polls, its Conservative successor accepted its terms. Quebec, on the other hand, was strongly in favour of NAFTA from the very beginning.

7. Environment

Acid rain and water pollution, affecting the Great Lakes and other shared waterways, were the main environmental preoccupations which governments, whether federal or provincial, have addressed particularly vigorously in Canada's relations with the United States.

The Reagan administration's rather detached approach to environmental concerns, which tended to drown acid rain, for instance, in scientific and statistical studies, did not of course make matters easier for Canada. So it is pleasant to note that its successor, the Bush government (1989-1993), was more mindful of the problem and willing to do something about it.

The United States *Clean Air Act* was signed into law by President George Bush on November 15, 1990. He and PM Mulroney signed the *Canada-United States Air Quality Control Accord* on March 13, 1991. This bilateral accord builds on the *Clean Air Act* and on the *Canadian Acid Rain Control Programme* of 1985. In addition to the control of acid rain precursors, the Accord provides for the prevention of air quality deterioration from transboundary air pollution, as well as the protection of parks and wilderness areas. This legislation has done much to improve matters regarding trans-border air quality problems generally, although certain problems in this area, affecting mainly southwestern Ontario, continue to build up.

Likewise, there is progress to be reported regarding water pollution. The quality of Great Lakes water is improving, thanks in great part to the Great Lakes Water Quality Treaty and the vigilance of the International Joint Commission. Several problems documented in earlier volumes, such as the Garrison Diversion, the flooding of the Skagit Valley, have been solved or are well on the way to being so. However, others, such as pollution by oil tankers, are still matters for concern. Nevertheless, progress has been such that rather less is heard today about the environment as shared with the United States than two decades ago.

Since the mid-1990s, the possibility of exports of water from Canada to the United States has attracted a good deal of attention. This question is dealt with in the next document.

Doc. 3.15   **[Bulk water exports]**

FINAL REPORT FROM THE INTERNATIONAL JOINT COMMISSION ON BULK WATER RE-MOVAL FROM THE GREAT LAKES. GOVERNMENT OF CANADA NEWS RELEASE NO. 45, MARCH 15, 2000. (EXTRACTS)[41]

FM Axworthy and Environment Minister Anderson stated, on receipt of the IJC Final Report, that it supports Canada's environmental concerns regarding the removal of bulk water from Canada's major drainage basins. Canada, they added, is already taking action in this respect. Under Bill C-15, now before Parliament, the Great Lakes and other boundary waters will be protected from bulk removals under Federal law.

They announced earlier, on February 10, 1999, (on the occasion of the IJC's Interim Report) that the government would introduce amendments to the International Boundary Waters Treaty Act which will enable us to prohibit bulk removals of water from boundary waters such as the Great Lakes.

In addition, the Federal government considered the IJC Interim Report to be the first component of a three-part Federal strategy to prohibit removals of water, including water for exports, announced on February 10, 1999. The other two components of the strategy are the amendments to the International Boundary Waters Treaty Act, and the development of a Canada-wide accord with the Provinces and Territorial Governments to prohibit removals, including removals for export, from Canadian watersheds. Discussions are ongoing with the Provinces and Territories. Alberta and British Columbia already have legislation prohibiting the bulk removal of water, including exports, and Ontario is currently finalizing such legislation.[42]

7.1. Acid Rain: A serious bilateral issue

Doc. 3.16   **[Canada-U.S. negotiations]**

ADDRESS BY ENVIRONMENT MINISTER JOHN ROBERTS, TO THE AIR POLLUTION CONTROL ASSOCIATION, NEW ORLEANS, LOUISIANA, JUNE 21, 1982. (EXTRACTS)

In Canada we are deeply disappointed with the state of negotiations

---

[41]For additional information, please visit Environment Canada's website on the Green Lane: www.ec.gc.ca/press/bulk_water_b_e.htm.

[42]A useful *Backgrounder* on the subject is attached to Government of Canada Press Release No. 23 of February 10, 1999, available on website: www.dfait-maeci.gc.ca.

between my country and the United States on acid rain. The foot dragging and interference in the development of scientific information has reached frustrating proportions.

The Reagan Administration's rejection of our proposal to reduce sulphur dioxide emissions in eastern North America by 50% by 1990 and a clear indication that it may be some considerable time before it will be able even to begin to discuss control actions are a bitter pill for us to swallow.

Remarks I made some time ago in favour of acid rain control were encapsulated in an October 16, 1981 editorial in the *Washington Post*:

> Enough is known about acid rain to put an end to the debate over whether the phenomenon is real, man-made, and damaging.
>
> It is all three. The important area for action now is how best to go about reducing sulphur and nitrogen oxide emissions, and how fast.

Yet, incredible as is may seem to you scientists and experts in the field, there are those who still insist that acid rain poses no immediate threat, and that it should be a subject merely for further research, not quick action.

Are we justified in taking immediate action? The answer can only be *yes*. Canada is already doing a lot to curtail acid rain. Of course we must do a lot more, and we are prepared to do so. In February of this year, my provincial colleagues and I committed ourselves to reduce sulphate deposition by 20 kilograms per hectare a year by 1990. We urged the United States to initiate control programmes also.

I will be the first to admit that Canada does not have clean hands when it comes to acid rain. Yet in Canada as a whole 50% of our acid rain originates in the United States. In Ontario, as much as 75%.

On the Canadian Shield, the area most sensitive to acid rain, tourism is a $700 million a year industry. Tourists do not like dead fish and dead lakes. In eastern Canada damage to buildings and other structures caused by corrosion from acid rain is conservatively estimated at $500 million annually. Our fresh water fisheries, our eastern forest products industry, are all seriously threatened by acid rain.

This, very briefly, is the Canadian case against acid rain. The gravity of the problem has been recognized by both our countries and the need for swift action has been embodied in the U.S./Canada Memorandum of Intent. This document, if lived up to, will set us well on the way towards eliminating cooperatively the threat in the only way that matters: reducing — at source — the pollution that causes it.

Canadians are disappointed with developments in the United States. We find that regulations in the United States are being relaxed, with two excuses. First, that ambient air quality standards are being met or improved. But air quality is by definition, local. It is not a standard relevant to long-range pollution transportation. Second, we are told that existing regulations permit exemptions.

That is not what we expected when we signed the Memorandum of Intent.

7.2. The Quebec Summit

[The environment]

JOINT STATEMENT ON THE ENVIRONMENT, MARCH 18, 1985.

During their *tête-à-tête*, the President and the Prime Minister discussed environmental matters at some length. They took note of the 75-year history of environmental cooperation between the two countries as exemplified by the Boundary Waters Treaty, the Great Lakes Water Quality Agreement, and the recent Skagit River-Ross Dam Treaty. They expressed their determination to continue to deal with U.S.-Canadian environmental issues in a responsible and cooperative spirit.

In the spirit of cooperation, and in recognition that the actions of one country are of concern to the other, there was agreement that a high level Special Envoy would be appointed by each government to examine the acid rain issue and report back to the President and Prime Minister by their next meeting.

The Envoys will:

(a) Pursue consultation on laws and regulations that bear on pollutants thought to be linked to acid rain;

(b) Enhance cooperation in research efforts, including clean-fuel technology and smelter controls;

(c) Pursue means to increase the exchange of relevant scientific information; and

(d) Identify efforts to improve the U.S and Canadian environment.[43]

8. Fisheries

Maritime boundaries and fishing concerns are very old problems with the United States going back to the Halibut Treaty of 1923, the first international treaty signed by Canada in its own right. Recently discussions have concentrated on two main subjects: Pacific salmon and the Georges Bank area of the Gulf of Maine.

The discussions concerning the Georges Bank area of the Gulf of Maine stemmed mainly from the extension in 1977 by both

---

[43]Foot-dragging of this sort prevailed until the end of the Reagan administration, despite persistent efforts by SSEA Clark and the Canadian Embassy in Washington to get things moving along. Matters progressed more expeditiously during President Bush's term of office (1989–1993).

countries of fisheries jurisdictions from 12 to 200 miles, as sanctioned by the UN Law of the Sea Convention.

This extension of jurisdictions caused two problems. The first was how to draw the boundaries between the fishing-zones of the two countries and how to deal with fishing in the disputed area pending an agreement on the boundaries. The second resulted from the fact that large areas that had previously been high seas, where both countries had fished, now fell under the exclusive jurisdiction of either Canada or the United States.

Despite fisheries and boundaries agreements signed by both countries in 1979, settling most problems, it was not possible to reach an understanding on the Gulf of Maine boundaries. The parties agreed to submit the dispute to the International Court of Justice in The Hague for a binding settlement. Its decision was announced in October 1984. Both the agreements with the United States and the Court's decision are documented below.

Canada/U.S. fisheries and boundary agreements
Doc. 3.18

DFAIT COMMUNIQUÉ, OTTAWA, MARCH 29, 1979.

Four agreements will be signed with the United States this afternoon: two relating to the Atlantic Coast and two concerning the Pacific Coast.

The East Coast Fishery Resource Agreement establishes a Canada-U.S. Fisheries Commission and provides for cooperative management, and for access and entitlements, to specific stocks of mutual concern.

The Treaty to submit the delimitation of the maritime boundary of the Gulf of Maine to binding dispute settlement and the Special Agreement provide for the submission of the dispute to a five judge Chamber of the International Court of Justice for a final decision on the placement of the boundary.

The two Pacific Coast Agreements include a Protocol to the International Pacific Halibut Convention, which will permit continued Canadian access to halibut off the coast of Alaska for the next two years and an Exchange of Notes giving the United States access to groundfish off British Columbia for a similar period.

Gulf of Maine boundary case
Doc. 3.19

OPENING STATEMENT BY JUSTICE MINISTER MARK MACGUIGAN, TO THE INTERNATIONAL COURT OF JUSTICE, THE HAGUE, APRIL 2, 1984. (EXTRACTS)

Canada has claimed less than half of the Georges Bank, since it first began to issue oil and gas permits in the Gulf of Maine area in 1964. The United States has claimed the whole of the Bank since 1976. The difference in the extent of the claims of Canada and the United States is thus more than a simple quantitative difference. Whatever may be the outcome of the present proceedings, the United States will not cease to be present on Georges Bank, since the Canadian claim leaves more than half the Bank to the United States. If the Court were to accept the U.S. claim, however, the result would be Canada's eviction from the Bank as a whole.

The boundary proposed by Canada for the Gulf of Maine is a reasonable and balanced one whose origins date back to 1964. It results from the application of the law to geography. Its equitable character is confirmed by non-geographical relevant circumstances that are rooted in legal principles proper to the zones to be delimited. The conduct of the parties attests to these facts.

Doc. 3.20 **Gulf of Maine Case: International Court's decision**

SUMMARY OF DFAIT COMMUNIQUÉ, OCTOBER 12, 1984.

Although the full implications for Canada of the Court's decision are still being examined, the Ministers concerned with the case have noted with satisfaction that the boundary confirms Canadian jurisdiction over a substantial part of Georges Bank.

In accordance with the terms of the Special Agreement, both parties have accepted that the decision of the Court is final and binding. The Department of Fisheries and Oceans is currently notifying Canadian fishermen of the geographical coordinates of the new boundary.

The case centred in a dispute over the rich fishery resources and the potential hydrocarbon resources of Georges Bank, a large detached bank lying seaward of the Gulf of Maine off the coasts of Nova Scotia and Massachusetts.

8.1. *Pacific Salmon*

If 20th century fisheries relations with the United States started with halibut in the 1920s, they closed with salmon. Roughly a decade ago, serious problems arose regarding the Pacific salmon fisheries. They were reminiscent of those affecting cod stocks on the East Coast and stemmed from much the same causes: overfishing and declining stocks, competition, and boundary problems.

In 1996, Canada announced that discussions for a new Pacific Salmon Treaty would be conducted with the United States on an ongoing basis, since in the phraseology of the announcement "Canada is committed for the long term to solving the problem in order to meet the interests of British Columbia fishers, particularly against Alaskan competition, and to ensure the well-being of the resource". The 1985 Treaty had expired and, without its conservation and other protective as well as enforcement provisions, Alaskan interests began removing on a large scale salmon headed for British Columbia's rivers. Matters became fairly violent at one time when B.C. fishing interests retaliated against the Alaskans. Many competing interests are involved: in Canada, both federal and provincial, at times in disagreement; in the United States likewise, notably Alaska, which has been more generally assertive in the matter than Washington. Talks among the parties concerned — frequently interrupted — are continuing.

9. Arctic Sovereignty

There is one particular problem in Canada's relations with the United States that is of very long standing but rather sporadic in occurrence: transit through the Northwest Passage. The United States does not recognize Canada's sovereignty over these waters. For Canada, they are internal waters. The United States claims that they are international waters and every so often sends a ship through.

In the late 1960s and early 1970s, when the United States tanker *Manhattan* and two icebreakers went through, the Trudeau government dealt with the issue by passing legislation which made it clear that the Northwest Passage was open for the passage of shipping of all nations, but subject to conditions required to protect the delicate balance of the Canadian Arctic.

In 1985, when the U.S. Coast Guard vessel *Polar Sea* went through, the response took a rather different turn. The Mulroney government opted *inter alia* to build a Polar Class 8 icebreaker, the largest of its kind in the world, to assert sovereignty over the Passage by keeping it open.

Policy on Canadian sovereignty in the Arctic   Doc. 3.21

STATEMENT BY SSEA JOE CLARK, HOUSE OF COMMONS, SEPTEMBER 10, 1985. (EXTRACTS)

The voyage of the *Polar Sea* demonstrated that Canada, in the past, had not developed the means to ensure our sovereignty over time. During that voyage, Canada's legal claim was protected, but when we looked for tangible ways to exercise our sovereignty we found that our cupboard was nearly bare.

The policy of this government is to maintain the natural unity of the Canadian Arctic archipelago. Arctic sovereignty has long been upheld by Canada. No previous government, however, has defined its precise limits or delineated Canada's internal waters and territorial sea. This government proposes to do so.

In summary, these are the measures we are announcing today:

1) Immediate adoption of an Order-in-Council establishing straight

baselines around the Arctic archipelago, to be effective January 1, 1986;

2) Immediate adoption of a Canadian Laws Offshore Application Act;

3) Immediate talks with the United States on cooperation in Arctic waters, on the basis of full respect for Canadian sovereignty;

4) An immediate increase of surveillance overflights of our Arctic waters by aircraft of the Canadian Armed Forces, and immediate planning for Canadian naval activity in the Eastern Arctic in 1986;

5) The immediate withdrawal of the 1970 reservation to Canada's acceptance of the compulsory jurisdiction of the IJC;

6) Construction of a Polar Class 8 icebreaker.[44]

10. St. Lawrence Seaway and Power Development

The St. Lawrence Seaway, one of the great engineering projects of the 20th century, became a prominent feature in Canadian-United States relations during the 1950s. Discussions with the United States on the subject had been interrupted by the Second World War and resumed almost immediately thereafter. The United States was generally hesitant about the project and it is only after Canada announced in 1952 that it was prepared to go ahead on its own that it decided to join in. The power aspects of the Seaway are still extremely valuable, but its maritime transportation side has been experiencing considerable difficulty lately as a result of competition from faster container transport by ship, truck, and rail.[45]

---

[44]The icebreaker, an extremely costly initiative, did not survive subsequent budget cuts.

[45]Regrettably, it is not possible to document the Seaway here, owing to space limitations. Interested researchers should consult R.A.M., Chapter VIII, pp. 259-276, for an extensive and detailed account of the subject.

4

The Far East

1. Japan

1.1. Peace Treaty

THE SECOND WORLD WAR CEASED IN EUROPE IN EARLY MAY, 1945, but continued until August in the Far East. During the interval Japanese forces were on the defensive everywhere. On July 26, President Harry S. Truman and the newly-elected Labour Party leader, PM Attlee, meeting in Potsdam, issued a proclamation calling upon the Japanese to surrender, if they wished to avoid the destruction of their country, and setting forth surrender terms. The terms were tough but the Allies did not refuse to deal with the existing government, as has had been the case with Germany. Although they contemplated fostering a democratic system of government for Japan, they did not call for the abdication of Emperor Hirohito. This turned out to be very important, both in expediting surrender and in carrying out its terms afterwards.

At first the Japanese government was deadlocked over surrender, but new catastrophes were in the offing. On August 6 the first atomic bomb was dropped over Hiroshima; two days later the U.S.S.R. formally declared war against Japan; on August 9, a second atomic bomb was dropped over Nagasaki.

The cabinet accepted the advice of the Emperor to surrender and did so unconditionally on August 14. On September 2, an Instrument of Surrender was signed on board the U.S.S. *Missouri* in Tokyo Bay. All states actively at war with Japan, including Canada, were invited to be represented and to sign it.

After the surrender in Europe, Canada had been rapidly organizing a force to take part in the Pacific hostilities but no units had been sent forward before the Japanese surrender. The government decided against participating in the occupation of Japan on the ground that it had commitments in Europe, and the Pacific Force was accordingly disbanded on September.

In 1946, by arrangement with the United States whose forces were in occupation of Japan, Canada sent a civilian liaison mission to Tokyo to maintain contact with the occupation authorities and to look after Canadian commercial and other interests.

After the surrender Japan was immediately occupied by American forces under General MacArthur thereby forestalling division of the country into separate occupation zones as had happened in Germany. Although the U.S.S.R. pressed for a share in occupation, this was avoided. Unlike Germany, Japan was never without a government after defeat, and the United States from the first held the Japanese government responsible for carrying out the terms of surrender instead of attempting to set up a military government as had been done in Germany.

In 1947 the United States proposed a peace conference. Decisions were to be taken by a two-thirds majority vote. The Soviet Union argued that the treaty should be drafted by the Great Powers alone and that the other allied powers should be brought in afterwards to approve the draft. A stalemate resulted and it was only several years later that a final peace treaty finally emerged.

The treaty laid the foundations for Japan's current political structure and institutions, as well as the tremendous industrial and commercial development that have made of Japan the world's second most powerful economy.

Doc. 4.1 **Comment on the treaty**

STATEMENT BY SSEA L.B. PEARSON, HOUSE OF COMMONS, APRIL 8, 1952. (EXTRACTS)

The treaty is a generous one. It has been represented by one of its main architects as a treaty of reconciliation, and that, I think, is what it is. Last October, when we were discussing this matter I referred to it as a good treaty, and I still believe it is a good treaty. It is, of course, not a perfect one, but I doubt if we had had months of discussion at San Francisco that we would have made it a better one. It restores Japanese sovereignty, but that sovereignty will be confined to the four main islands of the Japanese empire. It places no restrictions on Japan's economy or on Japan's ability to defend itself. Most important of all, the treaty sets Japan free to pursue a peaceful destiny, as we all must hope, and gives her an opportunity to contribute to the security and stability of the whole Pacific area.

The treaty was negotiated, as I explained last October, through diplomatic channels rather than through the more normal conference procedure. That was unusual procedure admittedly, but it was one which was made necessary by the circumstances. As early as 1947, the United States government had proposed to its allies a conference for the signing of the Japanese peace treaty in the usual way. This procedure was impossible because of the attitude taken at that time and subsequently by the Soviet union, which insisted that any such treaty should be negotiated not by a conference where all those who participated in the war against Japan would be present, but in the presence of the council of foreign ministers which would have given the U.S.S.R. and other members of the council a veto.

To avoid this procedure and the use of the veto in this connection, in September 1950 I believe it was the President of the United States initiated diplomatic discussions with the other countries represented on the Far Eastern commission with a view to negotiation by such discussion of a treaty, the final text of which we have before us today. The Canadian government participated in those discussions and was given ample opportunity to express its opinions on the various drafts as they were presented. These opinions of ours were not always accepted, Mr. Speaker, but the text which we have before us now does not represent the complete views of any one country which participated in those discussions, and is essentially a compromise document.

The Soviet union was kept fully informed of these discussions while they took place, but contributed little to them except abuse. When the conference was called in San Francisco to put the finishing touches on this process, not to negotiate a treaty but to sign one and go over the text of the draft which we have before us, the Soviet union and its satellite states were represented. As hon. members know, they refused, as indeed some other countries refused, to sign the draft.

The territorial adjustments are outlined in the treaty. The Potsdam proclamation ... provided that Japanese sovereignty would be limited to the four major islands and such minor islands as the allied powers would determine. Chapter II of the peace treaty carries out those surrender terms. Japan renounces all rights, title and claim to Korea, Formosa, the Pescadores, the Kurile Islands and South Sakhalin. In addition she renounces any rights she had with respect to the islands which she had under the terms of a league of nations mandate. Under article 3 of the treaty Japan retains residual sovereignty in the Ryukyu islands and other islands to the south and southeast of Japan which were after the surrender of Japan under United States administration. Japan has agreed to concur in any proposal to place those islands under United Nations trusteeship, with the United States as the administering authority.

It might have been better, and it certainly would have been neater, if the final disposition of the former Japanese territories had been defined precisely in the treaty, but it was not possible for the allied powers to reach agreement on this score. It was decided, therefore, in order that the peace treaty should not be further delayed, to have Japan simply renounce her rights in these territories, as she was required to do, and to leave to future international agreement the final disposition of the territories in question — including, incidentally, Formosa.

In addition to our general Canadian interest in a peace settlement which would return Japan to normal and friendly relations with the free world, Canada had certain special concerns which were made known at every stage of the negotiations and indeed at San Francisco itself. My colleague the Minister of Fisheries (Mr. Mayhew), who was with me at the San Francisco conference, gave the house a full account on March 11 last of the — as we think it to be — successful agreement on North Pacific fisheries which was reached with Japan and the United States in December of last year. Under article 9 of the treaty of peace Japan undertook to

> enter promptly into negotiations with the Allied Powers so desiring for the conclusion of bilateral and multilateral agreements providing for the regulation or limitation of fishing and the conservation and development of fisheries on the high seas.

The promptness with which Japan entered into these negotiations is, I think, an encouraging evidence of Japan's interest in living up to the trust which has been placed in her by this treaty of peace. I think it is also a good sign for future Canadian-Japanese relations which will be entering a new chapter when this treaty is ratified.

I do not intend to go into the substance of this convention since the house has already been given the details concerning it by my colleague the Minister of Fisheries. I would remind the house, however, that until the peace treaty comes into effect Japan will not be in a position to sign the fisheries convention. We can, therefore, by ratifying the peace treaty, assist in enabling Japan to sign and ratify this important convention.

A further question in which Canada was especially interested was that of Japan's undertaking with respect to commercial practices and agreements. I made clear the views of the Canadian government on this important matter in my statement in San Francisco. Possibly it would be desirable if I now put on the record what I then said. At the San Francisco conference I said:

> Japan agrees in the treaty to conform to internationally accepted fair trade practices. It is the confident hope of my government that Japan, in the future conduct of its commercial relations with other countries, will avoid certain prewar practices which were widely condemned at that time by other trading nations. Canada has no wish to see any discrimination against or any unnecessary obstacles to normal Japanese trade. On the contrary, as a trading nation ourselves we wish to see Japan develop its full trading possibilities. It is only common sense for us to wish for a prosperous rather than a poor Japan. Such prosperity, however, can never, in the long run, be established or even assisted by

General de Gaulle meeting a group of Canadian Embassy officers, Paris, 1964. Ambassador Jules Léger, later Governor General, is immediately to the left behind General de Gaulle. (Courtesy: M.F. Yalden)

The current editor discussing Canadian-Tunisian relations with President Habib Bourguiba in 1981. (Courtesy: President Bourguiba)

SSEA Paul Martin with his French colleague, Maurice Couve de Murville, at an OECD meeting in Paris, 1963. (Courtesy: OECD, Paris)

Trade and Commerce Minister (later Finance Minister and SSEA) Mitchell Sharp, with James C. Langley, Head of the Canadian OECD mission, during a ministerial meeting of the OECD in Paris, 1964. (Courtesy: OECD, Paris)

Finance Minister Paul Martin with Ambasssador Vernon G. Turner at a recent gathering in Ottawa of local University of Toronto graduates. (Courtesy: FM Martin and Amb. Turner)

Canadian Commissioner to the ICSC, Blair Seaborn (second from left), with his Indian and Polish colleagues, during a call on the President of the Republic of (South) Vietnam, Saigon, 1964. (Courtesy: Blair Seaborn)

Ambassador Arthur Menzies explaining the size of farms on the Canadian Prairies to the Chairman of the Chinese Communist Party at the Canadian Agricultural Machinery Exhibition in Beijing, 1978. (Courtesy: Amb. Menzies)

PM Diefenbaker and SSEA Howard Green with President John F. Kennedy, Ottawa, 1961. (Courtesy: Diefenbaker Canada Centre)

trading practices considered unfair by other countries and against which those countries have no alternative but to protect themselves if unhappily they should be adopted.

The peace treaty itself, as hon. members no doubt know, is not designed to settle questions of commercial policy but leaves this policy to be decided by the individual signatories of the treaty and Japan. Canadian attitudes and Canadian policy with respect to future commercial relations with Japan will, to a large extent, be influenced by whether or not Japan adheres to the declaration made in the preamble to the treaty of her intention, and I quote from that preamble:

... in public and private trade and commerce to conform to internationally accepted fair practices.

Another important section of the treaty deals with reparations. Critics of the treaty of peace in some countries have concentrated their attentions on the reparations clauses which represent an attempt to make this treaty an important step toward breaking the vicious cycle of "war-victory-peace-war." The allied powers recognize in the treaty that Japan should in principle pay reparations for the devastation and suffering she caused during the war. They recognize in addition, however, that Japan lacks the physical capacity to recompense her former victims if at the same time she is to achieve a viable economy and contribute to the economic health of the Pacific area. For certain nations represented at San Francisco, who had not only lost property valued in billions of dollars but also countless lives, as a result of Japan's military activities, the very limited reparations clauses could not but appear unsatisfactory. For others it was easier to understand that the exaction of even just reparations might impose such an economic burden on the defeated state as to vitiate the objectives of the treaty as a whole.

In the treaty Japan undertook to compensate those allied powers whose territories she had occupied, and I quote from article 14 of the treaty:

... by making available the services of the Japanese people in production, salvaging and other work.

Negotiations are already under way at the present time on this matter between Japan and Indonesia and Japan and the Philippines. Japan further agreed in the treaty to make available certain of her assets to indemnify members of the allied forces who had suffered undue hardships while prisoners of war of Japan. This matter is covered in article 16. The details of this scheme are at the present time being worked out between the allied governments concerned and the international committee of the Red Cross which is to be responsible for the distribution of the funds in question.

Finally, the treaty provides that Japan shall return all allied property which she held during the war years upon application to be made within nine months of the coming into force of the treaty.

A highly important section of the treaty deals with security. Under article 5 of the treaty Japan undertakes to settle its international disputes by peaceful means, to refrain in its international relations from the threat or the use of force and to give the United Nations every assistance in action taken in accordance with the charter. In return, the allied powers recognize Japan's sovereign right of individual or collective self-defence.

Article 6 provides for the termination of the occupation not later than 90 days after the treaty comes into force. However, it is stated explicitly in the treaty that there is nothing in this provision to prevent the stationing or retention of foreign armed forces in Japan under the terms of any agreement made between Japan and one or more of the allied powers. The peace treaty simply recognizes for Japan the principle which article 51 of the charter of the United Nations recognizes for all sovereign states. Hence, on the very day of the signature of the peace treaty, a security treaty between the United States and Japan was signed under the terms of which Japan granted to the United States the right, upon the coming into force of the treaty of peace, to dispose United States land, air and sea forces in and about Japan. That is an exceedingly important provision. These forces are to be utilized to contribute to the maintenance of international peace and security in the Far East and indeed to the security of Japan itself against an armed attack. A United States-Japan administrative agreement implementing this security treaty was signed last month in Tokyo.

2. Canadian-Japanese Relations

Political relations with Japan are of long standing. Tokyo was the site of one of the first Canadian diplomatic missions: a legation established in 1929. Since the Second World War, they have been friendly, indeed cordial.

Both countries share much the same basic approach to international affairs, viz., support for liberal multilateral trading arrangements; joint membership in several specialized international organizations, such as the Organization for Economic Cooperation and Development (OECD), international aid programmes, such as the Colombo Plan or the Development Assistance Group (DAG), peaceful applications of atomic energy; the intelligent use of the resources of the high seas, and so on.

Fisheries questions were a frequent theme of discussion and negotiation between Ottawa and Tokyo. Nevertheless, trade has been the predominant characteristic of Canadian relations with Japan since the end of the Second World War.[46]

Commercial exchanges between both countries have shown voluminous and continuing growth since the early 1950s and, except for the odd year, have produced extremely favourable trade balances for Canada. However, they developed a pattern early on that has generally favoured Japanese rather than Canadian industrial growth, that is, Canadian raw materials in exchange for labour-intensive Japanese finished goods.

Despite vigorous efforts by ministers, officials, the business community, the pattern of Canadian trade with Japan has not changed that much over the years. Canada is still exporting mainly raw materials, while importing finished products.

By 1955, for instance, Japan was well established as Canada's third largest trading partner and trade has been the mainspring of Canadian-Japanese relations ever since. Total trade between the two countries has mounted steadily over the years with the balance decidedly in Canada's favour. Japan is still the third largest Canadian export market.

Canada trades as much with Japan today as it does with Britain, France, and Germany combined.

Trading patterns evolve of course and certain problems with Japan in earlier years seem utterly archaic today. They concerned primarily exports to Canada of cotton and other cheaply-produced yarns, which threatened to disrupt Canadian markets. These were the subject of voluntary restraints by Japan and its exports were kept under review by Ottawa, with adjustments mutually agreed to.[47]

A particular problem with Japan arose somewhat later: exports of automobiles to Canada. The importation of Japanese automotive vehicles became the subject of regular, often annual, "understandings", whereby it was mutually agreed that exports of Japanese passenger cars to Canada would not exceed a set number of units over a given period of time, usually one year.[48] However, when Japanese automobile manufacturers began to set up plants in Canada, the problem diminished a good deal.

---

[46]See Section 2.2. below for details regarding early Canadian relations with Japan on fisheries questions after the Second World War.

[47]See A.E.B. II, pp. 151-156, for an outline of Canadian-Japanese trade relations during the 1960s, with particular emphasis on textiles.

[48]See A.E.B. III, p. 81, for background.

2.1. Trade

The 1954 trade agreement with Japan

STATEMENT BY TRADE AND COMMERCE MINISTER C.D. HOWE, HOUSE OF COMMONS, MAY 12, 1954. (EXTRACTS)

Japan has already become our third largest customer. It seems probable that Japan will continue in the future to increase in importance as a market for our exports.

This new agreement provides, among other things, for the exchange of most-favoured-nation treatment. This is the normal and established treatment which we extend to other friendly countries with which we trade. Quite clearly, we could not continue for much longer to withhold most-favoured-nation treatment from a country such as Japan, which is one of our largest customers.

In recent years we have been imposing the high rates of our general tariff upon imports from Japan. In consequence, we have imported very little from there, even though we have been selling large and increasing amounts of our exports to that country. It has become more and more difficult in these circumstances to justify the fact that we were not extending most-favoured nation treatment to Japan. In the new trade agreement we are now proposing to correct this anomaly.

In negotiating this new agreement, we set out to obtain and consolidate advantages in the Japanese market, and at the same time to safeguard in a reasonable way the position of our own Canadian manufacturers in our home market. The negotiations were carried on in Ottawa, over a considerable period of time, with representatives of the Japanese government. At each stage, the various aspects were given careful consideration by my cabinet colleagues and myself. The negotiations were recently concluded in a friendly way and both sides regarded the results as satisfactory. Good trade relations and effective trade agreements are based on the willingness of countries to recognize each other's difficulties. They are based also on the desire to make well-balanced arrangements which will operate to the advantage of all concerned.

Let me give a short outline of the essential features of the agreement, and I will then go into some explanatory details. Briefly, there are three important ways in which this agreement will facilitate the access of Canadian goods to the Japanese market. In the first place, our exports will be guaranteed most-favoured-nation treatment in Japan. Secondly, we will be assured that there will be no discrimination whatsoever against Canada and in favour of any other hard currency country with respect to quantitative restrictions, exchange controls, or any other matters. Thirdly, with respect to a list of nine important Canadians export products, Japan undertakes not to discriminate against Canada in favour of any other country regardless of its currency position. This list of products includes wheat, barley, woodpulp, flaxseed, primary copper, lead in pigs, zinc spelter, synthetic resins and milk powders. These are all very important concessions to have received. I shall return to these points a little later, to explain them more fully.

On our side, we undertake to make certain concessions to Japan. The agreement provides that Canada will extend most-favoured-nation treatment to Japanese goods. This means that imports from Japan will be entered under our most-favoured-nation rates of duty, which are generally applicable to the non-commonwealth countries with which we trade. This will involve reductions in the duties on imports from Japan, which have hitherto been subject to the much higher rates set forth in our general tariff. It is, of course, to be predicted that imports from Japan will increase under these new arrangements.

Canadian imports from Japan have increased in value as compared with pre-war years, but they are still relatively small. Last year, they included a range of items such as iron and steel, toys, oranges, pottery and chinaware, silk and other fabrics, tuna fish and a variety of manufactured products. Only in two items did our imports from Japan amount to as much as $1 million. Aside from these items, the value of individual import items from Japan was in each case considerably below a half million dollars.

In case injurious competition should materialize for particular Canadian industries out of such imports, careful safeguards have been provided in the agreement. We have been mindful of the fact that a sudden influx of low-priced imports might seriously affect some particular Canadian industry. In the agreement Canada therefore reserves the right to apply special duties on Japanese goods in legitimate cases of emergency where, as a result of increased imports, there is a serious threat of injury to domestic producers.

I hope, however, that Canadian trade with Japan will develop in such a way as not to create serious problems for Canadian industry. Japan, like ourselves, is vitally dependent on foreign trade. The Japanese government is no doubt fully aware of the fact that no lasting trade relations can be built up except on the basis of mutual good will and of adherence to fair trade practices. It is reasonable to expect that Japanese exporters will try to avoid creating problems which would undermine good relations. Japan has in recent years instituted a comprehensive system of control and inspection for its exports, in a positive effort to prevent dumping of goods, misrepresentation of trade marks and patents and other undesirable methods, and to abide by internationally accepted fair trade practices.

In fact, Japan, with her 85 million population and with her highly developed industries, is one of the world's largest markets for foodstuffs and raw materials, and for other products which we can supply. The maintenance of high levels of exports of these products is of fundamental importance to the whole Canadian economy. It is of direct benefit to our agriculture, our forest and our mining industries. By contributing to a buoyant economy and a prosperous domestic market in Canada, it is of vital importance to our own manufacturing industries which sell their products in the Canadian market. We have no monopoly on the supply of such products, of course, and other countries are also anxious to expand their share of the Japanese market.

Ratification of our agreement should open a new era of fruitful trade relations between Canada and Japan. Our two economies are to a large degree complementary and have much to gain from close and constructive co-operation. We are happy to play our part in helping Japan to take her place as a partner in the world trading community.

Editor's note: At the end of 1994, heralding trade policy for the 21st century, International Trade Minister MacLaren unveiled a revised version of *Canada's Action Plan for Japan* in a statement to the Canada-Japan Society in Toronto. Produced in cooperation with provincial governments and the private sector, it targets seven sectors where Canada is particularly well placed to excel: building materials, food, fish, and seafood products, automobile parts, information technologies, tourism, and aerospace. A current feature of Canadian trade relations with Japan are the annual meetings of Canadian and Japanese officials and businessmen aiming, on the Canadian side, at increased exports not only in the traditional sectors but especially in technology. Recently there has been some improvement and our exports of telecommunications and transportation equipment, software, prefabricated housing have been on the rise.[49]

2.2. Fisheries

Doc. 4.3   **The 1952 Fisheries Convention**

STATEMENT BY FISHERIES MINISTER R.W. MAYHEW, HOUSE OF COMMONS, MARCH 11, 1952. (EXTRACTS)

For some time it was thought that there would be something in the peace treaty with Japan referring to fisheries, not only on the west coast of Canada, but in other parts of the Pacific as well. Early in the spring of 1951, the deputy minister, Mr. Stewart Bates, and I were invited to Washington to discuss with Mr. John Foster Dulles this problem. Soon after we met him and began talking about the problem we were convinced that an attempt to include a fishery agreement in the peace treaty itself would mean endless work and delay. It would mean a separate agreement between Japan and all our allies, particularly in the Pacific. We were convinced after our talk with Mr. Dulles that he was right and that our best plan was to work out a separate fisheries agree-

---

[49]DFAIT News Release No. 245 of December 5, 1994, carries a "Backgrounder" providing a useful summary of the Action Plan.

ment. Again after a great deal of consideration and after discussing it with the fishing industry and fishermen of the west coast, it was thought that a tripartite agreement with Japan and the United States and Canada was the only really sensible sort of agreement. His Excellency the prime minister of Japan had already indicated by letter to Mr. Dulles that he would enter into a fisheries agreement with us and other nations promptly after the signing of the main peace treaty.

I think it is advisable for me at this point to indicate why an agreement of any sort was necessary. Those living on the Pacific coast have for a good many years been very deeply concerned about the danger of Japanese fishermen coming to British Columbia to fish our salmon, halibut and herring. The Japanese expedition to Bristol Bay before the war demonstrated that this was possible and that they were actually thinking along this line. This trip also created a great deal of resentment against the Japanese fishermen. While the Japanese fishermen had never fished along our coast, yet there was no reason why they could not, and very sound reasons as to why they would do it. For many years Japan has been the leading country in the world as far as fisheries are concerned, taking first place in the volume of her catch before the second world war. In addition to that, Japan needs what she gets from the sea to feed her people, probably more than any other nation. I understand that about eighty per cent of her protein is harvested from the sea. She also needs some of the other valuable species such as salmon and tuna for export purposes, and her fisheries have been considerably reduced as a result of the recent war, since Russia is now in command of the very valuable salmon fisheries formerly enjoyed by her. It was therefore necessary, if we wanted to add stability and security to the fishing industry on the British Columbia coast, to make some agreement with Japan.

The basis of this agreement involved two questions of principle which were difficult to reconcile: the right of all nations to the freedom of the seas and the reverse of that, to restrict Japan from fishing near Canadian or American shores. However, the solution to the problem was readily available. Canada and the United States both have a long history of conservation of certain species — salmon, halibut and herring — and it is quite true to say that these fisheries would probably have been lost to the world's food supply had we not over the years taken very rigid conservation methods. For many years we have restricted our fishermen as to the time they could commence seasonal fishing, when they would cease fishing, restricting all fishing for two or three days a week, regulating the length of their nets and the size of the mesh, and on many occasions leaving idle fishing gear and plants while these regulations were being applied. In addition to that, the government of Canada has spent large sums of money year after year for the scientific study of these species. Industries locating on our rivers were obliged to prevent pollution and to construct, at their own expense, dams and fishways to meet our regulations in order to provide easy ascent to the spawning grounds and safety in the spawning grounds. Likewise, the taxpayers of Canada have paid for both river and sea patrols to see that these regulations were carried out. We have also made international agreements between the United States and Canada for the conservation and propagation of the sockeye salmon on the Fraser river as well as for the halibut fishery, so that Canada as a whole, and the fishermen and fishing industry of British Columbia in particular, had a capital investment in the three species — salmon, halibut and herring. The fact that we had been doing this work for years made it comparatively easy and gave us a reasonable argument to use with Japan as to why they should waive their rights, not to the freedom of the high seas, but to fish these species in the waters of the east Pacific.

In gaining this concession, we obtained for the fishing industry of British Columbia what it has been most anxious to obtain and what it has been insisting on for some years. It was obtained not as a punitive measure nor because Japan was a defeated nation. It was obtained because it was a reasonable and fair request to make, one that in the same circumstances we would be ready to grant to any other nation in the Pacific.

Some of those who are opposing this agreement, and I believe others who are not opposing it but have not given it very serious consideration have asked the question, and I might say we have asked the question ourselves — why not just a simple agreement between Japan and Canada, each agreeing not to fish within a certain radius or area of each other's shore line? That sounds very simple and I am sure quite reasonable to a lot of people. But I would ask you to take just a second look at it. If you do you will see that such an agreement would mean the zoning of the Pacific ocean. Both Japan and ourselves would have to enter into separate agreements with other nations on a similar basis, and what would be the result? ... You would probably be surprised to know that the mileage of the coast line of Japan is approximately five times that of the coast line of British Columbia from point to point. If the whole of the Pacific area was divided up as suggested, Canada would suffer since she has one of the shortest shore lines of any country in the Pacific basin.

Others claim that this is by no means a perfect agreement as far as Canada and the United States are concerned. With that we agree, because it is not an agreement with the United States at all. It has not changed our relationship with the United States and we enjoy all the rights and privileges that we have ever had with that country. This is expressly stated in our agreement, and in this agreement we used the same wording as was used previously in the convention for the northwest Atlantic fisheries. I quote:

> Nothing in this convention shall be deemed to affect adversely the claims of any contracting party in regard to the limits of territorial waters or to the jurisdiction of a coastal state over fisheries.

4 — The Far East

We have made no concession whatever to the United States.

However, the United States and Japan realized and so stated that the stocks of fish on the North American coast are so intermingled that it would be impossible to segregate them in any way that would be practical of administration. Therefore the conference agreed that under no condition would Canada and the United States be asked to abstain from fishing any species of fish from and including the Gulf of Alaska southward to the Gulf of Mexico. That is a recognition which is very valuable to the Canadian fisherman ...

In this agreement we have established a principle that can easily be applied to a fourth, fifth or any other number of nations that want to accept it. I cannot say that this has been secured without cost. It has been secured at the cost of many millions of dollars, the millions of dollars which we have spent in conservation in the past, but it is certainly costing us no additional money or rights at this time. In that connection, if we had not been engaged in conservation and propagation on the west coast we would not have had this basis for asking the Japanese to waive any rights. That is the only cost. There is no new cost. All three countries are firmly convinced that the conservation of the fisheries on the high seas is a necessity, and that more and more the nations of the world will come to depend on the sea for more of their food. This agreement will allow the maximum of exploitation and at the same time a sustained yield of fish.

2.3. The North Pacific Treaty Negotiations

[First phase] Doc. 4.4

STATEMENT BY FISHERIES MINISTER H.J. ROBICHAUD, HOUSE OF COMMONS, JUNE 10, 1963. (EXTRACTS)

Mr. Speaker, on Friday last I advised the house that I would make a statement today on the series of meetings which are now taking place in Washington, and which opened last Thursday, to review the provisions of the north Pacific treaty.

In 1952 Canada, Japan and the United States entered into a treaty, the international north Pacific fisheries convention, the principal basis of which was the abstention principle. Under this principle it was agreed that any stocks of fish which are fully utilized by any one or more of the participating countries, and which are under regulation based on scientific investigation, will continue to be exploited only by the countries which have developed those fisheries to their full exploitation. Also any country which had not, for 25 years preceding the entry into force of the convention, exploited such stocks of fish agreed voluntarily to abstain from fishing such stocks.

Under this principle Japan, which had never participated in the exploitation of salmon, halibut and herring fisheries of North American origin, agreed to continue abstaining from fishing these stocks.

131

Canada, which had never exploited stocks of salmon in the Bering sea, also agreed to abstain from fishing those stocks.

The treaty was made for a period of 10 years following its ratification on June 12, 1953, after which time any of the parties to the convention could terminate the convention by giving 12 months notice. Before the expiration of the 10 year period this June Japan had requested that the three countries enter into discussions to review the convention and to consider the possibility of revisions.

The three parties met on Thursday of last week at the opening session in Washington, and stated their positions. From the statements made it is evident that the three parties are agreed on the fact that a treaty is needed for the protection of the fishing resources of the north Pacific. The differences between the parties are as to the kind of treaty that would give this protection. The Japanese position was stated by the Japanese chairman of the delegation, Mr. Masayoshi Ito, as follows:

> The implementation of the convention for 10 years has revealed that the formula of abstention contains in itself a number of difficult problems such as the difficulty of proving the existence of the conditions for abstention.

> Therefore, the government of Japan hopes to conclude, in place of the present convention which will shortly have run its initial ten-year period, a new convention the objective of which is to ensure the rational conservation and exploitation of the fishery resources of the north Pacific ocean by cooperation between our three countries, Canada, the United States and Japan.

> Japan is heavily dependant on fishery resources so that the conservation of resources is a matter of greatest concern to us. The government of Japan, while urging the discard of the formula of abstention, has no wish adversely to affect fishery resources and is prepared to give due consideration to the past efforts of the countries concerned for the conservation of those resources.

Secretary of the Interior Stewart L. Udall expressed the views of the United States government and its delegation as follows:

> It is our view in the United States that the convention has served well as a mechanism for the solution of common fishery problems and in so doing has contributed substantially to a pattern of harmonious relations among the three governments.

Further on he said:

> In short, we are convinced of the fundamental value of the principle of abstention for the solution of what are today

unique fishery problems, but problems which may in the future be all too common.

We are strengthened in our conviction by the manner in which this convention has served the three governments during the past 10 years. None of the governments has found in the functioning of the convention all that it might have hoped for. Japanese fishermen find defects in the convention, and so do Canadian and American fishermen. But, within its framework it has been possible for the three national fishing industries to prosper.

I shall quote two paragraphs of what I said, speaking for the Canadian delegation:

> Speaking for my country, I may say that the government is deeply conscious of the arduous work put in by the commission to demonstrate that the principles on which the international north Pacific fisheries convention is founded are sound. The abstention principle, on which the convention is based, is meant to cover a unique situation to protect certain fisheries which without it could not long survive.

Further on I said:

> One of the emerging problems in conservation of sea fisheries, which requires an urgent solution, is the intermingling of various stocks of fish. One state may be interested in exploiting a certain stock of fish which may be intermingled with a stock or stocks of fish which another state may be desirous of exploiting in the same region. This probably is the knottiest problem to be resolved in the fisheries of the north Pacific.

I concluded with the following remarks:

> In closing I express the hope that your deliberations will be successful, and successful they must be if we want to preserve the rich resources of our north Pacific high seas for the common benefit of future generations of our respective countries.

[Second phase]   Doc. 4.5

STATEMENT BY FISHERIES MINISTER H.J. ROBICHAUD, HOUSE OF COMMONS, OCTOBER 1, 1964 (EXTRACTS); AND COMMENT BY MR. F.A. MACLEAN, M.P.

Mr. Speaker, hon. members will recall that when the estimates of the Department of Fisheries were before the House last week I promised that at the conclusion of negotiations which were taking place here in Ottawa among Canada, Japan and the United States for the revision of the North Pacific fisheries convention I might be able to make a statement to the house.

At the opening session of the Ottawa negotiations I expressed the hope on behalf of the Canadian delegation that this third meeting of the parties to the international north Pacific fisheries convention would resolve the remaining differences and would culminate in a successful conclusion of the protracted negotiations. Three weeks of uninterrupted negotiations have brought the parties very close to agreement, but it has not been possible to reconcile all the remaining differences, and the delegations have agreed to a recess in the discussions in order to study and recommend to their respective governments other approaches to the unsolved problems.

We had hoped that final agreement could have been reached for the revision of the existing convention which, of course, continues in force but which may be terminated upon 12 months' notice by one of the parties. At the same time we realize that the problems with which the delegations have been faced are very complex, and that all must be solved before agreeing on a convention which we hope will remain in force for many years. The frank and co-operative attitudes of the delegations have permitted much progress and encourage us to hope that we shall reach agreement at our next meeting.

I should like to give, for the information of the house, a very brief résumé of the Canadian position. The salmon runs to our streams are of the very highest importance to the fisheries of Canada's Pacific coast. We believe that through scientific study, strict regulation and positive fish culture methods we have maintained these stocks which would otherwise have disappeared. We believe that the salmon resources can be greatly increased by the application of scientifically based techniques which are now emerging. But this maintenance and increase of the runs require not only that we continue out intensive efforts in research, regulation and culture, but that we also continue, at considerable cost to our economy, the protection of our rivers from other uses which would make them unsuitable for salmon. To justify all these costs of maintaining and, we confidently expect, increasing the salmon resources the benefits must accrue to the Canadian economy.

During the past three weeks much progress has been made toward agreement which would meet our needs in an acceptable manner. It seems that, on the one hand, the basis for the Canadian position is now well understood and is given sympathetic consideration. On the other hand we realize that recognition of our special interests must be contingent on continuation of our special efforts to maintain and increase the salmon stocks and on continued full utilization by our fishery, and that the situation must therefore be subject to review by the commission established by the convention. We have been very close to agreement which would embody these essential points.

4 — The Far East

The greatest unsolved problem is concerned with conservation measures for those stocks of North American salmon which now are fished on the high seas. Although the problem applies especially to sockeye of Alaska origin, Canada has a potential interest in a solution which could be applied to other stocks fished on the high seas although to a much more minor degree. We are also concerned by the growing scientific evidence that the high seas fishing of salmon stocks which are intensively fished inshore may be wasteful.

It appears that we are close to agreement on a formula which would be acceptable in so far as the major halibut producing areas are concerned. This formula would recognize the long history of research and regulation by the international Pacific halibut commission on behalf of the governments of Canada and the United States, and the resulting successful restoration and maintenance of the important halibut fishery. We had hoped that similar protection could be extended to other areas where the stocks have been the subject of similar study and regulation and are utilized by our fishermen. This must now be a matter for further discussion.

Regarding herring, we hope that a satisfactory solution can be reached as herring is not of significant importance to Japan.

I am encouraged by the valuable progress that has been made toward the solution of the remaining differences, and hope that these may finally be reconciled at the next meeting.

Hon. J.A. MacLean: Mr. Speaker, no doubt the house listened with interest to the rather lengthy statement of the minister on this very important subject. I regret that it was not quite as reassuring as we might have hoped it would be, because it is obvious that agreement has not been reached as yet on terms under which the north Pacific fisheries treaty could be extended for another lengthy or indefinite period of time. The minister neglected to say how long this recess in negotiations is going to be, but I hope it will not be too lengthy and that negotiations can be recommenced at an early date.

The problem is, of course, that there is a conflict of interest between Japan on the one hand and the United States and Canada on the other, because Japan depends on high seas fisheries and has very few streams which contribute anything to the stocks of salmon which are commercially exploited in the north Pacific. I would hope that the Canadian delegation, as they no doubt did, pointed out to Japan the possibility of Japan developing artificial spawning beds and other means whereby that country itself might make a worthwhile contribution to these stocks of fish, based on methods that have been developed in Canada.

We will look with interest to the reconvening of negotiations on this treaty, and we assume there will be no possibility of any of the parties giving notice that they intend to withdraw. The minister did not specifically say so, but we would hope that these negotiations will be reconvened at an early date and that a satisfactory agreement will eventually be reached.[50]

3. China

Missionary activity and some trade were the main characteristics of Canadian-Chinese relations down to the Second World War that brought the two countries into alliance against the Axis powers.

Reflecting wartime alliances, diplomatic ties began in 1943, when a Canadian legation was established in Chungking, China's wartime capital. It later became an embassy and moved to Nanking with the Nationalist Government of Chiang Kai-shek. A Canadian Government Trade Commissioner's Office had been established in Shanghai as early as 1908.

Communist armies defeated Chiang Kai-shek in 1949, and Mao Tse-tung established his administration in Beijing. The Chinese intervention in the Korean War and United States' opposition to China's presence at the United Nations placed serious limits on the development of Sino-Canadian relations.

From 1949 down to recognition in 1970, these relations were largely limited to trade, especially in cereals of which China was an extensive importer. This should not be taken to mean that Beijing did not loom large as a factor in Canadian foreign policy. It did, but to a much greater extent at the United Nations and as a facet of Canadian relations with the United States than with Beijing.

The question of Chinese membership in the United Nations was a recurring issue at each General Assembly until resolved in Beijing's favour during the fall of 1971. Successive Canadian governments held off from supporting Beijing's accession to the United Nations in view of United States hostility to Chinese membership and its threat to withdraw from the United Nations if Beijing were admitted. Diplomatic relations with the Peoples Republic were established in 1970 and embassies were again exchanged by the two countries early in 1971.

The first tangible move towards better relations with China took a very Canadian twist in 1961: the beginning of large-scale grain sales. This development, and others, eventually helped to pave the way for full recognition by the Trudeau government in the early 1970s.

---

[50]The Treaty's 10-year validity came due in 1963 and Japan requested that the three parties concerned enter into discussions to review its provisions and consider the possibility of revisions. Negotiations took placed during 1963 and 1964. They were inconclusive and the treaty's basic provisions remained in force.

4 — The Far East

Announcement of sale of grain to China Doc. 4.6

STATEMENT BY AGRICULTURE MINISTER ALVIN HAMILTON, HOUSE OF COMMONS,
MAY 2, 1961.

Mr. Speaker, the house will recall that on February 2, I informed hon. members that a sale of 40 million bushels of wheat and barley, valued at approximately $60 million, had been contracted between the Canadian Wheat Board and the China Resources Company.

I now inform the house that there was an additional sale to China of 2.2 million bushels of wheat, valued at $3.7 million, for shipment during March to May, 1961. Those connected with shipping grain through the west coast ports have made a fine effort to meet these commitments. As a result, the grain sold to China for delivery between March and August is being loaded ahead of schedule.

Simultaneously with the fulfilling of the first order there have been discussions and finally negotiations between the Canadian Wheat Board and the China Resources Company concerning further amounts of grain that could be made available. Because of the quantities of grain involved and other factors, the Canadian Government felt there should be an over-all agreement to facilitate orderly marketing.

I am now pleased to report that a long term agreement has been signed. This long term agreement covers the period June 1, 1961, to December, 1963. Under this agreement we have committed ourselves to provide up to six million tons of barley, wheat and flour. Of this amount approximately one million tons will be barley. To put this into approximate bushels and value, it would provisionally be 186.7 million bushels of wheat and 46.7 million bushels of barley, worth approximately $362 million.

If one adds the previous order for 28 million bushels of wheat and 12 million bushels of barley, valued at $60 million, then the total transaction that could provisionally be expected for the three calendar years 1961, 1962 and 1963 will be 217 million bushels of wheat and 58.8 million bushels of barley, with a total approximate value of $425.6 million.

I mentioned earlier that the first order of 40 million bushels was being moved satisfactorily. As an extension to the order now being filled, a contract to provide additional grain from June 1 to November 30 of this year has been signed. It is the first contract under the long term agreement. The amounts are 750,000 long tons of wheat, 360,000 long tons of barley and 32,500 tons of flour, to be shipped mainly from west coast ports. The equivalent in bushels is 28 million bushels of wheat, 17 million bushels of barley and 1.5 million bushels of flour. The estimated value of this order is $66 million. The terms of payment under the long term agreement are 25 per cent cash and the balance in 270 days.

Hon. members will appreciate that it is beyond the resources of the Canadian Wheat Board to extend credit facilities for the quantities involved in these transactions. Accordingly the government, reflecting its intensive efforts to sell grain in volume to new markets, is prepared to guarantee to a maximum of $50 million the credit necessary for the Canadian wheat board to conclude these transactions on a short term credit basis. I have made it clear that there is a long term agreement. Under that agreement one contract has been signed. Each future contract will be negotiated in respect to price and quantity.

A sale of this order will spread substantial benefits through the Canadian economy. Not only will it provide a welcome increase in western farm incomes, but this in turn will release new purchasing power for the goods and services required by farmers from the business community at large. Additionally the sale will generate increased employment for country and terminal elevator operators, railway and dock workers, and others engaged in the domestic handling and export movement of grain and flour. It is apparent that new grain sales of this magnitude will add significantly to Canada's total earnings from exports. Business activity in general will therefore be stimulated to a marked extent by the conclusion of this new sales contract with China.

Doc. 4.7 **Establishment of diplomatic relations with the People's Republic of China**

STATEMENT BY SSEA MITCHELL SHARP, HOUSE OF COMMONS, OCTOBER 13, 1970.

I am pleased to announce the successful conclusion of our discussions in Stockholm with representatives of the People's Republic of China, reflected in today's joint communiqué which records our agreement on mutual recognition and the establishment of diplomatic relations. The joint communiqué of the Government of Canada and the Government of the People's Republic of China concerning the establishment of diplomatic relations between Canada and China is as follows:

1) The Government of Canada and the Government of the People's Republic of China, in accordance with the principles of mutual respect for sovereignty and territorial integrity, non-interference in each other's internal affairs and equality and mutual benefit, have decided upon mutual recognition and the establishment of diplomatic relations, effective October 13, 1970.

2) The Chinese Government reaffirms that Taiwan is an inalienable part of the territory of the People's Republic of China. The Canadian Government takes note of this position of the Chinese Government.[51]

3) The Canadian Government recognizes the Government of the People's Republic of China as the sole legal government of China.

---

[51]This "Canadian" formula was later used by other countries. SS 72/21 of October 14, 1972, gives useful background regarding the negotiations that led to recognition and also provides a summary of the recent history of Sino-Canadian relations.

4) The Canadian and Chinese Governments have agreed to exchange ambassadors within six months, and to provide all necessary assistance for the establishment and the performance of the functions of diplomatic missions in their respective capitals, on the basis of equality and mutual benefit and in accordance with international practice.

Officials from my department and from Industry, Trade and Commerce will be leaving for Peking very shortly to begin administrative preparations for the opening of a Canadian embassy in Peking. We hope to have the embassy in operation within two or three months.

The establishment of diplomatic relations between Canada and China is an important step in the development of relations between our two countries, but it is not the first step, nor is it an end in itself. We have opened a new and important channel of communication, through which I hope we will be able to expand and develop our relations in every sphere. We have already indicated to the Chinese, in our Stockholm discussions, our interest in setting up cultural and educational exchanges, in expanding trade between our two countries, in reaching an understanding on consular matters, and in settling a small number of problems left over from an earlier period. The Chinese have expressed the view that our relations in other fields such as these can only benefit from the establishment of diplomatic relations between our two countries. They have also agreed in principle to discuss through normal diplomatic channels, as soon as our respective embassies are operating, some of the specific issues we have raised with them.

Status of Taiwan — Canadian Explanatory Note

As everyone knows, the agreement published today has been under discussion for a long time. I do not think it is any secret that a great deal of this discussion has revolved around the question of Taiwan. From the very beginning of our discussions the Chinese side made clear to us their position that Taiwan was an inalienable part of Chinese territory and that this was a principle to which the Chinese Government attached the utmost importance. Our position, which I have stated publicly and which we made clear to the Chinese from the start of our negotiations, is that the Canadian Government does not consider it appropriate either to endorse or to challenge the Chinese Government's position on the status of Taiwan. This has been our position and it continues to be our position. As the communiqué says, we have taken note of the Chinese Government's statement about Taiwan. We are aware that this is the Chinese view and we realize the importance they attach to it, but we have no comment to make one way or the other.

There is no disagreement between the Canadian Government and the authorities in Taipeh on the impossibility of continuing diplomatic relations after the Government of Peking is recognized as the Government of China. Both Peking and Taipeh assert that it is not possible to recognize simultaneously more than one government as the Government of China. Accordingly, the authorities on Taiwan and the Canadian Government have each taken steps to terminate formal diplomatic relations as of the time of the announcement of our recognition of the Government of the People's Republic of China.

3.1. Canada and China in the 1970s and 1980s

The main feature of Sino-Canadian relations since recognition in 1970 has been trade, which has been expanding voluminously, particularly over the last two decades. As is the case with Japan, annual meetings grouping together Canadian and Chinese officials and businessmen became a regular feature of the relationship.

Doc. 4.8   **Canada and China**

STATEMENT BY INTERNATIONAL TRADE MINISTER, MS. PAT CARNEY, TO THE CANADA-CHINA TRADE COUNCIL, VANCOUVER, DECEMBER 12, 1986. (EXTRACTS)

When the new government took power in 1984, we were determined to turn Canada's economy around. Canada is a trading nation and we naturally focused on expanding international markets as the main engine of our economy. We therefore undertook a series of discussions with the provinces and the private sector and established the National Trade Strategy. Its objective is to revitalize the Canadian economy and to create more jobs in Canada by increasing Canada's success in the international market place.

As part of the Strategy, we determined that we should focus our efforts on priority markets. The first of these is, of course, the United States, our largest trading partner.

The expanding economies of the Pacific Rim represent the other priority focus of our trade policy. Canada is a Pacific Rim nation. In 1985, for the first time, our total exports to the region were greater than those to West and East Europe combined. This trend has continued, making it our second most important market area.

There are four messages that I bring to you today. The first is that our policy of expanding trade relations with China is an integral part of the government's focus on trade. The second is that we have established some major new tools to help the private sector in trading with China. The third is that the market in China for British Columbia remains exciting. The fourth is that China is a tough market to penetrate, but attention to some basic guidelines will help.

China has been chosen as a priority market within our Trade Strategy. Why China? The reason is simple. China is our fifth largest export market. Of all the countries seeking to ensure themselves a place in the Chinese market, Canada is the first largest supplier to that country.

In order to provide more tools and a better framework for our commercial success in China, we have expanded contacts at the highest levels in both governments. Senior Chinese ministers have provided us with some advice for Canadian firms wishing to increase their relations with China. I would like to pass them on to you:

Canadian firms do not appreciate the huge size of the Chinese market for power projects. Canadians do not understand the cut-throat nature of international competition in China.

Canadian firms will not be able to sell to China without the support of the Canadian Government to put forward a Canadian team approach to China.

We have taken a number of steps to encourage a team approach to China and to ensure that competitive tools are available.

We have decided to provide financing for projects in China. We have concluded a double taxation agreement with China. We have funded studies by Canadian firms on projects in China where downstream benefits can create jobs in Canada. Some of these are already paying off in the hydroelectric and industrial fields.

We have put these tools in place to make Canada more competitive in China, and the emphasis is on competition What we have done is necessary but not sufficient. It ensures that the door to China is as open to us as to others. We are fifth in China, and fifth has to try harder, to be more active in pursuing the market, to have the right technology and products, and to offer the best price. There is another requirement. We must work closely together.

China is a difficult, but not impossible market. The keys to opening it up are: preparation, approach, perseverance, and patience. Do your homework in advance. Try to understand the inter-relationships of Chinese organizations of interest to you. Find our where the decision-making authority is. Use all the contacts you can. City and provincial "twinning links" have proven helpful. Be willing, indeed eager, to include existing Chinese capabilities and components in your bids. Be ready to make available some technology transfer and training. The Chinese are in a hurry to develop.

3.2. Canada and China in the 1990s

The major development Sino-Canadian relations recently has been the Agreement reached between the two countries on a wide range of market access issues related to China's entry into the World Trade Organization.

Doc. 4.9 **Canada-China Trade Agreement**

DFAIT NEWS RELEASE NO. 256, NOVEMBER 26, 1999. (EXTRACTS)

In the Agreement, Canada's fourth largest trading partner, has committed itself to reducing tariffs on imports of Canadian industrial products and to liberalizing access into China's burgeoning services market, including telecommunications and financial services. China will also improve access for many Canadian agricultural goods including wheat, barley and malt, canola and canola oil. In 1998, Canada's exports were valued at $2.5 billion. The top items being grains, seeds, fruit, wood pulp, cereals, and fertilizers.[52]

4. The "Tigers"

As with Japan and China, trade has been the dominant thrust in Canada's relations with the rapidly emerging industrial states of East and Southeast Asia, colloquially known as the Tigers.

Ten of Canada's top export markets are now Asia-Pacific economies, among which can be found such countries as Korea, Malaysia, Singapore, Thailand. While Canadian policy is aimed at increasing exports to all Pacific Rim countries as much as possible, as with Japan there are constant reminders that the trade mix should change: that a higher proportion of Canadian manufactured goods and technological products should be imported and not just our wheat, coal, copper nickel, or lumber.

4.1. Hong Kong[53]

Doc. 4.10 **Trade Action Plan for Hong Kong**

NEWS RELEASE BY INTERNATIONAL TRADE MINISTER, MS. PAT CARNEY, MARCH 1, 1988, AT THE ANNUAL MEETING OF THE HONG KONG/CANADA BUSINESS ASSOCIATION.

The Trade Action Plan has four main objectives:

1) To increase Canadian awareness of the size, openness, and Western style business environment present in Hong Kong;
2) To encourage Canadian exporters to take advantage of the active Hong Kong re-export market as a gateway to many major Asian markets;
3) To position Canadian businesses in Hong Kong in order to enhance

---

[52]The news release comes with a useful "Backgrounder" giving details about the Agreement.

[53]**Editor's note:** Although Hong Kong has now been returned to China, it is included here as an indication of its importance as a priority in Canada's Pacific Rim trade. The statistics given in the following document reflect Hong Kong's previous status.

our trading prospects with China; and

4) To increase business relationships with Hong Kong entrepreneurs.

Hong Kong is the third largest import market in Asia, as well as the world's busiest container port and sixth most active air freight terminal. In 1987, Hong Kong recorded 12% growth in GNP and a 40% growth in imports. In 1986, Canada ranked only 23rd among suppliers to the Hong Kong market, although since 1977 Canadian exports to Hong Kong have increased more than seven-fold, to an annual total of nearly $500 million in 1988.

4.2. Korea

Canadian-Korean trade has increased prodigiously over the last two decades. Korea is currently Canada's sixth-largest export market. By the end of the 1990s, Korea was importing roughly $3.5 billion worth of Canadian products annually and two-way trade was in the vicinity of $6 billion.

Despite these improvements, a number of problems remain to be solved. Korean markets are not as open as they might be. Our exports in the technological sector are on the rise, notably in telecommunications and transportation, yet generally remain heavily weighted in raw materials. While a number of Canadian firms are present in Korea, we have nothing there to rival such names as Hyundai, Daewoo, Samsung, here.[54]

Canada and Korea   Doc. 4.11

ADDRESS BY INTERNATIONAL TRADE MINISTER JAMES KELLEHER, TO THE CANADA-KOREA AND THE KOREA-CANADA BUSINESS COUNCILS, VANCOUVER, OCTOBER 3, 1985. (EXTRACTS)

I am very pleased to note that over the past year the Korean Government has launched a number of measures to open up its market for foreign investment. The recent revisions in its Foreign Capital Investment Act, providing for new investment incentives and tax benefits were particularly welcome.

Let me touch on some of the opportunities for Korean investors in Canada. You are all aware that we have scrapped FIRA, the old Foreign Investment Agency, and replaced it with Investment Canada. The mandate of the new Agency is to attract new investment and the opportunities are broad. They range from entrepreneurial immigration through joint venture production to corporate investment. Corporate investment can of course serve a variety of strategic purposes: the sim-

---

[54]DFAIT Statements 97/2 and 97/37 of January 13, 1997 and September 30, 1997, respectively, provide details regarding the state of the current relationship.

ple acquisition of equity, securing long-term supplies of raw materials, or business development to gain export access. We encourage them all.

Industrial cooperation, in fact, is an important element of our export development strategy for Korea, as is clear from the recently signed Joint Industrial and Economic Understanding between the two governments. This will mean that both Canada and Korea will allocate more resources to support private sector efforts to take advantage of the opportunities made possible by the Joint Understanding. And now is the time to do so.

There is a push on in Korea to diversify the economy into high technology and export-oriented products. So let me call on Canadian companies to make their own push into this market.

Another exciting possibility is cooperation in the construction of nuclear reactors in third countries.

However, the subject of trade imbalance between our two countries is a matter for concern. It has now grown to proportions that can no longer be defended. Korea has argued in favour of improved access in the Canadian market for automobiles, footwear, textiles and clothing. We have argued for improved access in Korea for Canadian products where we are particularly competitive. We are waiting expectantly for results.

In total frankness, it will become increasingly difficult to look favourably on Korea's further commercial aspirations in the Canadian market unless Canada can be encouraged by new inroads in some of the sectors we are trying hard to penetrate, sectors in which we are totally confident that we can compete.

Let me mention some specifics. Korea now applies a 20% tariff on softwood lumber. There is a 40% tariff on canola seeds. There is also an outright embargo on canola oil. There is a de facto import ban on alfalfa. For Canada, penetration of these markets, and for the markets for many of our manufactured goods, is essential to restore the imbalance in our trade and to increase the ratio of value-added products in our exports to Korea.

4.3. Canada and the Association Of Southeast Asian Nations (ASEAN)

ASEAN has been growing over the years and now has 10 member countries (Burma, Brunei, Cambodia, Indonesia, Laos, Malaysia, Philippines, Singapore, Thailand, and Vietnam), as well as ten "dialogue partners" (Australia, Canada, Korea, Japan, New Zealand, United States, the European Union, India, China, and Russia. Canada has been a partner since 1977. Dialogue partners are often invited to ASEAN meetings.

4 — The Far East

Canada and ASEAN Doc. 4.12

SPEECH BY SSEA JOE CLARK, DURING THE "SIX-PLUS-ONE" MEETING OF THE ASEAN POST-MINISTERIAL CONFERENCE, JAKARTA, JULY 28, 1990. (EXTRACTS)

Both Canada and ASEAN can be very pleased with the efforts of our private sectors in advancing trade and investments between us.

Bilateral trade reached $3 billion in 1989, more than double the level of 1986. Bilateral investments present a similar picture. The value of Canadian investment in ASEAN reached $1.5 billion in 1989, up from $800 million in 1980. I am particularly disappointed that we have not seen more ASEAN investment in Canada, despite the opportunities resulting from the Canada-United States Free Trade Agreement.

What governments do best is to develop frameworks for trade and investment. Canada initiated bilateral trade consultations with ASEAN governments in the spring, focusing particularly on market access issues with the multilateral trade negotiations now going on. The successful conclusion of the Uruguay Round offers the best means of advancing long-term prospects of greater trade between Canada and ASEAN.

4.4. Asia-Pacific Economic Cooperation (APEC)

APEC was set up in Canberra, in 1989, to provide a vehicle to channel the regional investment interests of Australia, the United States, and Japan, and also to provide a link with growing subregions such as the Greater South China Economic Zone. It brought together the six ASEAN "dialogue partners" of the day: Australia, Canada, Japan, South Korea, New Zealand, the U.S., and added thereto the "three Chinas": Beijing, Hong Kong, and Taiwan. Since then, it has been enlarged to include such new additions as Brunei, Chile, Indonesia, Malaysia, Mexico, Papua New Guinea, the Philippines, Singapore, Thailand. Membership is expected to continue growing, particularly since APEC's major goal is free trade among participants by the year 2020. In the circumstances, it has overtaken ASEAN to a large extent, although ASEAN still meets regularly. Incidentally, it will be recalled that APEC's fifth summit meeting in Vancouver, in 1997, gave rise to a number of incidents as the RCMP sought to move demonstrators into designated areas.

Although the Chrétien government has been paying somewhat more attention to APEC recently, it has continued its predecessor's approach to ASEAN.[55]

---

[55]See DFAIT statement SS 99/45 of July 27, 1999, for details.

Doc. 4.13   **APEC**

<small>STATEMENT BY INTERNATIONAL TRADE MINISTER ART EGGLETON, AT THE CANADA-CHINA BUSINESS COUNCIL'S ANNUAL GENERAL MEETING, SHANGHAI, NOVEMBER 26, 1996. (EXTRACTS)</small>

I have just come from Manila, where I attended the APEC meeting. One of the distinguishing features of APEC is its determination to incorporate the views of business into its work. Canada is chairing APEC in 1997 and one of our major objectives is to help small andf medium-sized enterprises to do business in these exciting and dynamic markets.

To that end, we will be placing particular emphasis on trade facilitation by working on things like making customs processes easier and pushing ahead with work on comparability of standards for products and services.

These sorts of efforts by APEC members will go a long way to making their markets both accessible and profitable for Canadian businesses.

Doc. 4.14   **Canada: A Pacific Rim country**

<small>SPEECH BY SSEA JOE CLARK, TO THE ASIA PACIFIC FOUNDATION, VANCOUVER, OCTOBER 22, 1988. (EXTRACTS)</small>

Asia is on the move. For Canada, the changes are real, fundamental, and of direct national concern.

Canada is a Pacific Rim country. Today, the Asia-Pacific region accounts for some 43% of our non-USA trade, compared to 34% for Europe. Five years ago, the figures were reversed.

A full fifty percent of our immigration now comes directly or indirectly from Asia.

Investment from Japan, Hong Kong, Korea, and Taiwan is growing rapidly: in the automobile industry, in resources, pulp and paper, in electronics and advanced technologies. It results in more jobs, new technologies, and a more promising future for our children.

Japanese tourists have increased by some 450% over the past five years. They are the highest-spending visitors we have.

The Government is responding actively to the opportunities that Asia offers to Canada:

- We have developed and implemented national strategies for managing our relations with Japan, China, and India;
- We have opened new offices in Osaka, Shanghai, Bombay, and Auckland;
- We have applauded the opening of the Taiwan trade office of the Canadian Chamber of Commerce;
- We have established effective mechanisms for cooperation with ASEAN;
- In Japan, we have pursued new initiatives in financial services and

investment promotion, in scientific collaboration and technology transfer. In 1986, we signed a science and technology agreement with Japan;

- We have embarked on a programme to open up new air services to the Asia-Pacific region.

There are five broad areas where we should be developing new programmes aimed at making Canada an important economic and political partner to Japan and other key countries in the Asia-Pacific region.

First, we must improve the teaching of Asian studies in Canada, particularly languages and culture. That includes every aspect of Asian society: history, culture, economics, language, politics, the way they think and the way they act.

In Australia, today, more than ten times as many young people are studying Japanese as in Canada. The U.S., Britain, France, Germany, outpace us as well.

Second, we need more effective scientific and technological cooperation.

Third, we must strengthen the trade and investment efforts that we began with the National Trade Strategy.

Fourth, we need more programmes to help Canadians to learn about Asia and vice-versa. For example, we should encourage and assist research on Asia-Pacific issues by our universities and foundations; fund visits to Canada by young Asian leaders and prominent journalists; support internships by young Canadians in Japan and vice-versa.

The final element, I believe we should be pursuing is the question of Pacific institutionalization. There is no Pacific equivalent to the network of North Atlantic organizations and institutions that link the European and North American countries politically, economically, and in the preservation of peace.

Canadian partnership in Pacific 2000   Doc. 4.15

SPEECH BY SSEA JOE CLARK, TO THE CORPORATE HIGHER EDUCATION FORUM, EDMONTON, MAY 16, 1989. (SYNOPSIS)

The Pacific 2000 programme comprises:

(a) A Trade Strategy designed to maintain and improve our market share;

(b) A Japan Science and Technology Fund;

(c) An Asian Languages and Awareness Fund, and

(d) A Pacific 2000 Projects Fund, which will offer support to Canadian activities in the region.

Canada's objectives as a player whose trans-Pacific economic, political security, and cultural links are expanding dramatically are:

(a) Mustering support for liberalized global trade;

(b) Promoting common disciplines and rules on trade, investment, technology transfer, and intellectual property;

(c) Research and analysis of regional economic growth;

(d) Engaging in scientific cooperation in areas of common interest; and

(e) Ensuring that the Pacific Rim countries are integrated into the international economy.

The responsibility to meet the challenges which the Asia Pacific region offers belongs to all of us: Government, private sector, and academic community.

5

International Economic and Trade Policy

UNDERSTANDABLY, DURING THE SECOND WORLD WAR, the Canadian economy was progressively mobilized and organized for war purposes and there was some apprehension that, when the war ended, Canada would again be faced by conditions of widespread Depression.

Counter-measures against unemployment and economic dislocation were taken as hostilities were drawing to a close in Europe and, in April 1945, the government presented a comprehensive White Paper to Parliament outlining the broad economic policies it proposed to apply in the post-war period. It was entitled *Employment and Income, with Special Reference to the Initial Period of Reconstruction.*

The most immediate major domestic aim of government policy should be "the adoption of a high level of employment and income, and thereby higher standards of living." To achieve that goal it outlined its long-range policy and emphasized that domestic policy would have to be closely coordinated with international economic and financial policy as well.

1. Towards a multilateral trading system

Canada accordingly took part with other trading nations in setting up international institutions to establish the foundations for multilateral trade on the widest possible basis. Two such institutions emerged from the Conference held at Bretton Woods in 1944, where Canada played an active role.

They dealt with the financial aspects of the international economy: (1) the International Monetary Fund (IMF), designed to assure the stability and convertibility of currencies, and thus facilitate the settlement of international accounts, thereby helping to prevent the competitive manipulation of currencies that had seriously affected trade during the Depression; and (2) the International Bank for Reconstruction and Development (IBRD), more commonly known as the World Bank, designed to revive international investment in countries devastated by war and in under-developed areas.

A third institution—an International Trade Organization (ITO)—was also planned, but did not come into being at the time, an insufficient number of countries (the United States particularly) declining to accept the new organization. The charter of the proposed new body was worked out at conference in Havana during 1946 and 1947 that had been called by the United Nations. It would have dealt directly with trade regulations, especially those aimed at reducing tariffs and other barriers to trade, and also the creation of a code of good national behaviour in international trade.

However, a provisional arrangement called the General Agreement on Tariffs and Trade (GATT) was worked out, pending acceptance of an eventual world body. It took more than 40 years (1994) for the World Trade Organization (WTO) to emerge!

Meanwhile, GATT included most of the prohibitions against unfair practices embodied in the draft charter of the Organization, and an agreement for short term tariff reductions among nearly all members attending the conference. This provisional agreement came into force a few months after the Havana conference. GATT's provisions were regularly modified and brought up to date by successive conferences.

Following is a brief outline of the procedures followed by GATT: conferences of the signatories were held from time to time as required to give effect to or modify existing regulations. In addition, special conferences for the multiple reduction of tariff barriers are held.

Doc. 5.1   **GATT**

ADDRESS BY TRADE AND COMMERCE MINISTER C.D. HOWE, TO THE 6TH SESSION OF
CONTRACTING PARTIES, GATT, GENEVA, SEPTEMBER 17, 1951. SS51/33. (EXTRACTS)

It is barely four years since October, 1947, when the General Agreement on Tariffs and Trade was drawn up and signed by the representatives of twenty-three countries. Since then, the scope of the GATT has steadily increased. Prestige and experience have accrued to the work of the Contracting Parties. It is not too soon to say that this organization has demonstrated its usefulness. It has already more than paid for itself through the results which have been achieved. The GATT has earned its place in the front rank amongst international organizations. Today there are thirty-seven participating countries and most of them are represented here. Multilateral tariff negotiations have been organized on three occasions and have been carried through to a successful conclusion.

There have been various occasions on which outside observers have said that a crisis had been reached or that approaching difficulties would prove insurmountable. The General Agreement was itself the product of arduous negotiations and compromises. Many people wondered, prior to Torquay, whether it would be possible to arrange for the prolongation of the life of the tariff concessions which were negotiated at Geneva and Annecy. When the time came, it was found possible to continue the large bulk of earlier tariff concessions for a further period of three years, along with the new concessions negotiated at Torquay. Only a very small number of tariff items had to be renegotiated. Rather than a crisis or a defeat, this proved to be one of the major accomplishments of the GATT Similarly, there was disappointment at the failure of some of the participants at Torquay to conclude new tariff agreements, these including some of the countries most important in world trade. As the months have gone by, in spite of this, we have noticed that commercial relations amongst these same countries have continued on an amicable basis without noticeable impairment. The countries in question have all continued to adhere to the General Agreement and the results of their earlier tariff negotiations have continued in force.

The GATT was organized as a collective international effort to get rid of obstacles to trade, to reduce tariffs and to minimize the scope of quantitative restrictions. Surely these are objectives to which all countries could give their encouragement and support. However after having been a member of the Canadian Government for sixteen years one thing at least I have learned. Whether we have prosperity or depression and whether we have war or peace, there is always someone to clamour for tariff protection and quantitative restrictions to solve some immediate problem that besets the world. No matter what the contingencies, there are always some people who want to run for cover and protection, whether or not there is any real threat of trouble.

Nothing can be more short-sighted than to give way to the pessimists and to curtail trade. Some few individuals may be helped by import controls, but in the long run curtailment of trade is not the road to prosperity and higher standards of living. On the contrary, restrictions more often lead to mutual impoverishment. We have to bear in mind that import controls spread like an epidemic once they start and are very difficult to check.

Sometimes, of course, restrictions are unavoidable for brief periods of time, and the General Agreement contemplates circumstances in which countries are quite entitled to resort to them. Along with many other countries, Canada found herself in serious balance of payments difficulties during the period of readjustment which followed the last war. Our currency reserves were seriously depleted at that time and immediate action was essential to prevent a critical situation. In the circumstances, it was deemed necessary to impose import controls and this we did. The Canadian Government always regarded these controls as temporary and our industries were warned on repeated occasions that the protection offered by these controls would be withdrawn at the earliest possible date. This was in full accordance with our obligations under the GATT and it was also in the best interests of our national economy.

We knew that import controls would not provide of themselves a lasting remedy for the difficulties which beset us at that time. They merely provided a breathing space during which other methods could be made effective. The real solution to the problem was to increase the flow of trade. We stepped up our exports and we achieved a better balance of trade with each of the great currency areas of the world. I am happy to report that all of our emergency restrictions on imports were removed some time ago. Canada is now exporting and importing more than ever before ...

Within the GATT we have many countries with different systems of government. For myself, I have always found that production and trade are most efficiently organized by private people. On occasion, of course, the Canadian Government has shown its ability to organize production very efficiently. Some of the countries represented here have committed themselves, on the other hand, to a considerable degree of state control and state direction of their economic affairs. One of the great virtues of the General Agreement is that, from the beginning, it has represented a workable compromise between these points of view. If world trade is to flourish in the future, as it must, it will be necessary to continue this basis of common arrangements and common understanding between state trading and private trading countries.

It may happen on occasion that arrangements which have been made become impossible to continue. Where governments undertake the direct control of trade, there is always the danger that such devices will be used as political and economic weapons. In such circumstances, it is possible completely to frustrate trading relations as envisaged by the General Agreement. Extreme problems of this kind will not often arise, however, and when they do they can be dealt with as isolated cases.

It is essential that the vitality of this organization be preserved. My delegation is interested in the provision of machinery by which the Contracting Parties would carry on the details of technical work between sessions, so that these sessions can be made shorter and more efficient. Only in this way will it be possible to obtain the attendance of responsible and senior representatives from the participating countries.

I am sure that other delegations have come here with important problems. It is to be hoped that satisfactory solutions can be found for all of these, to enable the GATT to move forward to its future tasks. The achievements to date are unprecedented, in bringing together into a common agreement all of the countries which are important to world trade and in reducing the incidence of tariffs and trade restrictions. My delegation has come here prepared to support all measures which will strengthen this organization and help to maintain the substance of its accomplishments. On the other hand, we do not think it wise at this time to entertain proposals for expanding the activities of the Contracting Parties into new fields. The task of the Contracting Parties is already well defined and important in the field of tariffs and related trade controls. It would be unwise to endanger the whole structure by too wide a diversification of our efforts.

2. Tariff negotiations and reductions: The "Rounds"

Under the General Agreement on Tariffs and Trade (GATT), extensive and lengthy meetings began at Geneva in 1963, known as the "Kennedy Round" of Trade and Tariff Negotiations. These stemmed from the Kennedy administration's Trade Expansion Act of 1962 and the power contained therein to reduce most United States tariffs by half and remove altogether duties that were 5% or less. President Kennedy had actively encouraged this legislation and the resulting conference was called the Kennedy Round to honour his memory.

The Kennedy Round has been followed by a succession of substantive international tariff conferences, such as the Tokyo Round (1973-1979), the Uruguay Round (1986-1993), and currently the Seattle Round. Since subsequent Rounds have followed the pattern, the basic objectives, of the Kennedy Round quite closely, it is dealt with in detail below.[56]

Canada and the Kennedy Round: Preparations and initial position Doc. 5.2

STATEMENT BY TRADE AND COMMERCE MINISTER MITCHELL SHARP, HOUSE OF COMMONS, APRIL 14, 1964. (EXTRACTS)

In his budget speech the Minister of Finance referred to the prospect that these negotiations, known colloquially as the Kennedy round, would rank with the important trade negotiations that have taken place under the auspices of GATT since the end of the war. Hon. members may recall that the basis of these forthcoming negotiations was the decision of the GATT trade ministers last May when I attended the conference in Geneva on behalf of Canada. At that time several things were de-

---

[56]For details regarding Canada's objectives and the results we achieved at the Tokyo and Uruguay Rounds, see A.E.B. III, Chapter V, pp. 91-94. DFAIT News Release No. 99/59 of November 26, 1999, provides comprehensive coverage of "The Canadian Agenda in Seattle."

cided which, I should perhaps recall: First, that the trade negotiations should begin on May 4, 1964; that the negotiations should be based on the principle of reciprocity; that there should be the widest possible participation in the negotiations; that the negotiations should cover all classes of products, whether industrial or agricultural; that the negotiations should deal with both tariff and non-tariff barriers to trade; that they should be based on a plan of substantially equal linear tariff cuts for certain of the more highly industrialized countries; that the trade negotiations should provide for acceptable conditions of access to world markets for agricultural products, and that every effort should be made to reduce barriers to exports of the less developed countries. It was on the basis of these principles as agreed to last May in Geneva that a trade negotiating committee was established to work out or negotiate a plan to supervise the conduct of the negotiations.

This committee has been at work and it has been trying to work out the negotiating rules relating to the countries participating on a linear basis, and particularly the question of the depth of the tariff cut, and the way of dealing with this problem of tariff disparities.

Now, since these negotiating rules will have an important bearing on the results, one can say that the negotiations which we have been talking about as if they were to begin on May 4, have really already begun. These negotiations have, in fact, now been in progress for some months. Since this matter is of very considerable interest not only to the members of this house but to the community at large, I should like to deal briefly, and I hope clearly, with the problems that are now under discussion.

The essence of the problem of tariff disparities is to develop equitable rules for negotiations of equal linear tariff cuts between countries with differing tariff levels or structures. This problem, as hon. members may well recognize, arises particularly between the European Economic Community and the United States because the tariffs which now surround the European Economic Community are the result of an averaging process, a process which was necessary in order to make one community out of the six countries that entered into the European Economic Community. During this averaging process most of the tariff peaks were removed. The United States, on the other hand, has many low rates, but more particularly high rates in certain sectors, rates that are substantially above the rates of duty for the same items in the common market tariff. The six contend that where their tariff is significantly below the level of the comparable United States tariff an equal linear tariff cut would not yield an equivalence of benefit. Last May it was agreed that the trade negotiations committee should develop a criterion for determining where significant tariff disparities exist — that is disparities which are meaningful in trade terms — and to determine what special rules should be applicable for tariff reductions in such cases.

Since the likelihood is that where tariff disparities are found to exist there will be smaller cut in tariffs, the question of the number of items accepted for special treatment has an important bearing on the total scope of the negotiations and on the question of reciprocity of benefit. It may also have an important bearing on the exceptions which would be made to the general rule, and particularly upon the general position of countries other than the United States and the European Economic Community, who will be affected by the depth of the tariff cuts made by them. Although progress has been made, the chief countries concerned have not yet resolved these difficult issues. Further meetings are scheduled between now and the opening date of May 4.

The second and perhaps most important point that was referred to the trade negotiating committee was the depth of the tariff cut. The United States trade legislation allows for cuts of up to 50 per cent on an across the board basis and with few exceptions. It also permits the removal of United States tariffs where the rates are 5 per cent or less. The discussions that have been going on in Geneva have been going forward on the working hypothesis of a 50 per cent cut. Whether this will become the actual rule for tariff reduction remains to be agreed. How much of the tariff of the United States, of the European Economic Community and of other countries will, in fact, be reduced in these negotiations cannot be finally known until the end of the negotiations. It will depend on the extent to which the participating countries are prepared to exchange meaningful concessions. The actual average incidence of the cut will be determined, not only by the general rate, whatever that may be, but also by the number of disparities involved and the number of exceptions made.

We for our part, and I am speaking now on behalf of Canada, are hoping that our trading partners will be prepared to go as far as possible in offering reductions to barriers to our export trade. There is every evidence to suggest that the United States administration is determined to offer maximum concessions to other countries within the scope of the authority received from congress. The United Kingdom and the continental EFTA (European Free Trade Association) countries have indicated that they intend to make substantial and positive response and they are interested, like the United States, in keeping exceptions to the minimum and narrowing the list of disparity items. The European Economic Community, on the other hand, has reaffirmed its support for a major round of trade negotiations but attaches great importance to a satisfactory resolution, from its point of view, to the problem of tariff disparities and to other matters bearing on the scope and balance of the negotiations.

I have referred to exceptions. These are items which countries may consider it necessary to withhold from their linear offer. It was agreed by the ministers last May that such exceptions should be kept to a bare minimum; that they should be subject in each case to confrontation and justification. The United States, by its own trade legislation, is required to exclude from its tariff offer lead and zinc and petroleum.

Other countries do not have such legislative requirements. They may, however, be expected to come forward with certain items on which they do not feel able to offer tariff cuts. Such lists of exceptions and the scope of them might well become a key element in the negotiations themselves.

For example, it would clearly limit the value of the negotiations for Canada if items of particular interest in our trade were included in the exceptions lists of countries where we have important markets.

The working out of negotiating roles with respect to made in agriculture is also proving to be both delicate and difficult. It is agreed that trade in agriculture should be an integral part of the negotiations and that the negotiations are to deal with the creation of acceptable conditions of access to world markets for agricultural products.

Here, however, special measures of protection as most hon. members know, designed to support farm economies by one means or another make it difficult, indeed well-nigh impossible, to apply the same negotiating rules to basic agricultural products as can be applied to the negotiations in the industrial sector. In many cases, some very important for Canada as an agricultural exporter, the tariff is not the effective barrier to trade. In other cases, the tariff is used in combination with other restrictive devices. None the less, for efficient agriculture producers whose international trade has a substantial agricultural content, meaningful negotiations on agriculture will be a critical element in a successful negotiation.

This is so for Canada and for the United States as well as for Australia and New Zealand. The problem of finding a satisfactory negotiating base has had the added complexity that the European economic community is still in the process for formulating its common agricultural policy. It will require a good deal of imagination and good will to work out a solid settlement with the community in an area in which, for most basic agricultural products, the key element affecting production and therefore the scope for imports is the level of the support price, the system and the price being protected by a variable levy at the frontier which has the effect of bringing up the price of competitive imports to the level of prices prevailing in the domestic market.

While it is too early to be clear about the prospects in this sector, negotiations have been initiated for world cereals arrangements and there appears to be a readiness to bring agricultural supports and domestic production policies under international negotiation and confrontation. Meat groups and dairy products groups have been established to look into the possibility of special international arrangements for these products. Canada and other traditional exporters are placing the emphasis on access and satisfactory international prices. The Six tend to approach the question from the basis of acceptance of their agricultural system and a form of negotiation which would be related to it but which would emphasize the status quo rather than the expansion of competition between domestically produced and imported products.

Commonwealth countries generally have been playing an active role in the preparatory stages of the GATT trade negotiations. Whether they be developing countries, or chiefly agricultural exporters like New Zealand and Australia, or countries like Canada and the United Kingdom, each has made clear the important benefits for trade which they see possible through the Kennedy Round, and there has been very strong support throughout the commonwealth for the forthcoming round of tariff negotiations.

As in the past, any major world trade negotiations involving substantial reductions in barriers to international trade will inevitably involve adjustments in the commonwealth preferences. To the extent, for example, that the United Kingdom reduces its most favoured nation rates, the margins of preference of commonwealth countries in access to the British market would be reduced. Similarly, a Canadian participation inevitably involves adjustments in preferences that, for example, the British are accorded in this market. While no detailed discussions have been held with the British government on this matter, we have been in touch and the two countries will be consulting closely throughout the negotiations with a view to ensuring that, whatever adjustments in the preferences may be necessary, they are worked out in consultation.

Finally, Mr. Speaker, I would like to refer to the position of state-trading countries in relation to these international negotiations. As hon. members are aware, Canada has found some important and valuable markets within the Sino-Soviet bloc. There is every reason to believe that this area will continue to have substantial food import requirements that we should be in a position to supply. The framework for these commercial exchanges has generally been worked out through bilateral negotiations in which I had some participation, and in which, I understand, one of the ministers of the former government had also. It has so far not been found possible to bring state-trading countries into a multilateral trading framework.

One of the challenges of the future, as market economies seek to develop closer commercial ties with socialist planned economy countries, will be to see whether a broad and more or less continuing framework of multilateral trade can be developed, in which state-trading countries and the needs of market economies can be fitted together on a mutually satisfactory basis.

You will see, Mr. Speaker, from the problems I have discussed how difficult and complex a situation faces both the GATT conference, and the United Nations conference now in progress. The finding of the way through them will require patience as well as diligence. We should expect what appear to be delays and set-backs from time to time. This is in the nature of important world trade negotiations. However, I am encouraged by the progress that is being made, and look forward to the launching of the Kennedy round on May 4 next, and to the serious and worth-while negotiations that lie ahead. In them Canada will seek to play its full part.

Doc. 5.3 **Canada and the Kennedy Round: Final results**

STATEMENT BY TRADE AND COMMERCE MINISTER ROBERT WINTERS, HOUSE OF COMMONS, APRIL 29, 1967. (EXTRACTS)

The final act of the Kennedy Round is to be signed tomorrow morning in Geneva, thus bringing these negotiations to a formal conclusion. The resulting agreements, including the schedules of tariff concessions granted by all participating countries, can now be made public. I should make clear that these tariff cuts will not come into effect until January 1, 1968, and in many instances they will be staged over the next four years.

At the conclusion of my remarks I shall ask leave to table, on behalf of the Minister of Finance and myself, detailed information on the tariff and trade agreements of interest to GATT concluded during the Kennedy Round. Everything possible is being done to ensure that the Canadian business community is made aware of these results without delay ...

Mr. Speaker, as has been indicated on numerous occasions, the Kennedy Round constitutes by far the most important trade pact in history, the most comprehensive in coverage and the most significant in the extent and depth of tariff reductions.

Over $45 billion of goods and hundreds of thousands of tariff items are affected by the concessions exchanged; all aspects of world trade, including tariffs and certain non-tariff barriers, and agricultural as well as industrial goods, were within the ambit of the negotiations. Never before have trade negotiations of this scope, magnitude and far-reaching impact taken place.

It is fitting, on this final day, to pay tribute once again to the statesmanship and farsightedness of the late President Kennedy. To his initiative were due in large part the ambitious objectives which these negotiations set themselves and which have to such a high degree been attained.

It was to be expected that the Kennedy Round would be exceedingly complex and difficult, involving a great deal of intensive bargaining; indeed, there were occasions, through the nearly four years of negotiations, when the obstacles appeared to some too great to be overcome. However, despite crises and delays, and due to the perseverance and basic goodwill of all countries concerned, the issues blocking agreement were resolved.

For Canada, the success of the Kennedy Round has wide-ranging implications, opening new broad perspectives of expanded trade and benefiting all sectors and regions of the economy. Indeed, a dramatic and sustained increase in Canadian export trade is essential if we are to deal effectively with the common issues confronting us as regards standards of living, balance of payments, jobs and the like. The concessions granted in our own tariffs to gain greater access to other markets must be regarded in the light of the very great benefits which can accrue to Canada from expanded exporting opportunities.

Many sectors of industry, where Canadian tariffs are being reduced are also the sectors which stand to benefit most from export gains. In many instances, the cuts in Canadian tariffs are in areas which will help reduce the costs of production for Canadian processors and manufacturers, as well as for consumers. That, Mr. Speaker, is important.

The export benefits obtained by Canada from its agreements with major trading partners cover, including wheat, over $3 billion of our current export trade. In the United States and the EEC, most industrial tariffs will be reduced to levels of 10 per cent or less. As a result of the across-the-board tariff cuts made by our major trading partners, trade opportunities will become available for the first time to a very wide range of manufactured goods — many of which will be Canada's exports of tomorrow. For Canada, therefore, the Kennedy Round could contribute to the solution of many of our basic economic problems and set in motion the process of adaptation and restructuring which could, in time, reshape the character of the economy. There are many areas where we need more values added, more up-grading of our raw materials, and this should help.

It may well be that the Kennedy Round will be regarded in the future as a crucial turning-point in the transformation of Canada from a resource-based economy to one of the most advanced industrial nations of the world.

I have commented, on previous occasions, in some detail on the significance of the new cereals agreement for Canada's wheat trade, for the Western Prairie Provinces, and for the economy and balance of payments as a whole. The International Wheat Council is convening a special negotiating session in Rome on July 12, with a view to revising the International Wheat Agreement so as to incorporate the cereals commitments agreed to in the Kennedy Round.

Canada welcomes the participation of all countries with a significant interest in wheat trade in these negotiations, and would like to see the new agreement completed and put into operation as soon as possible.

Now that the Kennedy Round is concluded, it is vitally important that every sector of the Canadian economy should exploit the new export opportunities before us. The main initiative must rest with private enterprise itself. The department is being geared to provide maximum assistance to the Canadian business community in their export efforts. There will, of course, be areas and sectors which may feel a sense of greater exposure to competition because of tariff reductions made to gain access on a wider basis to the markets of the world for a very broad range of Canadian products. There are bound to be some local, negative reactions. But, in the overall, this is a great, positive step, and it can mean a very large net gain for the Canadian economy. I am sure our dynamic Canadian enterprise will ensure that result.

3. International Economic Policy

The mid-years of the century were creative ones in terms of new international agencies, regional groupings, and specialized conferences designed to foster trade and economic development. The beginnings of the European Union (formerly the European Economic Community) come to mind in this context. So too does the Organization for Economic Co-operation and Development (OECD), in which Canada played a particularly active role in broadening the membership and mandate of the Organization for European Economic Co-operation (OEEC) at the time.[57]

The first of the great UN conferences on Trade and Development (UNCTAD) goes back to this period also.

But events closer to home were also having an impact on our approach to world economics: the Canadian dollar.

Doc. 5.4   **The dollar floats again**

STATEMENT BY SSEA MITCHELL SHARP, JUNE 8, 1971, TO THE OECD MINISTERIAL MEETING IN PARIS. (EXTRACTS)

We meet at a time of considerable economic difficulty for many, if not most, of the members of our Organization. Problems of unemployment and inflation continue to plague us. The recent crisis in the international monetary system and its longer-term implications call for study and action by member governments if we are to bring about greater stability in the financial environment.

As a major trading nation, Canada attaches the highest importance to an orderly international system of trade and payments. While the current-account balances of some major countries moved some distance toward a better equilibrium in the light of stated objectives in 1970, I note the forecast that there will be little progress in 1971 toward a pattern of current-account balances that would support appropriate capital flows. The fact is, though, that the recent disturbances have come about primarily as a result of capital movements rather than current-account imbalances. The speculative flows early last month, which resulted in changes in a number of European exchange-rates, emphasized the need for improvement in the present system. This will not be a simple task.

---

[57]See A.E.B. I, pp. 355-357, for an account by Finance Minister Donald Fleming in the House of Commons on December 10, 1960, about the creation of the OECD and Canada's role in helping to bring it about.

5 — International Economic and Trade Policy

Let me recall the circumstances that led to the freeing of Canada's exchange-rate just over a year ago. In 1969, Canada had a sizable deficit on current account and there was a large outflow of short-term capital in response to a rise in interest-rates abroad. These out-payments were offset by the traditional inflows of long-term capital and only minor changes occurred in our official reserves during the year. Substantial shifts, however, occurred in our balance of payments during the first five months of 1970 and, as a result, our overall reserves rose at an accelerated rate and increased by $1,200 million (U.S.) during that period. Our exports increased to a much greater extent than could be accounted for by the rebound from the effects of strikes late in 1969. In addition, short-term capital outflows declined in response to lower interest-rates abroad and this combination left Canada exposed as a target for speculative inflows. We decided to act promptly before speculation became too heavy — thereby, we believe, making a contribution to the stability of the international monetary system.

Our situation in May 1970 was not quite comparable to that faced by others last month. In the first place, we had moved comparatively quickly from a deficit to an unexpectedly large surplus on current account. Secondly, our trading and financial relations with the U.S.A. are very close. Finally, the extreme openness of our economy to the movements of goods and capital causes us to experience unusual difficulty in maintaining a fixed exchange-rate within the margins prescribed by the IMF.

The classic prescription would have been to seek the concurrence of the Fund to a new and higher par value. Our problem was to determine a rate that would be sustainable for a reasonable period.

In taking the decision to move to a floating exchange-rate, we made clear our intention to resume our obligations under the par-value system as soon as circumstances permit. This remains our firm determination and, while we have reviewed the situation from time to time during the past year, the underlying situation, both internal and external, has not seemed to us sufficiently settled to re-establish a par value that could be defended over the foreseeable future. In terms of payments, we have been confronted by a need to bring about an adjustment in our capital account in line with changes that have occurred in our current account. Expansionary financial policies, which our domestic economic situation required, have been helpful, but we have had to reinforce the effect of these policies by appeals to Canadian borrowers to seek the funds they required in the Canadian market to the maximum possible extent. At the same time, we felt a sense of uncertainty about the impact of international developments — a sense that would appear to have been justified by recent events.

The extent of departures from the fixed-rate regime that have taken place raises very large issues. Our experience and that of others has underlined the inherent difficulties involved in combining a system of fixed exchange-rates and free capital flows internationally with the imperative demands placed upon our control instruments by the objectives of high employment and price stability domestically. There are a number of different ways of escaping from the dilemma — greater exchange-rate flexibility and control over the international flows of capital, greater international harmonization of monetary policies — but all these alternatives raise difficulties of a practical and policy nature.[58]

4. The World Economic Summits

The Summits have their origin in an informal meeting in 1973, when the United States Secretary of the Treasury invited the Finance Ministers of Britain, France, and Germany to Washington to discuss international monetary conditions. Japan was invited to their 1974 meeting.

As global trade and financial transactions became increasingly complex, the President of France, Valéry Giscard d'Estaing, a former Finance Minister and host of the 1975 meeting, decided that Heads of State or Government and not just Finance Ministers should receive an invitation, and he added Italy to their number.

The 1975 meeting took place at Rambouillet, near Paris. Canada was not invited, but after an intense lobbying campaign, supported by the United States, it attended the next one and has since been an active member of the Group. Participants became known, in this context, as the G-7 countries, to which Russia was recently added, making it the G-8. Summit meetings take place annually.[59]

The Summits started out well, with substantive discussions among the Heads of State or Government whose countries, taken together, account for more than half of the world's trade and in-

---

[58]For further information about the Canadian/United States dollar relationship, and that of other currencies, from the 1930s down to the early 1990s, see A.E.B. II, pp. 214-215, and A.E.B. III, p. 99. *A History of the Canadian Dollar* by James Powell, 1999 (published by and available from the Bank of Canada, Ottawa) provides the whole story from the beginnings (pre-1841) down to the end of the 1990s. Incidentally, the Canadian dollar reached its all-time low vis-à-vis the U.S. dollar on August 11, 1998: (.6304 U.S. intra-day trading; .6311 U.S. at close).

[59]Apart from the Group of 8, there is also a Group of 11 that meets occasionally. It comprises the G-8 countries plus Belgium, the Netherlands, Sweden, to which Switzerland is sometimes added. The leading developing countries, such as Argentina, Brazil, Chile, Indonesia, Malaysia, Mexico, among others, have created their own Group of 15 to protect and enhance their interests. Lately the Group of 20, a Canadian initiative under the leadership of Finance Minister Martin, has come into being. It groups together the G-8 countries along with such large economies as Brazil, China, India, Mexico, Spain, among others.

dustrial output. During the 1980s, however, the meetings were not always as substantive or as effective as earlier ones. They seemed to have become media events, taken over almost entirely by the television networks, particularly during the years that President Ronald Reagan was in office (1981–1989). An aura of frustration tended to surround them.

Recently, things have improved, but there may be some truth to the old Japanese saying that "there are two kinds of fools in this world: those who have never climbed Mount Fuji and those who have climbed it twice."

The Economic Summits   Doc. 5.5

SPEECH BY ALLAN GOTLIEB, UNDER-SECRETARY, DFAIT, TO THE CANADIAN INSTITUTE OF INTERNATIONAL AFFAIRS, WINNIPEG, APRIL 9, 1981. (EXTRACTS)

In considering why the meetings began, we must go back to the situation in 1975. Two years after the Yom Kippur War and the ensuing fourfold increase (by December 1973) in oil prices by the Organization of Petroleum-Exporting Countries (OPEC), it was painfully evident that the industrialized countries had not coped well or cohesively with the fall-out. They were confronting major and pressing economic problems (recession and unemployment, accompanied by inflation), many of which indeed originated before the oil shock, arising in part out of the persistent current-account deficits of the United States.

When the International Monetary Fund (IMF) Interim Committee in June 1975 failed to agree on how to approach major monetary issues (exchange rates, quotas, gold), the French President, Valéry Giscard d'Estaing, elected to his seven-year term little more than a year earlier and himself a former Finance Minister, suggested a monetary summit on the ground that it was largely the floating exchange rates which were destabilising the monetary system and causing the major economic problems.

After some hesitation, the other leaders agreed. They went to Rambouillet in November 1975, but only after agreement that the agenda should provide for consideration of over-all economic policies as well as monetary issues, and also look at North-South problems as well. The Summit was to take a policy-oriented, rather than a narrowly technical, approach. The emphasis was on coordination. The leaders felt constrained to consult together, to try to work together more closely, and to be seen to be doing so.

If we stand back and look at successive Summits, one is struck by a number of points:

The main economic problems identified by the leaders as requiring their attention have largely been the same mix over the years: low growth, inflation, unemployment, protectionist pressures, energy, the North/South dialogue.

There has been a growing appreciation of the degree of inter-dependence among developed countries, so much so that domestic policies in any major country have a growing effect on others and thus no one country can regulate its own economy alone. Accordingly, problems such as interest rates, economic stimulus or restraint, have to be tackled in concert.

There has been a shift from the more short specific issues of earlier Summits to the longer-term outlook current today. Also, the Summits have extended their purview beyond the basic economic issues. Terrorism and hijacking have been such issues, as well as refugees.

At a minimum, looking ahead, I find it hard to imagine that Summits in some form or another are not here for the foreseeable future. Indeed, if Summits did not exist, they would probably have to be invented. In my view, they are here to stay.

For our part, in Canada, we attach a good deal of importance to the Summits. They should continue to be available to do the sort of things they do now. They might even begin to take what I call the macro-political approach. Somehow, I believe, we in the industrial world need a manageable locus for concerting our views and objectives, our policies and activities.

It is particularly important, from a Canadian point of view, that this kind of consultation and concertation be effectively taking place among our closest friends, since we are placed in a very delicate position in the case of persistent and major unresolved differences, say, between the United States and the European Community countries, or Japan. We are accordingly anxious to overcome the current differences on economic and political strategy among the industrialized democracies and believe the Summits could be helpful in doing so.

5. Globalization: A 21st-Century Approach

Trade, finance, economies generally, transnational corporations, are becoming increasingly globalized. Canada is playing a leading role in seeking to ensure global economic growth and stability, to reduce the risk of financial crises, while also taking into consideration the need to respond to the requirements of the world's poorest and most vulnerable countries.

Finance Minister Martin has been in the forefront of this movement as Chair of the new Group of 20, comprising the G-8 countries, as well as such large economies as Brazil, China, India, Mexico, Spain, among others.

Doc. 5.6   **Six-point Canadian plan to deal with global financial problems**

STATEMENT BY FINANCE MINISTER PAUL MARTIN, OTTAWA, SEPTEMBER 29, 1998. FINANCE CANADA NEWS RELEASE. (EXTRACTS)

In a speech to the Commonwealth Business Forum, Finance Minister Martin laid out the challenges facing the global economy and urged the international community to take action on six fronts:

1) Ensuring appropriate monetary policy through G-7 central banks paying close attention and giving appropriate weight to the risk of a further slowdown in the global economy;

2) A renewed commitment by the merging market economies to sound macroeconomic and structural policy;

3) Expeditious action to strengthen national financial systems and international oversight;

4) Development of a practical guide or "roadmap" for safe capital liberalization in developing countries;

5) Agreement to work urgently towards a better mechanism to involve private-sector investors in the resolution of financial crises, including the possibility of an Emergency Standstill Clause; and

6) Greater attention to the needs of the poorest countries to ensure that they receive the resources and support that they need to reduce poverty and being growing.

The plan would address the most immediate dangers by ensuring that interest rates support continuing sustainable growth and promoting a sound policy environment in the merging markets. It would also address the underlying causes of financial instability by strengthening financial sector supervision and ensuring that "hot money" private investors bear their share of the financial burden during times of crisis.[60]

6. International Trade Policy

The vigorous encouragement of international trade has been a characteristic of all Canadian governments since the Second World War.

Both the St. Laurent and Diefenbaker governments pursued much the same positive approach to Canadian trade and emphasized exports consistently. One problem that they had to deal with at the time was Britain's initiatives in seeking to join the European Economic Community (EEC). A successful outcome of its moves towards Europe would — in their view — have severely cut into our trade with Britain. Its efforts culminated successfully in the 1970s when it did manage to join the EEC, now the European Union.

---

[60]The statement comes with a useful *Backgrounder* outlining the plan in greater detail. See also Finance Canada News Releases 99-051 and 99-052 of June 7, 1999, for further information about the Martin proposals with respect to "reforming the international financial architecture to limit the frequency and severity of financial crises."

However, any slackening in our trade with Britain was quickly taken up by the steep rise in our trade with the United States. In the 1950s, the percentage of trade with the United States, in terms of our world trade, was somewhat above 50%. Today, it has reached well above 80%. Trade with the expanded European Union (EU), including Britain, has of course also grown in volume over the years, but in terms of percentages it is around 10% currently.

The basic trade objectives of the Trudeau government were much the same: the promotion of a strong domestic economy and the development of an international trading environment favourable to Canadian exports, but with a twist.

In keeping with its philosophy of seeking a more detached relationship with the United States, it proposed a "Third Option", coupled with a Contractual Link and Framework Agreement with the European Union. Neither produced the hoped for results and trade with the United States continued to rise steadily.[61]

The Mulroney government concentrated on North America and concluded the two Free Trade Agreements that have set the basic pattern of Canada's trade policy from the late 1980s until well into the 21st century.

The Chrétien government has generally maintained its predecessor's trade policy, but one of its initiatives — Team Canada — aroused a good deal of attention. Initially, the idea was to encourage better federal-provincial exchanges by bringing together the Prime Minister and his provincial opposite numbers in settings abroad, where they could get to know one another better and feel more at ease than at home to discuss questions of interest and concern to them. To give the initiative a somewhat sharper focus, PM Chrétien proposed that it also include academics and businessmen. Thus "Team Canada" was born.

The Team Canada missions did not produce all the hoped for results, particularly on the trade side. That to Latin America, the largest one, and those to South and Southeast Asia took place just before the severe recessions that hit Brazil and other regions in Latin America, as well as several countries in Southern Asia: the so-called "Asian flu". Offsetting this, the federal-provincial and academic objectives were achieved.[62]

---

[61]During a visit to Europe in 1975, PM Trudeau met with the heads of member governments of EEC in Brussels and explained his Contractual Link project to them. See A.E.B. II, pp. 225-226. As for "Canada and the United States — the Third Option", A.E.B. II, pp. 106-111. carries the text of SSEA Mitchell Sharp's statement about this to the Canadian Institute of International Affairs, Toronto, September 18, 1972.

[62]For more complete coverage of the Team Canada project, see *DFAIT and*

For the record, the immediately following document rounds out the trade policy picture from the Trudeau government's standpoint during the early 1980s.

Canadian Trade Policy for the 1980s: A discussion paper

Doc. 5.7

BOOKLET PRODUCED UNDER THE AUTHORITY OF THE DEPUTY PRIME MINISTER MACEACHEN, AND MINISTER OF STATE FOR INTERNATIONAL TRADE GERALD A. REGAN. (SUMMARY)

The broad objectives of Canadian trade policy can be summarized as follows:

The development of a more efficient, productive, and and competitive domestic economy and the promotion of a more stable and open international trading environment within which Canadian and foreign firms alike are encouraged to plan, invest, and grow.

To a large extent Canadian trade policy has been, and will continue to be, developed as a trade-off between the objective of improved access to foreign markets, the need to promote efficiency and competitiveness, and the need to provide protection for those Canadian industries subject to intense competitive pressures, but considered important in terms of national or regional interests.

Within this broad context, more specific export trade policy objectives are: continuing to develop the adjacent U.S. market, while reducing the tendency towards the development of regional groupings through reductions of trade barriers on a non-discriminatory basis; advancing Canadian industrial development through expanding Canadian export opportunities for further processed food and industrial materials; and promoting long-term and stable markets for Canada's primary exports (agricultural, fisheries, and industrial).

On the import side, Canadian trade policy objectives are to provide an international framework which will facilitate the development of a competitive domestic economy, including specifically, an appropriate level of protection against injurious competition, as well as reasonable measures to safeguard Canadian agricultural producers.

Taking the export and import sides together, Canadian trade objectives seek to achieve a balanced development of trading opportunities which take into account regional and sectoral interests.

7. Canada and the Commonwealth Caribbean

A brief mention of Canadian relations with the countries now commonly grouped together under the general heading of the Commonwealth Caribbean might conclude this chapter. They are of very long standing and were once far more prominent than today.

Team Canada by the current editor in *Bout de papier*, pp. 3–5, Volume 16, No. 1, Spring 1999.

They go back to the sugar-rum-molasses for cod-cereal trade of the 18th and 19th centuries.

Trade was followed by investments. Canadian banks, insurance, and mining companies gradually acquired highly influential positions in many of the islands. The commercial aspects of the relationship were governed by the Trade Agreement of 1925. It came to an end some 50 years later when, in 1976, the Commonwealth Caribbean countries decided to adhere to the European Union's Lomé Agreement.

After the islands became independent in the 1960s, the pattern of relations with Canada changed a good deal. Most Canadian investments were nationalized. Aid, immigration, tourism, sugar, became the dominant features of the relationship, to which money-laundering and drugs can be added today. In the aid sector, for instance, Canadian allocations to the Caribbean countries have *per capita* surpassed by far those to all other recipients. India, Pakistan, and others receive much greater amounts overall of course, but not *per capita*.

With ups and downs, this pattern of relations is likely to continue well into the 21st century.[63]

---

[63] A.E.B. I, pp. 296-298, and A.E.B. II, pp. 175-183, go into the subject of Canadian relations with the Commowealth Caribbean countries in considerable detail.

6

North-South Issues

INITIALLY, THAT IS, AFTER THE SECOND WORLD WAR, North-South Issues were limited basically to aid, as development assistance was then called. Today, a much broader range of activities is included under the heading, for instance, narcotics, money-laundering, terrorism, woman and child abuse, and other such contemporary problems that were nowhere near as prominent fifty years ago.

1. Development Assistance: The Colombo Plan

Canada's development assistance programmes began shortly after the Second World War under the Colombo Plan: the result of a meeting of Commonwealth Foreign Ministers in that city in 1950.

Canada and the Colombo Plan   Doc. 6.1

STATEMENT BY SSEA L.B. PEARSON, HOUSE OF COMMONS, FEBRUARY 21, 1951. (EXTRACTS)

A little over a year ago the Foreign Ministers of the commonwealth countries met in Colombo to consider many of the urgent political and economic problems then facing Asia. Out of their discussions a consultative committee on south and south-east Asia was created which was charged with examining economic problems of the area and preparing appropriate recommendations. This committee, which drew its original membership from seven countries, United Kingdom, Australia, New Zealand, India, Pakistan, Ceylon and Canada, met in Sydney last May and in London last September. Its most recent meeting, in Colombo, Ceylon, ended yesterday.

The United States, with the unanimous agreement of the seven original members, recently joined the consultative committee. In announcing his government's acceptance of this invitation, the Secretary of State in Washington, on January 24 of this year, said that it afforded his country the opportunity "for further cooperation with the countries of south and south-east Asia in their efforts toward economic and social development." Representatives of the following non-commonwealth countries also attended the recent meeting in Colombo: Burma, Cambodia, Vietnam, Indonesia, the Philippines, and Thailand.

Canadian Foreign Policy 1945–2000

During 1950, when the United States was continuing to carry such a heavy burden of foreign aid, it was, I think, appropriate that the commonwealth countries should examine together some of the pressing economic problems of south and south-east Asia. These were not new problems, but they were ones to which the free world had not previously given adequate attention. The commonwealth countries did good work, therefore, in bringing together in one report an analysis of the needs of the countries which comprise four-fifths of the area of south and south-east Asia.

Since the Plan was drawn up there have already been significant economic changes which are bound to affect its progress, at least in its initial stages. The burden of rearmament, which the western countries have been forced to take on, is having major economic consequences. The prices of many of the raw materials produced in south and south-east Asia have gone up sharply. This advantage has been offset to some extent by the rising cost of the goods which the Asian countries must import. Even more serious are the difficulties in obtaining delivery of critically needed goods. Most regrettable, there has been a serious falling off in India's food supply owing to drought in some regions, floods in others, and locusts in still others. This has imposed a very real human and economic problem on India.

The Colombo Plan calls for a capital development programme in commonwealth countries of south-east Asia totalling about $5 billion over a six-year period starting this year. Of this $5 billion it is expected that about $2 billion will be raised internally and about $3 billion will come from external sources. Private capital is one source, though in the present international situation it cannot be as important as it should be. We also hope that the International Bank will be another source for financing some of the larger projects. So far as government contributions are concerned, the United Kingdom has announced that its contribution over the six-year period will take the form of sterling balance releases, at a high and fixed rate, grants for colonial development, and loans floated in London, amounting to well over 300 million pounds or more than 900 million Canadian dollars. Australia has announced that it will provide 7 million pounds sterling, that is nearly 21 million Canadian dollars, in the first year; and that over the six-year period its contribution will be not less than 25 million pounds sterling, that is, nearly 75 million Canadian dollars.

The Canadian government has been giving very serious consideration to the course of action which should be recommended to parliament. We have been conscious that Canadians, as individuals — and this has been clearly reflected in the press from one end of the country to the other — wish to contribute to the success of this plan. This desire of the people of Canada, to extend assistance, has also been clearly shown in the debate on the speech from the throne. It was reflected by the remarks of the leader of the opposition, (Mr. Drew) when he expressed his confidence that members of the house would support

170

all practical measures which will bring hope and encouragement to those who are in such great distress in so many parts of the world. It was reflected also in the remarks of the member for Rosetown-Biggar, (Mr. Coldwell) when he called the Colombo plan the most imaginative ever adopted by the commonwealth countries.

The government therefore authorized Mr. David Johnson, our high commissioner in Pakistan and our delegate to the recent meeting of the consultative committee, to state that the Canadian government would ask Parliament to appropriate $25 million as its contribution to the first year of the Plan, provided that it was clear that other contributing countries would be making appropriate contributions so that the broad objectives of the Colombo Plan might be realized.

The United States representative at the Colombo meeting said that his government welcomed the initiative of the countries participating in the Colombo plan; that the plan itself appeared to offer a basis for genuine economic progress and that the United States intended to co-ordinate to the greatest extent possible the programme it had undertaken, or might undertake, in the area with those programmes under the Colombo plan.

I should also inform the house that we are immediately opening discussions with the Indian government to see whether they would wish that some of the funds we provide this year under the Colombo plan should be spent on Canadian wheat for their famine-stricken country. As yet, we do not know exactly what types of wheat, available in Canada, will be of use to India, nor, of course, do we know what next year's crop will be. However, it is our hope that some wheat may be provided to the government of India in connection with the plan. This wheat, I imagine, would be sold by the Indian government to the people of India under its rationing system, where possible and the money so raised could then be devoted to capital developments. In the Colombo Report it is clearly recognized, especially in the case of India, that imports of food as well as imports of capital goods may serve in attaining the objectives of the plan. At the same time as we open discussions with the Indian authorities we shall open parallel discussions with the Pakistan authorities.

In conclusion ... perhaps I might read to the house the last sentence of the Colombo report which summarizes so eloquently our hopes for the success of the Colombo plan.

In a world racked by schism and confusion it is doubtful whether free men can long afford to leave undeveloped and imprisoned in poverty the human resources of the countries of south and south-east Asia which could help so greatly, not only to restore the world's prosperity, but also to redress its confusion and enrich the lives of all men everywhere.

2. From the External Aid Office to the Canadian International Development Agency

Initially aid, both policy and programmes, was under the jurisdiction of DEA's Economic II Division until a separate agency — the External Aid Office — was established in 1960 to run the programmes. Policy remained under the jurisdiction of the SSEA. Currently, the Canadian International Development Agency (CIDA) has separate representation in the Cabinet, but continues to remain under the ultimate jurisdiction of the Foreign Minister and of course the Cabinet for international policy matters.[64]

The pioneers of the Canadian Colombo Plan programmes would hardly recognize them today, so changed have they become in funding, in range, in scope, in objectives and complexity. The Plan's programmes stressed technical training and scholarships, the despatch of experts, the provision of emergency and other foodstuffs. It also included large-scale dam and road building projects, but with no studies of their potential impact on the environment since it was not the concern then that it has become today.

Our programmes continue to embrace such traditional subjects, but they are now also used as an instrument in financing trade, in assisting developing countries in dealing with their foreign debts, in helping to clear land mines, in supporting ex-communist countries in transition, in helping the under-privileged living in particularly difficult political situations, e.g., certain countries in Africa, with educational and other training. They are also applied in the cause of advancing human rights considerations of special concern to Canada, e.g ., the status of women, and generally taking into account the human-rights performance of recipient countries. The environmental impact of capital projects is now a basic aspect of Canadian aid policy. Aid budgets are also used in the government's campaign against international drug trafficking.

Canadian aid budgets have steadily increased over the years. Under the Colombo Plan, yearly aid allocations were in the vicinity of $25 million during the early 1950s. Programmes increased steadily, both in size and in area coverage. Aid disbursements peaked — in volume terms — at $3.2 billion in 1991-1992.

As budgets and programmes expanded, the Government decided in 1970 to create an entirely new agency when the External Aid Office was transformed into the Canadian International De-

---

[64]See R.A.M., Chapter X, Commonwealth Relations, pp. 364-372, for an account of the meetings at Colombo in 1950. Also A.E.B. II, pp. 231-235, for CIDA.

velopment Agency, CIDA for short, with a broader range of scope and activities.

Aid budgets have since dropped significantly as a result of Government deficit reduction policies. Currently, they are hovering around $2 billion. Reflecting these cuts, traditional forms of aid have changed recently. Instead of food and locomotives, for instance, the emphasis is now on improving efficiency, on encouraging institutional reform in crucial parts of developing countries' economies and, in this way, to better prepare for the future by emphasizing long-term rather than immediate benefits.

A basic aspect of Canada's aid programmes (and those of many other donor countries as well) has been the policy of insisting that aid be given in the form of Canadian goods and services, that is, tying aid funds to procurement in Canada. Tied aid percentages have dropped over the years, but continue to be a feature of our programmes. A significant proportion of Canadian aid — roughly one-third — is channelled through the multilateral agencies of the UN system, through the World Bank or regional banks, and as such is untied.

Despite its generosity Canada (along with most donor countries) has never reached the UN target of 0.7% of GDP for assistance to developing countries set in 1969. Currently, the percentage is about 0.27%

Down to the early 1960s, Canadian aid programmes were almost entirely Commonwealth-oriented. It was not possible to provide aid to the French-speaking countries of Africa at the time. They were still under colonial rule, although the former French colonies in Indochina became recipients of Canadian aid through the Colombo Plan after independence in 1954. Canadian development activities started in Francophone Africa after independence and accelerated rapidly when the former French colonies became caught up in the turmoils of Canada's constitutional problems and mounting difficulties with France towards the towards the end of the 1960s.[65]

A new approach to aid   Doc. 6.2

STATEMENT BY PM TRUDEAU TO A CONVOCATION CEREMONY MARKING THE DIA-
MOND JUBILEE OF THE UNIVERSITY OF ALBERTA, EDMONTON, ALBERTA, MAY 13, 1968.
(EXTRACTS)

Never before in history has the disparity between the rich and the poor, the comfortable and the starving, been so extreme; never before have

---

[65] This aspect of Canada's assistance programmes is covered in Chapter 9 on the provinces, where Canada, Quebec, and *La Francophonie* are dealt with.

mass communications so vividly informed the sufferers of the extent of their misery; never before have the privileged societies possessed weapons so powerful that their employment in the defence of privilege would destroy the haves and the have-nots indiscriminately. We are faced with an overwhelming challenge. In meeting it, the world must be our constituency.

I can find no better words to express this view than those employed in General Principle Four of the Final Act of the 1964 United Nations Conference on Trade and Development: "Economic development and social progress should be the common concern of the whole international community and should, by increasing economic prosperity and well-being, help strengthen peaceful relations and co-operation among nations".

Pope Paul VI in his fifth encyclical was even more concise "the new name for peace is development".

These references to assistance and to co-operation relate not only to economic assistance. They relate to assistance in any form that will create the political, economic and human climate most conducive to the nurturing of human dignity. International activities of this breadth are a far cry from the earlier and more primitive concepts of direct financial assistance. In their impact and in their value, they are also a long way from charity and philanthropy. If the Canadian goal is to assist other states in this way, then we are involved with humanity. And we are involved for our mutual benefit.

I emphasize this because when one benefits from an activity one is less likely to object to its cost. How do we benefit? In several respects:

(a) A world community of nations freely co-operating should result in a lessening of international tension. This would lead to a world less susceptible to war. Canada and Canadians would become more secure, and in this troubled world, that would be benefit beyond measure.

(b) A multiplicity of nations possessing expanding economies would mean that standards of living would rise and world markets would multiply. Canadian products would find more purchasers, and for a trading nation such as Canada, that would be a benefit of great value.

(c) In times of peace, men have turned their attention towards the development of their cultures, and the enrichment of life. Canadians live more meaningfully by enjoying the works of artists and scholars of whatever national source, and that is a benefit of unquestioned value.

These interests and these benefits submit to no national boundaries. The social, economic, and political betterment of any man anywhere is ultimately reflected in this country. If at the same time our consciences — our humanitarian instincts — are served, as they are and as they should be, then so much the better. Unquestionably the concept of international assistance is appealing because it is one of the most uplifting endeavours in which man has ever engaged. But we must never forget that in this process Canadians are beneficiaries as well as benefactors.

Any discussion of development assistance tends to lead eventually to a complex of issues which can conveniently be grouped under the word "strings". The very mention of this word prompts cries of "foul" from those whose interest in aid programmes is essentially philanthropic since it suggests Machiavellian political motivation on the part of the donor. The situation, as with any problem which has defied final solution over the years, is very complicated. A frank and open discussion of it by the Canadian public could do nothing but good. Our assistance programme, and the way in which it is conducted, must respond to the wishes and wisdom of those upon whose support it depends.

Canadians, I think, expect a certain selectivity in these programmes. We all feel instinctively that our help should go to those in the direst need, to those who will make the best use of it and to those making an honest effort to promote democratic institutions and personal liberties. Beyond this, however, difficult questions arise. Should aid be given unconditionally or should it be dependent on some concept of performance? For example, if land reform or tax revision are in our view necessary for economic or social development in the recipient country, should this "string" be attached to our aid? More difficult, perhaps, in domestic terms at least, is the problem of "Canadian content". It is widely held that "tied aid" diminishes the real value of development assistance by increasing costs. Yet an element of tying, with the immediate benefit it implies for Canadian production, may be an important factor in assuring wide domestic support for the aid programme.

These are difficult matters of judgment, not absolutes, and informed attention to them by people such as yourselves can help us to make choices more intelligently and more closely attuned to the deepest feeling of our people.

The long-range benefits cannot be over-emphasized. As Canadians we must realize that international co-operation, particularly in the field of economic assistance, in order to remain effective must take on a new form. From the present pattern of commodity and food assistance, of gifts of manufactured goods and loans of money, we must, in response to the economic needs of the developing countries, turn more and more to preferential trade arrangements. The two United Nations Conferences on Trade and Development have made clear that economic aid, in order to be effective, must increasingly take the form of trade.

The Secretary General of the United Nations, U Thant, concisely described this change in 1962. He said:

The disappointing foreign trade record of the developing countries is due in part to obstacles hindering the entry of their products into industrial markets, and in part to the fact that production of many primary commodities has grown more rapidly than demand for them. It is appreciated that "disruptive competition" from low income countries may be felt by established industries in high income countries. Yet, precisely because they are so advanced, the high income countries should be able to alleviate any hardship without shifting the burden of adjustment to the developing countries by restricting the latters' export markets. A related problem to be solved is that of stabilizing the international commodity markets on which developing countries depend so heavily.

Progress could certainly be made if the main industrial countries were to devote as much attention to promoting as to dispensing aid.

This kind of aid, these preferential trade arrangements, have no glamour attached to them. They cannot be illustrated by stirring photographs of rugged Canadian engineers posing before massive dams in remote places. This kind of aid doesn't offer a ready market to Canadian manufacturers, nor does it reduce our base metal or other commodity surpluses. In short, this kind of aid is competition, and bears little evidence of the sweet philanthropy which we have sometimes employed in the past to coat the cost of our aid "pill". Unless Canadians are aware of the vital goal our aid is seeking to achieve, they may not be sympathetic to a change of this sort. It is my opinion that Canadians will understand, and will accept the challenge. Economic aid, unless effective, will be useless. In order to be effective it will, in all likelihood, be costly. Yet we and the other developed nations have no alternative. The world cannot continue to accommodate mutually exclusive blocs of rich nations and poor nations.

We must recognize that, in the long run, the overwhelming threat to Canada will not come from foreign investments, or foreign ideologies, or even — with good fortune — foreign nuclear weapons. It will come instead from the two-thirds of the peoples of the world who are steadily falling farther and farther behind in their search for a decent standard of living. This is the meaning of the revolution of rising expectations. I repeat, this problem is not new. But its very size, involving some two-and-a-half billion people, makes it qualitatively different from what it has been in the past.[66]

---

[66]Many of the ideas broached in this statement are to be found in the White Paper on "International Development" in *Foreign Policy for Canadians*. It is one of the six booklets to emerge from the foreign policy review of 1968-1970. (Available from the DFAIT or CIDA websites under "Suggested Reading', below'.) See also *Charter: Official Development Assistance* and its accompanying booklet, *Sharing our Future*, issued by CIDA in 1987 for an update.

6 — North-South Issues

2.1. Democracy and Respect for Human Rights: Good Governance and Aid

Foreign policy themes and priorities: 1991–92. Update.   Doc. 6.3

BOOKLET ISSUED BY DEA, OTTAWA. (EXTRACTS

Objectives

- Encourage respect for human rights, the rule of law, and fundamental democratic principles;
- Encourage good governance and sound economic policies in partner countries;
- Maintain commitment to policies aimed at poverty reduction;
- Retain a strong and active commitment to humanitarian assistance.

The value of democracy and respect for hunan rights have triumphed not only in the revolutionary transformation of Central and Eastern Europe, but also in the more evolutionary process of democratic change in much of the developing world. The increasing acceptance of these values by people around the globe is a strong endorsement of the fundamental values which have driven Canadian foreign policy for the past 50 years. A new and hopeful international consensus is building: a consensus that may be the finest legacy of the 20th century — a consensus of democratic, universal human rights.

Our foreign policy, including development assistance, should continue to make clear our abiding commitment to respect human rights, the rule of law, and economic and political freedom.

Sustainable economic growth, led by the private sector, is necessary for all societies to improve the quality of their citizens. Economic conditionality will remain central to evaluating requests for official development assistance and debt relief, with ongoing consultations among donor countries on how this can be best achieved. Good governance considerations must also play a role in allocating development assistance.

Good governance includes: respect for human rights, democratic development, probity in government, basic social programmes accorded priority, poverty alleviation, acceptable levels of defence spending, and market-based economies.

Aid and trade — The challenge of exportation   Doc. 6.4

STATEMENT BY MINISTER OF STATE FOR EXTERNAL RELATIONS PIERRE DE BANÉ, TO THE MONTREAL CHAMBER OF COMMERCE, FEBRUARY 23, 1982. (EXTRACTS)

The government actively supports trade development. We work closely with the trade development departments of provincial governments. Federal trade officers abroad, in Ottawa, and in the regions are prepared to help in the identification of markets and potential buyers. We have treated export assistance programmes such as the Programme

177

for Export Market Development (PEMD) and the Promotional Project Programme with budgets for trade development and for participation in trade fairs and missions abroad.

We are also adapting programmes as required to meet changing world conditions. An Export Trade Development Board has been established to advise the government on all matters relating to exports. My comments would not be complete without mentioning the crucial role of export financing. Last year, the Export Development Corporation (EDC) helped exporters to conclude sales of $1,4 billion through their export insurance and loans programmes. The government does not support the predatory financing that has been offered by some competitor countries. However, we are prepared to offer a blending of commercial and aid funds, if there is evidence that foreign competitors are offering *crédit mixte* financing to secure trade deals.[67]

3. The UN Conference on Trade and Development (UNCTAD)

The first UN Conference on Trade and Development (UNCTAD) took place in Geneva from March 23 until June 15, 1964. It had been convened by the United Nations to consider and seek solutions for the trade and development problems of the less-developed countries of the world. All members of the United Nations and the specialized agencies were invited. It is estimated that some 1,500 participants and observers attended.

Canadian UNCTAD policy and objectives have remained constant from the beginning: support for multilateral institutions such as the GATT, the IMF, the World Bank; substantial contributions to international development to hasten economic and social progress in the world; the promotion of economic development through financial and technical assistance; the removal of restrictions on imports from developing countries, and similar programmes. These themes, with variations taking into account current developments, have recurred at every subsequent UNCTAD meeting, usually held at four-year intervals.

---

[67]France was an early user of *crédit mixte*: hence the term. It is a device that can take many configurations and forms, but is basically a combination of commercial and aid funds for financing trade deals. Generally, it entails a mix of export development loans from public sources and on occasion private corporations such as the major banks, along with a component involving funds from aid agencies. These may vary in amount, according to the size of the deal, and may involve interest-free or reduced-interest funding, accompanied by varying periods of grace and time-frames for repayment, and so on. *Crédit mixte* or variations thereof are widely used by many countries today.

6 — North-South Issues

STATEMENT BY SSEA PAUL MARTIN, TO UNCTAD, GENEVA, MARCH 24, 1964. (EX-
TRACTS)

Since its foundation, the United Nations has played an important and
constructive role in the vital sector of economic and trade co-operation
among nations. Member countries have joined together to dismantle
the barriers to world trade with the aim of ensuring the best use of the
world's resources and raising the living standards of the world's peoples. In the interests of expanding world trade, rules have been fashioned as safeguards against the restrictive and discriminatory practices of the past. The General Agreement on Tariffs and Trade, the International Monetary Fund, the International Bank and other United
Nations institutions were set up to buttress the new framework of
world trading relationships. This new and more liberal trade system
has brought benefits to all the countries of the world. No country is
more indebted to these accomplishments than my own, which is so
vitally dependent on foreign trade. Canada supports the preservation
and development of the basic trade rules and institutions which have
been fashioned over the past two decades.

A great co-operative endeavour over the past two decades has
been the economic development of new countries and countries seeking to reach new economic and social goals. The United Nations and
its Agencies have not only aroused world support for these efforts,
but have also given us many of the tools to work with. Massive resources have been transferred by way of aid directly and through international agencies to reinforce even greater efforts of the developing
countries themselves. That the efforts of these countries are bound
to be paramount was emphasized yesterday in your speech, Mr. President when you pointed out that, in this "endeavour for rapid economic
growth to offset the increase in population and to keep up with the development trends in advanced countries, the developing countries bear
the main responsibility for their economic and social progress". The
same point was made by the present Prime Minister of Canada some
years ago when he was speaking of the role of external aid. He went
on, however, to develop this point in the following way:

> The fact that external aid may often be marginal does not,
> however, make it unimportant. Many a garment might un-
> ravel if it were not for the hem. In much the same way, the
> fabric of economic and social life in many of these countries
> is strengthened by the function which outside assistance per-
> forms and by the evidence which it brings of widespread in-
> terest, sympathy and support.

Since the war Canada has made substantial contributions to international development efforts. From the start, Canada actively encouraged the formation of United Nations programmes and we backed

up our support with substantial contributions. We were among the founding members of the Colombo Plan in 1950 and since then we have annually transferred Canadian resources to countries in South and Southeast Asia, and more recently to Africa and countries in the Caribbean area. Through Canadian and United Nations programmes we have provided substantial development resources, by far the greater part of which has been on a grant basis requiring no repayment.

The Canadian aid effort is part of a broad co-operative endeavour to hasten economic and social progress throughout the world. My Government recognizes both the new sense of urgency behind this endeavour and the growing determination to achieve development goals. We have, therefore, decided to increase Canada's economic aid by more than one-half. Our expanded effort includes a new programme of long-term loans on liberal terms. We expect our aid expenditures during the next twelve months to reach $180 to $190 million.

Until recently, the main emphasis in international arrangements has been to promote economic development through financial and technical assistance. We must now add another dimension to the great effort to support economic development. We must examine how trade can make a fuller contribution. The developing countries are rightly seeking through trade expansion to accelerate their economic development and to raise their living standards. World trade is still too much fettered by restrictions, high tariffs, trade discrimination and other barriers. The terms of trade have deteriorated for exporters of raw materials and foodstuffs. These basic products, moreover, are subject to sudden and unforeseen price fluctuations which can result in serious setbacks for development plans and for the efforts of producing countries. The developing countries are rightly seeking to diversify their economies, to create soundly based processing and manufacturing industries and to sell the products of these industries in the markets of the world. Their efforts deserve and require the encouragement of advanced countries. All of these countries represented here today stand to gain by increases in the productive capacity and prosperity of the less-developed world. As I see it, the task before this conference should be the establishment of a framework of world trade in which developing countries can achieve a satisfactory rate of economic growth and improved standards of living.

To achieve all these objectives will not be easy and will require adjustments and fresh efforts by all of us. Our task will be eased if we work together and share in the inevitable adjustments. By acting together within the United Nations, we can create in all our countries conditions and the political will necessary for progress. Indeed, the only way to move forward effectively is by joint action.

Mr. President, the issues before this conference have been ably analyzed in the report presented by the Secretary-General, Dr. Raul Prebisch. His report presents us with many challenging proposals. I should like to take this opportunity to pay tribute to the distinguished services which he has already rendered to this conference.

My Government — and I am sure each of the governments represented here — has given most serious thought to the issues facing this conference. Each of us will be making a contribution to the consideration of these problems in the days ahead. It may be helpful if I were to outline at this preliminary stage in a more specific way the Canadian approach on how these objectives can best be attained.

First, Canada will work with other developed countries in eliminating, wherever practicable, tariffs and other restrictions which obstruct trade in tropical foodstuffs and industrial raw materials traditionally exported by developing countries. The new round of tariff negotiations coming up in the GATT, known as the "Kennedy round", will complement this conference. These negotiations should reduce or eliminate barriers to many important exports from developing countries. To free world trade in food and raw materials would be a major accomplishment, from which all countries in the world will benefit. At present, Canada has no quantitative restrictions on imports of products of interest to developing countries, and our tariffs on tropical products and raw materials are generally low or have been removed altogether; we have no internal taxes inhibiting the consumption of these products.

Canada has been a party to all major commodity agreements concluded since the end of the last war. We have always been prepared to explore with other countries the possibility of other agreements on a commodity by commodity basis. However, it would not be in the interest of the developing countries to encourage unduly high prices for primary commodities. High prices are likely to generate unsaleable surpluses by stimulating production and reducing consumption through the use of natural or synthetic substitutes.

Canada will work with the developing countries and others in trying to improve the conditions of world trade for temperate agricultural products. Agricultural protectionism in certain developed countries has been growing; it is tending to increase uneconomic production in these countries. It has curtailed the markets of efficient suppliers in developed and developing countries alike.

Canada had advocated that, in the forthcoming "Kennedy round" of tariff and trade negotiations, developed countries should ensure that products of interest to developing countries, including manufactured goods and semi-processed materials, are included in the scope of negotiations. As has been recognized in the GATT, this should be done without expecting full reciprocity from developing countries for benefits they may derive from these negotiations. We are hopeful also that successful negotiations of reduction of tariffs on semi-processed materials will go a long way to reducing differentials between tariffs on raw arid processed commodities which have created problems for developing countries.

Canada strongly supports a general removal of quantitative restrictions now impeding imports into developed countries of manufactured goods from developing countries. It has been noted that exports of manufactures by developing countries are of limited variety and are exported in volume to only a few markets. Developing countries need the greatest possible freedom of access to the widest number of markets if they are to establish a diversified and expanding industrial structure. The likelihood of market disruption would be lessened if these exports were less unevenly distributed among developed countries through the establishment of more uniformly favourable conditions of access.

While Canada is approaching the question of preferences with caution, we should be prepared to consider proposals for the exchange of regional tariff preferences among developing countries for a limited period and under conditions which took reasonable account of the interests of outside countries.

Canada would be prepared, during the course of the "Kennedy round" of tariff negotiations, to examine carefully any tariff preferences now enjoyed by Canada in the markets of the developing countries which may be regarded as prejudicial to the trade of other developing countries.

Canada recognizes that development plans and efforts may be prejudiced by adverse changes in the terms of trade or by other occurrences beyond the control of developing countries. Accordingly, we supported the recent decision of the International Monetary Fund to increase its help to countries suffering from temporary declines in export receipts. As regards longer-term declines, we are prepared to join with others at this conference in studying ways of improving bilateral aid programmes and relating them more closely to the changing economic and trading circumstances of the individual developing countries.

It will be clear from my presentation that we believe that much more can be done and must be done to free the channels of trade. We think that, if this were done, the developing countries would have a better opportunity of competing on terms which would bring into play their natural advantages as efficient producers of certain commodities and manufactures The freeing of trade channels would also help overcome the effects of undue protectionism in the developed countries and lead, of itself, to some of that international division of labour to which reference has already been made in this conference. But I do not want to suggest that the freeing of the channels of trade is all that requires to be done. The range of problems which we have come to consider is vast and no single nor simple solution for them is likely to be possible.

As regards the basic question of future institutional arrangements, it is our belief that we can only see clearly what will be required when we approach the end of our deliberations. We shall then have a better idea of what is likely to emerge as a result of the conference. In general, we are not in favour of setting up a new organization of a more or less independent character. Rather, we should be more inclined to adapt the existing machinery to make it more responsive to the problems of the developing countries. Indeed, encouraging progress is already being made in that direction.

4. South Africa

Before Nelson Mandela's release from prison and return to South African politics in the 1990s, culminating in his resounding victory at the polls, South Africa's racial policy — summed up in the Afrikaans word *apartheid* (in rough translation: apartness, separate development) — had been a problem of long standing, at the UN, the Commonwealth, and elsewhere. The entrance of new members into the UN during the 1950s and 1960s, particularly from Africa and Asia, brought it to a head.

Before then, Canada's approach to the question had been based on one of the UN Charter's fundamental principles, that is, that the internal affairs of member states were not subject to discussion; and that it was generally preferable to have South Africa within the UN, where world pressure could be brought to bear upon it, rather than absent where it could go ahead unhindered by outside prodding. It was also held that outside intervention against South Africa would have detrimental effects on the very people within that country whom it was designed to help.

After 1960, however, when the theories of *apartheid* and its accompanying practices intensified in South Africa, successive Canadian governments exerted continuing and mounting pressure against South Africa both at the UN, in the Commonwealth, and directly upon South Africa in a broad range of activity, both public and private, encompassing commercial, financial, political, and cultural measures, including sports. PM Diefenbaker and later SSEA Clark were in the forefront of this campaign during their terms of office. South Africa left the Commonwealth in 1961.

South Africa — Meeting of the Commonwealth Prime Ministers   Doc. 6.6

REPORT BY PM DIEFENBAKER ON THE COMMONWEALTH PRIME MINISTERS' CONFERENCE, HOUSE OF COMMONS, MAY 16, 1960. (EXTRACTS)

I came back from the London Conference feeling that, bearing in mind the difficult circumstances arising from the situation in South Africa, the Conference was generally useful and successful.

Many observers have, of course, pointed out that the proceedings of the meetings did not result in any perceptible change in the attitude of the South African Government. It was not to be expected, however, that magic improvements could take place in a situation of such tension and complexity. I believe that those who in future will examine and judge this period in Commonwealth history will decide that this meeting did not fail to respond to the stern test to which it was put.

I would be the last to say that everything was achieved that I would have desired. I do not contend that, in so far as the communiqué is concerned, it can convey the full nature and substance of the deliberations that took place. On occasions in the past I have heard my predecessors, Right Hon. Mackenzie King and Right Hon. Louis St. Laurent, report on conferences they had attended. In every case it was made perfectly clear that while no decisions were made or can be made in these informal circumstances, there is a oneness of mind that comes about through the exchange of ideas. There was no disposition on the part of any of the representatives to evade this issue, and there was no lack of frankness in private and informal discussions. I underline the fact that only in unanimity can there be a final communiqué issued. Everything that is included therein represents the agreement of all. To bring together the representatives of one quarter of the world's population, belonging to many races and being of many colours, I think it is quite an unusual result that several conclusions were arrived at unanimously which cannot but result in the possibility of change along the lines generally desired.

Despite the profound differences which prevailed and persisted throughout, it was possible for a communiqué to be issued. This was difficult with two inherently conflicting elements to be reconciled. First, it had become essential that a way be found for Commonwealth governments to make clear their intentions on this central question of racial relations. Second, it was desirable that this should be done without violation of the traditional practice of these meetings that the internal affairs of member countries are not the subject of formal discussion. I believe now more certainly than I did when I spoke here on April 27 that any departure from this last principle would mean the end of the Commonwealth as we know it, because if we ever arrive at the point where we will discuss the internal affairs of other countries and determine the course by a majority, then there will be problems that will arise and it could only mean that several countries in the Commonwealth could not accept the decisions of the majority. I need not go into particulars in that regard; I think a number would come to mind immediately, including the question of migration. Personally, as the House knows, I was of those who thought it worth while to try to achieve the first objective of enabling the views of Prime Ministers to be expressed without sacrificing the principle of non-interference, which is one of the elements of the Commonwealth association. I took the view that notwithstanding the depth of feeling on this racial issue — my views throughout the years and now are a matter of record — I believed it would be wrong and damaging to the spirit and fabric of the

Commonwealth partnership if a majority of the Commonwealth governments, finding themselves allied in condemnation of one or more of their number, were to constitute themselves as a court of judgment. I saw, as I said a moment ago, in that trend an end of the association as we know it. The seed of mutual recrimination would threaten the partnership whose essence has always been tolerance, restraint and free cooperation.

Strong feelings were held in the informal meetings. Men like the President of Pakistan, the Prime Ministers of India, of Malaya and of Ghana, accepted this view as essential to the preservation and maintenance of our relationship. There was unanimous acceptance of the principle that internal affairs of free states are not to be the subject of formal discussion, and that any action in that regard would damage the strength and ultimately the preservation of the institution itself.

I cannot reveal, in the tradition of those meetings, the substance of the talks. They were at times bilateral, at times in small groups, and at other times all the representatives took part in an informal and private exchange of views. For my part, I had two lengthy and private personal conversations with Mr. Louw; I participated in other informal discussions. I left Mr. Louw in no doubt that in Canada there is no sympathy for policies of racial discrimination, on whatever grounds they may be explained, and that such policies are basically incompatible with the multiracial nature of the Commonwealth association. I made it clear to him that the policy of South Africa was a denial of the principle that human dignity and the worth of the individual, whatever his race and colour, must be respected, and that there could be no doubt as to our views in that connection. Indeed, those views are being generally expressed now.

A few weeks ago there were those who felt that what we required was condemnation by various parliaments. I think the events during the days of the Conference were an answer to that contention. Our views, the views of all of us in other parts of the Commonwealth, or most of the people in other parts of the Commonwealth, were set out only a few days ago by the Archbishop of Canterbury when he said:

> But the tragedy is that so far they (South Africa) have seemed to pay little or no regard to the burdens they are imposing on the hearts and consciences and political principles of those who are their brethren in the Commonwealth, in culture, in Christian faith and in common humanity.

Only in the last 24 hours I have received from the Primate of the Anglican Church of Canada the declaration of that Church, which represents the views expressed at the 1958 Lambeth Conference:

> The Conference affirms its belief in the natural dignity and value of every man of whatever colour or race as created in the image of God. In the light of this belief the Conference

185

affirms that neither race nor colour is in itself a barrier to any aspect of that life in family and community for which God created all men. It therefore condemns discrimination of any kind on the grounds of race or colour alone.

I would be less than frank if I did not say that I cannot report that there was any indication in Mr. Louw's attitude, representing his Government, that he was moved by the arguments or concerned about the force of international opinion. However, he learned the viewpoint, he recognized that of all those present there no one, in the informal meetings or elsewhere, could give support to racial discrimination in a multiracial Commonwealth.

It is clear that the issue of racial conflict will continue to pose a fundamental problem for Commonwealth countries and, indeed, for the world community. My hope is that by this meeting we have assisted in the process of change. The matter was not on the agenda but it was discussed with clarity and frankness, and above all, by those from whom you would have expected the expression of violent opinions, with a dignity, a restraint and a recognition of the tremendous issues at stake that must give heart to all of us as to the meaning of the Commonwealth as such.

International concern has been demonstrated in the United Nations. In the last few days the Secretary-General, Mr. Hammarskjold, has been holding talks in London with Mr. Louw. Whatever the results may be, I am sure they will be aided in their talks by what took place at the Conference. I hope the people of South Africa can work their way out of the dreadful impasse to which they have been brought. I hope their isolation on the continent of Africa will give them thought and a realization of the situation. It was a great South African, Field Marshal Smuts as he subsequently was, who as long ago as December 1918, reminded us of this fact:

There is no doubt that mankind is once more on the move. The very foundations have been shaken and loosened and things are again fluid. The tents have been struck and the great caravan of humanity is once more on the march.

He was pointing to the need of new institutions, new ways of thought, new kinds of international behaviour if the world was to avoid the catastrophe of another war. His words were of prophetic application to his own continent.

It was made very clear in the communiqué that racial equality was of the essence. The communiqué had this to say:

Whilst reaffirming the traditional practice that Commonwealth Conferences do not discuss the internal affairs of member countries, Ministers availed themselves of Mr. Louw's presence in London to have informal discussions with him about the racial situation in South Africa. During the informal discussions Mr. Louw gave information and answered questions on the Union's policies, and the other Ministers conveyed to him their views on the South African problem. The Ministers emphasized that the Commonwealth itself is a multiracial association and expressed the need to ensure good relations between all member states and peoples of the Commonwealth.

We know the results of the assertion of racial superiority only a few years ago and the effects that followed from it. It is my hope that the South African Government will heed, and heed quickly, the appeal that was made to it, not only in the communiqué but in personal conversations.

The Government there has been planning to hold a referendum on the question of changing the present status of South Africa from a monarchy to that of a republic. In that regard it was pointed out that the choice between a monarchy and a republic is entirely the responsibility of the nation concerned. Then there are these significant words. I am not going to interpret them, because they require no interpretation; their significance lies in the fact that they were accepted unanimously by all who were there:

> In the event of South Africa deciding to become a republic and if the desire was subsequently expressed to remain a member of the Commonwealth, the meeting suggested that the South African Government should then ask for the consent of the other Commonwealth governments either at a meeting of Commonwealth Prime Ministers or, if this were not practicable, by correspondence.

This established clearly that membership in the Commonwealth is not a formality. These words speak for themselves. They make clear that the Prime Ministers were not prepared to give an advance assurance that South Africa might remain a member of the Commonwealth in the event that a decision was made to adopt the status of a republic. Therefore the important point is that if a change of status does take place as a result of the referendum, the consent of the other Commonwealth governments will be required as a precondition of continued membership. Again I emphasize the fact that this was accepted by all.

The attention given to the South African problem, however, should not be allowed to obscure the deliberation which took place on many other subjects. The nature of those deliberations is fairly reflected in the communiqué, but I am going to make a few general references thereto. The multiracial nature of the Commonwealth was underlined by the admission of Ghana three years ago at the last meeting, by the participation of the Prime Minister of Malaya this year and by the fact that the federation of Nigeria, with a population of 35 million, will join the family on the 1st of October and that Sierra Leone and other countries with various colours and races will, it is expected, soon be applying for membership.

What has taken place here is a recognition that there is no automatic membership in the Commonwealth, and I believe it is also suggestive of the possibility that the time is not far distant when acceptance by custom rather than by declaration of certain basic principles, including equality of all races, colours and creeds, will be assured. This view is underlined in various editorials to which I could refer. I draw the attention of the House to the fact that Canada's views were known, but the fact that we had not had a resolution placed Canada's representative in a position to speak to Mr. Louw in a way that did not arouse his antagonism. What happened here is well set out in the *London Financial Times*:

> If the South African Government carries through its plan for making the country into a republic ... Important constitutional matters will arise. ...
>
> More important even than these constitutional considerations is the simple truth expressed by Mr. Diefenbaker last week that a Commonwealth in which the majority of the population is coloured must unequivocally accept racial equality.
>
> The seriousness of racial problems varies widely from member country to member country. Not all of them have an untarnished record. Yet the position today is that the truth of Mr. Diefenbaker's proposition is accepted in theory at least everywhere in the Western world except in South Africa. Refusal to accept it would mean losing the struggle against Communism by default.

And so I might go on in that regard. This was an important step forward, and in that connection it is important internationally.

Doc. 6.7   **Canada's measures against *apartheid***

STATEMENT BY SSEA JOE CLARK, HOUSE OF COMMONS, OTTAWA, SEPTEMBER 13, 1985. (EXTRACTS)

I am guided in this statement by two realities: first, that Canadians are offended by and abhor the practice of institutionalized racism by a society that claims to share our values; and, second, that Canada's influence is limited, but real.

I will be reviewing today the actions Canada has taken, and announcing some new initiatives. Before doing so, I think it would be helpful to indicate some of the changes we seek to bring about, which would prove that South Africa is moving away from *apartheid*.

In terms of broad principles, we would look for the introduction of common citizenship in South Africa; an end to the laws which classify South Africans according to race and colour; freedom for all South Africans to live, move, and work unimpeded by arbitrary restrictions; and independence for Namibia under UN Resolution 435.

None of these is as important, however, as the final principles that I would cite, which are the release of political detainees and prisoners and the release of the African National Congress and the United Democratic Front leaders; the initiation of a process of consultations and negotiations with the leaders of the blacks, coloureds, and Indians; and finally the initiation of a process of reform based on consent, not opposition or coercion.

Canada's contribution in helping to bring about change has been significant. Our policy, through several administrations, has been one of consistent opposition to *apartheid*.

On July 8, I issued a statement of policy on behalf of the government, introducing ten steps including certain economic sanctions to strengthen our opposition to *apartheid* and two measures to foster peaceful change.

We ended the programme for market development in South Africa (PEMD) and the global insurance policies written by the Export Development Corporation (EDC) in so far as they apply to South Africa.

We have broadened and tightened application of the UN arms embargo so as to include a broader range of high technology items, including computers.

We have been the only government to announce the abrogation of our double taxation agreement with South Africa.

We drew the attention of Canadians to the UN Security Council's resolution prohibiting the sale of *kruggerrands* and sales in Canada have come virtually to a halt.

We developed and clarified policies on sporting contacts and official contacts and cooperation.

We announced the assignment of an officer, charged with responsibility for labour affairs, to our embassy in South Africa, to maintain direct contact with South African workers who are agents of reform. That officer will be chosen in consultation with the Canadian Labour Congress.

We more than tripled the funds available for education and training for the black community, including the award of 40 scholarships in the current fiscal year.

Other levels of government in Canada have also sent strong signals. A number of provinces have seen this as a special case and have taken steps within their jurisdictions to oppose *apartheid*. Private companies have voluntarily announced that they will no longer purchase South African goods. Canadian labour has consistently spoken out against *apartheid*.

We are taking a number of further measures:

First, I am meeting a group of representatives of Canadian business and finance in order to examine areas of cooperative action against *apartheid*. I believe that there is a very real possibility that, where governments may not have influence on some levels of the business community and the bureaucracy of South Africa, Canadians active in business and financial circles could well have the influence that could do what governments, parliaments, and public officials are trying to do.

Second, the government is introducing a voluntary ban on loans to the government of South Africa and its agencies. We are asking the Canadian banks to apply such a ban. Some have already acted on their own and we have welcomed that.

Third, I am announcing the appointment of Mr. A.F. Hart as administrator of the Canadian Code of Conduct for the employment practices of Canadian companies operating in South Africa. Mr. Hart has had a distinguished career in the Canadian foreign service, including assignments as High Commissioner to Ghana, with simultaneous accreditation as ambassador to several nearby states.

Fourth, the government will apply a voluntary ban on the sale of crude oil and refined products to South Africa.

Fifth, we are bringing in an embargo on air transport between Canada and South Africa. It will cover both freight and passenger flights, particularly charter flights, since there are no regularly scheduled flights between the two countries.

Sixth, a register has been opened for the voluntary measures which Canadian provinces and municipalities as well as private institutions, organizations, and firms have taken against *apartheid*. Thousands of Canadians have acted quietly on their own.

Seventh, in view of the increasing numbers of arrests of non-violent opponents of *apartheid* in South Africa, an additional $1 million will be allocated on humanitarian grounds to assist the families of political prisoners and detainees.

5. The Decline of the Commonwealth

Between its birth as the British Commonwealth of Nations under the 1931 Act of Westminster that reflected developments in the British Empire during and shortly after the First World War and the 1960s when Britain sought closer relations with Europe, the Commonwealth was an important feature not only in world affairs, but of Canadian foreign policy as well. Today, with the United Kingdom now absorbed in European affairs, it has pretty much faded as a factor in Canadian foreign policy and also as a force in international affairs, although its Heads of Government continue to meet for a few days every two years.

Most Commonwealth-related problems during the period following the Second World War resulted from the racial situation in Southern Africa, Rhodesia's unilateral declaration of independence, civil war in Nigeria, the violent birth of Bangladesh as an outcome of war between India and Pakistan.

It is symptomatic of Canada's dwindling interest in the Commonwealth that Canadian Governments were generally content to follow the leadership of others in these questions, except for the racial situation in South Africa about which strong views existed here. Indeed, for several of the problems, leadership came less from within the Commonwealth than from outside.

This does not mean to say that from the Canadian point of view the Commonwealth has become inactive or futile. The Colombo Plan continues to provide a substantial outlet for Canadian aid. After initial expressions of scepticism, PM Trudeau became a strong supporter of Commonwealth Prime Ministers' meetings. He sought to modernize and streamline them and, with mixed results, also to guide them into new and more useful channels of activity, especially in the field of comparative administration and the technique of government.

Nevertheless, the fact is that the Commonwealth today is no longer the focal point in Canadian external relations that it was not so long ago.[68]

6. The Organization of American States (OAS)

This a very old story, going back to the turn of the 20th century. When the Pan-American Union — the ancestor of the OAS — came into being, Canada was fully expected to join. Among the chairs made especially for the executive board table at the time, one was set aside for Canada with its name on it. The names of the heroes of the Americas engraved on the walls of its headquarters building in Washington include that of Champlain, along with those of Bolívar and San Martín, among others. Canada's Coat-of-Arms *a mari usque ad mare* adorns one of its façades.

In 1942, the Pan American Union organizers invited Canada to a special conference, scheduled to be held in Rio de Janeiro, regarding defence matters in the Americas. The invitation was vetoed by President Roosevelt and, after that episode, Canadian governments were understandably wary about joining.[69]

Instead, as a feature of the Trudeau government's foreign policy review *Foreign Policy for Canadians*, Canada opted for the status of Permanent Observer at the OAS in 1972.

The issue was finally resolved in 1990, when the Mulroney government's decision to seek full membership in the OAS was unanimously accepted by hemispheric governments.

---

[68]It is regretted that space considerations do not permit fuller treatment of Canada and the Commonwealth. See R.A.M. Chapter X; also A.E.B. I and II, Chapter V, respectively, for detailed coverage.

[69]See J.C.M. Ogelsby's *Gringos from the Far North* (Toronto, Macmillan, 1976) for a detailed account of the early history of Canada's relations with the Pan American Union; also A.E.B. III, pp. 107-109.

Doc. 6.8   **Canadian membership in the OAS**

ADDRESS BY PM BRIAN MULRONEY, AT THE MEETING OF HEMISPHERIC LEADERS, SAN
JOSÉ, COSTA RICA, OCTOBER 27, 1989. (EXTRACTS)

The Government of Canada has concluded that the time has come for
Canada to occupy the vacant chair at the Organization of American
States that has been reserved for us all these years.

On behalf of the Government of Canada, I am pleased to announce that I have instructed the Permanent Observer of Canada at
the OAS formally to notify the Secretary General that Canada is prepared to sign and ratify the Charter of the Organization. I hope you
will welcome us.

In an age of interdependence, the well-being of the peoples of
this Hemisphere is indivisible.

We realize that Canadians' rights will not be secure while the
rights of others are denied; that Canadian prosperity will not be assured while the prosperity of others is diminished; that Canada's environment will not be safeguarded until the environment of everyone is
protected; and that Canadian society will not free itself from the evil
of drugs while others remain in its grip.

On all these issues, hemispheric cooperation is integral to Canada's interests and the OAS holds the key to that cooperation. Canada's
presence here today signals a new departure in our relations with Latin
America. We recognize that our interests are directly engaged here. We
will no longer be apart.

Our decision to join the OAS symbolizes our determination to be
full and constructive citizens of the Americas.

7. Drugs

Drugs are a growing problem in international relations in the Americas and elsewhere, and not just among countries. There are more
Canadians in jail for drug offenses around the world today than
for any other crime. In addition, not only is it a dangerous business in itself among traffickers and users, but in some countries
trafficking in narcotics is viewed so severely as to entail the death
penalty.

Related to drug trafficking is the problem of money-laundering and both are increasingly dealt with together. For instance, in
the context of the 1998 G-8 meeting, a number of steps related to
money and drugs have recently been taken in Canada, with effect
towards the end of 2000. Essentially, they are aimed at making it
more difficult to transfer funds around the world.

Reporting of large transactions to a new federal agency by
Canadian chartered banks, credit unions and other financial institutions, such as foreign exchange houses and brokerages, as

well as businesses such as casinos, even lawyers, has been broadened and will become mandatory. Until now such reporting was
voluntary. Penalties for non-compliance will be high. The thresh-
old to be reported is expected to be set at $10,000. Suspicious
transactions, even if for less money, will also have to be reported
to the new agency, whose mandate will include scrutiny of offshore tax havens. The Canadian $1,000 bill is being withdrawn
from circulation.[70]

The international component of the National Drug Strategy   Doc. 6.9

COMMUNIQUÉ BY SSEA JOE CLARK, MAY 28, 1987. (EXTRACTS)

In general, the National Drug Strategy is aimed at solving domestic
problems. However, illicit trafficking is an international industry and
it is clear that Canada cannot solve its drug abuse and trafficking problems in isolation.

Many of the drugs consumed in Canada, such as cocaine and
heroin, are brought into our country illegally by well-organized trafficking networks based overseas. In 1985, the RCMP and Customs seized 62 kg of heroin, 1090 kg of cocaine, and 19,000 kgs. of hashish.
These are the last statistics available and probably understate the dimensions of the problem today. Furthermore, Canadian territory often
serves as a transit point for narcotics being sent by these trafficking
networks to other countries. In addition, illicit psychoactive substances
are produced in Canada to feed the addictions of citizens of other
countries. Clearly, we must act to stem this traffic, not only because
Canadians are its victims, but also because we have a role to play as
responsible citizens of the world.

Drug abuse is not new, but its dimensions are. As early as 1909,
Canada helped to prepare an international Convention to control the
traffic in Opium. We also played a leading role in drafting the 1971
Psychotropic Convention and we continue to play a prominent role in
organizations such as the UN Commission on Narcotic Drugs. Yesterday, Canada was elected to that important commission, which in the
past has concentrated on reducing the supply of drugs. Canada and
other countries have introduced a new focus on the other part of the
problem: trying to reduce demand.

We are also seeking to take account of the new sophistication
of international networks trafficking in drugs, whose tentacles now
stretch around the world.

The government is now working internationally on three fronts:

1) The UN Fund for Drug Abuse Control, which sponsors projects
   to assist producer countries to develop and finance programmes

---

[70]For a summary of the new provisions, see the *Ottawa Citizen* and the *National
Post*, July 11, 2000.

to help farmers to move away from drug production; to improve local standards of living; and to train local police to deal with the extremely well-organized drug traffickers. Canada, through CIDA, has made substantial contributions to this body's general fund. That is a new policy direction for CIDA, since 1985. As well, we will continue to consider on a case-by-case basis, requests from narcotics-producing countries for development assistance.

2) Our contribution, through CIDA, to the UN Fund for Drug Abuse Control will be raised to $500,000 this year and to $1 million by 1991, to demonstrate our commitment to international cooperation.

3) We are expanding the Consular Awareness Programme in External Affairs, to make Canadian travellers more aware of the dangers of drug purchase, possession, trafficking and use abroad. More Canadians are in prison abroad for drug offenses than for any other crime.

7.1. *Drugs and Human Security*

The Chrétien government has been active among G-8 countries in opposing drug-trafficking. Canada agreed at the Santiago Summit of the Americas in April 1998 to host a group of hemispheric foreign ministers on drug issues. Canada was elected to chair the Inter-American Drug Abuse Control Commission Working Group that will develop the multilateral evaluation mechanism for monitoring national and international anti-drug efforts.

FM Axworthy has been a leader in the struggle against narcotics. By viewing it in human security terms, his approach has been both novel and imaginative.

Doc. 6.10   REMARKS BY FM AXWORTHY, JANUARY 8, 1999.

Drug abuse in the Americas is intimately linked to poverty, urban decay, and criminal elements, and threatens democratic development, sound economic management, and even relations between states. The problems associated with illicit drugs will only be solved by moving beyond legal approaches and viewing them from a broad human security perspective, by seeing how the drug problems affects individuals and communities.[71]

---

[71]News Release No. 35, February 19, 1999, has a useful *Backgrounder* on Canada's aims and objectives, both in the UN and OAS contexts, regarding drug-trafficking, and related problems such as money-laundering and small-arms trafficking. FM Axworthy's quote is from DFAIT News Release No. 1, January 8, 1999.

7

The Environment

THE DEGRADATION OF THE ENVIRONMENT through air and water pollution is largely a feature of the last half century. It stems in great part from industrial growth, the rise in the number of automobiles, the use of chemicals, massive oil spills, nuclear waste, among other causes. In particular, massive oil spills in the oceans served to galvanize public attention, as has deteriorating air and water quality in many cities around the world.

This concern has embraced such problems as population growth and housing; the protection of the living resources of the land and of the sea; the cleanliness of the atmosphere; the preservation from pollution of the Arctic and Antarctic regions, as well as the oceans and outer space.

These questions have been dealt with mainly at large-scale international conferences conducted under the auspices of the United Nations. Canada has been in the forefront of such meetings from the very beginning. Owing to provincial experience and expertise in many of these fields, stemming from constitutional responsibilities under the constitution, provincial participation in Canadian delegations attending international environmental conferences has become a matter of course.

This chapter begins with some of the world's great environmental developments over the last few decades, in which Canada played a leading role.

1. Law of the Air

STATEMENT BY SSEA PAUL MARTIN TO THE SECOND INTERNATIONAL CONFERENCE   Doc. 7.1
ON AIR AND SPACE LAW, MCGILL UNIVERSITY, MONTREAL, NOVEMBER 3, 1967.

Your meetings today must have prompted you to reflect on the work of those nations which met in Chicago in the winter of 1944.[72] That was a time when those with foresight were preparing for peace and were recognizing the urgency of radical changes to meet the immediate needs

---

[72]The meetings led to the creation of the International Civil Aviation Organization (ICAO), whose headquarters are located in Montreal.

of a vastly different world. Perhaps in no single industry had the effects of war been felt more strongly than in aviation. The war proved beyond doubt the tremendous potential of the airplane, both as an awesome and devastating carrier of destruction and a swift and reliable means of transport. It is said that the Second World War telescoped a quarter century of normal peacetime technological development in aviation into six years. If anything, the pace of this development is accelerating. Due to the ingenuity of the scientist, engineer and businessman, the airplane is now a major instrument of commerce and — what is significant for the lawyer — a creator of major international problems.

Aviation today is mainly an international activity requiring, for safety's sake alone, the most complex co-ordination of techniques and laws. Air law is the result of a compromise between national drives and international imperatives. It is a conglomeration of specific branches of national and international law, both private and public.

Aircraft of one nation travelling through the air space of several states, landing in others and carrying large numbers of passengers, create many problems of conflicting legal systems. Without determined and imaginative efforts on the part of those concerned with air law, it will be increasingly difficult for the law to keep pace with social and technological development.

But I am not saying anything startling, or even new. The facts are obvious. Nevertheless, the extent of the danger due to the unprecedented growth of the industry has been seriously underestimated.

The Chicago Convention of 1944 was a major step towards international legal standardization. It is often called "the Constitution of Air Law" or "The Charter of the Air". At Chicago, the strong Canadian delegation, headed by C.D. Howe, then Minister of Reconstruction, played an active role in support of an international air authority. We were strong proponents of the "freedoms of the air" — a term which the Honourable Adolf A. Berle, then head of the American delegation, attributed to Canada. In fact, "Freedom of the Air", the title of your present meeting, is what the late Mayor LaGuardia referred to at Chicago as the "meat" of the Convention, for it lay at the very centre of the problem of the number of services that ought to be permitted on a particular route and the share each country should have in these services.

The Chicago Convention was but the first chapter, albeit a successful one, in the work of international co-operation which Franklin Roosevelt described then as part of "a great attempt to build enduring institutions of peace". The Canadian Government continues to subscribe fully to this ideal, for as C.D. Howe said, "if we cannot devise a working system of co-operation and collaboration between the nations of the world in the field of air transport, there will be a smaller chance of our enjoying peace for the remainder of our lives".

What are the problems of the future of aviation to which we should all address ourselves? The trend today is towards greater aircraft productivity and more and longer passenger trips. This means larger, faster, costlier and more complex aircraft flying more often over greater distances. Foreseeable technological developments include "jumbo" jets, supersonic transports, hovercraft, vertical and short take-off aircraft and, eventually, hypersonic vehicles propelled partially by rocket motors with speed and performance characteristics akin to those of spacecraft. Large investments will be required by all governments and airlines, not only for these more sophisticated vehicles but also for related facilities to accommodate the expected increase in traffic. In Canada, we are acutely aware of these problems and are having to revalue estimates we made only a few years ago. The new Canadian Transport Commission is part of our general effort to improve methods of study and co-ordination in the whole field of transportation, including aviation.

The Chicago Convention was a dual-purpose treaty. It contained an international civil aviation code and it established the International Civil Aviation Organization (ICAO) There are now over 115 member states in ICAO. It is a continuing source of pride to Canadians that ICAO should have its headquarters in this city. Every day ICAO assists in matters of coordination, technical assistance and education, to help its members with difficulties which are often beyond their individual ability to overcome. Considerably more could be done, however, to utilize ICAO for the general benefit. Greater use of ICAO machinery for the settlement of disputes should be actively encouraged. The economic necessity of using the large and costly aircraft to their fullest capacity, and therefore of international airlines obtaining traffic rights in as many places as possible, underlines the desirability of having impartial means of arbitrating disputes and a larger degree of standardization and unification in the rules, regulations and laws governing the international use of air space. The international legal implications of aircraft now in the drafting and experimental stages of development also require our urgent attention. Take the hovercraft, for example. Is it a surface vessel or an airplane? The legal arguments need resolution since this vehicle has a potential for international commerce.

In 1964, Canada faced domestically something similar to what is now a common international problem: the competing claims and interests of large airlines. The Government decided that the international air services provided by Canadian airlines should be integrated into a single plan which would avoid unnecessary competition or conflict. This means that outside Canada neither of our two major airlines (Air Canada and Canadian Pacific Airlines) serves any point served by the other. The Government also made it clear that any development of competition in domestic main line services must not put the Government airline, Air Canada, "into the red". In addition, Canadian regional air carriers were given an enlarged role in relation to domestic main line carriers. The application of these three principles has strengthened Canada's position in world aviation. For instance, since

1964 there have been successful negotiations with several countries, designed to achieve international route extensions and improvements for both Air Canada and Canadian Pacific Airlines.

Projecting this domestic example onto the international scene, would be to suggest that perhaps the logical course for public and private international air law is in the direction of one set of rules to govern all flight at whatever altitude.

If international air law is to abandon the techniques of bilateral negotiation, with its jungle of complicated agreements based on the narrow application of national sovereign rights, then it could probably take a lesson from developments in the law of outer space. A new frontier for the law of the air figuratively and literally lies at the fringe of outer space. In 1963, the UN Declaration of Legal Principles Governing Activities by States in the Exploration and Use of Outer Space marked the end of the speculative phase in which the "general pundits" conjectured on whether certain maritime and air-law principles of national sovereignty and freedom of the seas were applicable in outer space. Events since then, such as the recent Outer Space Treaty, suggest that a new legal order is emerging — that of the world community acting for the common good and welfare of all mankind.

The main provisions of the Outer Space Treaty are that outer space, the moon and other celestial bodies shall be explored and used for peaceful purposes only. Like the Limited Test Ban Agreement of 1963, it is part of a series of international agreements leading towards general and complete disarmament. Hopefully, more agreements are on the way — a non-proliferation treaty and, interestingly, an item now before the General Assembly calling for a treaty on the peaceful use of the sea-bed and the ocean floor and their resources in the interests of mankind. First outer space, now the sea-bed and ocean floor. What environment will be next? Air space? What a blessing it would be if by universal agreement the use of the air were reserved exclusively for peaceful purposes, in the common interest of all men.

The main thrust of outer space law is today towards two conventions — one on assistance and return of astronauts and space vehicles, the other on liability for damage caused by the launching of objects into outer space. The implications of these conventions for air law are obvious. Considerable attention is also being given to defining outer space in legal terms. Again, this cannot but affect the law of the air for, apart from drawing a boundary between air and space, there is the related problem of defining spacecraft and hybrid-air-and-spacecraft in legal terms and of co-ordinating international regulations for their use in air space. We must avoid the confusion of having different and possibly conflicting regulations for space vehicles and aircraft flying in the same environment. In this regard, it seems a pity that there is not more contact between air lawyers and space lawyers.[73]

---

[73] See also "Canadian Participation in Space Programmes" by C.M. Drury, Presi-

7 — The Environment

Let us look for a moment at a few problems which will require international legal action. A major problem facing us all in this machine age is noise. We are continually bombarded with noise, and despite our increasingly elastic thresholds of tolerance, jet aircraft have multiplied this attendant disturbance to the point of nuisance. Unless there are some major technological improvements, the larger and faster jets with their greater power take-offs and shallower landing paths will compound this problem. There are several possible solutions: airport curfews, to enable some quiet periods; relocation of airports and runways and restrictions on building near them; and better insulation of dwellings and offices — but each of these national solutions will require some kind of international agreement to be made completely effective. I hope that the fifth Air Navigation Conference of ICAO, starting in Montreal soon, will succeed in agreeing on an international standard unit for noise measurement as the first step towards an international agreement on aircraft noise. Perhaps international air lawyers could then produce regulations and provisions for their world-wide enforcement. The time may come when all new aircraft will be required to demonstrate that they do not exceed a set of internationally accepted noise levels.

One of the agreements signed at Chicago was the International Air Services Transit Agreement — commonly known as "the two freedoms agreement" — in which freedom of mutual overflight was guaranteed. Such flights, if at supersonic speeds, promise to disturb and annoy those on the ground under the SST's flight path. Consequently, if overflight is to be permitted, international agreements will have to be reached on the level of the noise from the sonic boom to be tolerated.

Domestically, old common law conceptions of property ownership from the soil upwards *usque ad coelum,* have been limited legislatively and judicially to meet the requirements of country-wide air travel. To have recognized private claims to air space would have interfered with development of aviation in the public interest. The extent to which airlines will be able to take advantage of technological progress in aviation, will depend upon the willingness of countries to exchange "freedom of the air" on a multilateral basis.

Another specific problem is that of liability. In 1965, the United States denounced certain provisions of the Warsaw Convention of 1929 limiting the liability of air carriers for personal injury or death of passengers in international air carriage. This denunciation was withdrawn last year when most of the world's major airlines entered into an agreement in which they accepted considerably increased limits of passenger liability. It would not seem advisable, however, that a matter of this nature, which is really one of governmental responsibility, should continue to function for too long as an agreement between carriers. It is

dent of the Treasury Board, Canadian Aeronautics and Space Congress, Montreal, November 17, 1970.

time some fresh attempts were made to draft new protocols, perhaps introducing some flexibility in the amount of the limits of liability. I might mention that the draft convention on liability now under active consideration in the UN Legal Sub-Committee on Outer Space will probably adopt criteria of absolute liability for damage caused on earth or in the air space. Urgent thought should, therefore, be given by air lawyers as to how this may affect private international air law.

Still another problem which may require action internationally is that of integration. There is a growing tendency towards private arrangements for international co-operation. There are pooling arrangements, airline unions and various regional efforts at multilateralism, such as the Scandinavian Airlines System and Air Afrique and the proposed Air Union in Europe. The enormous cost of the next generation of aircraft will accelerate the merging process and, in turn, cause further difficulties in the negotiation of traffic rights, particularly if each of these new organizations considers its individual members to be one entity. Many bilateral agreements will become obsolete and require complicated renegotiation. On the brighter side, however, these same joint operational arrangements may well be regarded as useful precedents for future, far-reaching multilateral conventions.

The airplanes of the past will serve the common interests of the future no better than will the law of the past. Therefore, we must effect a breakthrough in legal attitudes every bit as impressive and functional as the everyday wonders in which we fly. More effort should be made by governmental policy makers, by the academic community and the legal fraternity, to insure that international civil aviation realizes its full potential for the economic and cultural development of our world.

There is a requirement for multilateral agreements regulating the scheduled commercial operation of international civil aviation. A serious attempt was made at Chicago in the International Air Transport Agreement and in the forthright proposal by Australia and New Zealand, supported I understand by France, to plan for the internationalization of civil aviation. We should not, nor if the predictions are accurate can we, continue to say that the time is not yet ripe for such a development. Nevertheless, whatever international arrangements are made, they must, ideally, be both fair and functional and allow for profitable commercial operations and future expansion. Moreover, they should bring to the industry a far larger amount of certainty than that which exists today, thereby enabling airlines and governments to effect more orderly planning and programming to avoid such troublesome matters as excess capacity.

2. Law of the Sea

Canada has been a pioneer in this field going back to the late 1950s, as documented in earlier volumes in this series. The main developments took place during the 1960s and early 1970s, *viz.*, the regulation of our coastal waters through the extension of the then traditional internationally-accepted 3-mile territorial sea to 12, including a fishing zone, in 1964; its expansion to a 200-mile exclusive economic zone first proposed in 1970 and put into effect in 1977.[74]

Law of the Sea questions culminated in the Third Law of the Sea Conference of the United Nations that began in 1973 and ended in 1982, when the UN Law of the Sea Convention was adopted on April 30 of that year by a vote of 117 states (Canada) in favour and four against (Israel, Turkey, the United States, and Venezuela). The Convention was opened for signature on December 10, 1982, at Montego Bay, Jamaica, when 119 states signed. By December 1984, 159 states had signed.

Canada signs Law of the Sea Convention   Doc. 7.2

DFAIT COMMUNIQUÉ, OTTAWA NOVEMBER 22, 1982.

SSEA Allan J. MacEachen announced today that Canada will sign the UN Convention on the Law of the Sea, when it is opened for signature at the final session of the Third Law of the Sea Conference in Jamaica from December 6 to 10.

In making the announcement, Mr. MacEachen underscored the important role which Canada played in the Conference in providing leadership and in generating ideas to resolve the vast range of laws which the Conference had before it. These included: the limits of the territorial sea; the establishment of exclusive economic zones providing coastal state control over important fishing stocks; the limits of the continental shelf; marine scientific research; protection of the marine environment and deep seabed mining.[75]

Canada as a leading coastal state is a major beneficiary of the Conference, having obtained recognition of its right to control offshore living and non-living resources, as well as to take measures for the prevention of marine pollution, particularly in Arctic waters.

The Convention, in its 320 articles and nine annexes, provides a clear set of rules for the management of ocean affairs, for the protection of the interests of developing as well as developed states, and for the resolution of disputes which might arise. A major benefit of the Convention is the important contribution it can make to world peace

---

[74]Owing to space considerations it is not possible to document all early Law of the Sea questions here. These are covered in A.E.B. I, pp. 85-95, and A.E.B. II, pp. 280-296. The immediately following document provides a summary of previous developments.

[75]Reflecting conference negotiations at the time, Canada declared a 200-mile fishing zone as of January 1, 1977.

and security.[76]

Doc. 7.3 **Sovereignty in the Arctic**

STATEMENT, APRIL 8, 1970, HOUSE OF COMMONS, ANNOUNCING THE GOVERNMENT'S
INTENTION OF INTRODUCING TWO BILLS CONCERNING CANADA'S MARINE ENVIRON-
MENT AND THE LIVING RESOURCES OF ITS TERRITORIAL SEAS.

Mr. Trudeau tabled at this time a copy of a letter that had been delivered to the Secretary General by the Canadian Ambassador to the
United Nations, in which a reservation was submitted to Canada's acceptance of the compulsory jurisdiction of the International Court of
Justice. The Prime Minister stated that this reservation was meant to
obviate any litigation of certain features of the two new bills.

The text of the letter follows.

Your Excellency,

On behalf of the Government of Canada,

1) I give notice that I hereby terminate the acceptance by
Canada of the compulsory jurisdiction of the International Court of Justice hitherto effective by virtue of
the declaration made on September 20, 1929, and ratified on July 28, 1930, under Article 36 of the Statute of
the Permanent Court of International Justice, and made
applicable to the International Court of Justice by paragraph 5 of Article 36 of the Statute of that Court.

2) I declare that the Government of Canada accepts as
compulsory *ipso facto* and without special convention,
on condition of reciprocity, the jurisdiction of the International Court of Justice, in conformity with paragraph
2 of Article 36 of the Statute of the Court, until such
time as notice may be given to terminate the acceptance, over all disputes arising after the present declaration with regard to situations or facts subsequent
to this declaration, other than:

(a) disputes in regard to which parties have agreed or
shall agree to have recourse to some other method
of peaceful settlement;

(b) disputes with the Government of any other country which is a member of the Commonwealth of
Nations, all of which disputes shall be settled in
such manner as the parties have agreed or shall
agree;

---

[76]A four-page annex accompanying the communiqué provides details about
the Convention's benefits for Canada under the following headings: territorial
sea, exclusive economic zone, continental shelf, deep seabed mining, and settlement of disputes. It is available from DFAIT, Ottawa.

(c) disputes with regard to questions which by international law fall exclusively within the jurisdiction of Canada;

(d) disputes arising out of or concerning jurisdiction or rights claimed or exercised by Canada in respect of the conservation, management or exploitation of the living resources of the sea, or in respect of the prevention or control of pollution or contamination of the marine environment in marine areas adjacent to the coast of Canada.

3) The Government of Canada also reserves the right at any time, by means of a notification addressed to the Secretary-General of the United Nations, and with effect as from the moment of such notification, either to add to, amend or withdraw any of the foregoing reservations, or any that may hereafter be added.

It is requested that this notification may be communicated to the governments of all the States that have accepted the Optional Clause and to the Registrar of the International Court of Justice.

Accept, Excellency, the assurances of my highest consideration.

Yvon Beaulne,
Ambassador.

His Excellency U Thant
Secretary-General of the United Nations
New York, New York

In his statement to the House, the Prime Minister said:

Canada strongly supports the rule of law in international affairs. Canada has made known to other states that it is prepared to participate actively in multilateral efforts to develop agreed rules on the protection of the environment and the conservation of the living resources of the sea.

Canada is not prepared, however, to engage in litigation with other states concerning vital issues where the law is either inadequate or non-existent and thus does not provide a firm basis for judicial decision. We have, therefore, submitted this new reservation to Canada's acceptance of the compulsory jurisdiction of the International Court relating to those areas of the law of the sea which are undeveloped or inadequate.

It is well known that there is little or no environmental law on the international plane and that the law now in existence favours the interests of the shipping states and the shipping owners engaged in the large-scale carriage of oil and other potential pollutants. There is an urgent need for the development of international law establishing that coastal states are entitled, on the basis of fundamental principle of self-defence, to protect their marine environment and the living resources of the sea adjacent to their coasts.

In spite of this new reservation, Canada's acceptance of the compulsory jurisdiction of the Court remains much broader than that of most other members of the United Nations, and it is the hope of the Government that it will prove possible to reach agreement with other states on the vital need to develop the law to protect the marine environment and its living resources so as to make it possible for Canada again to broaden its acceptance of the court's jurisdiction.

The following background notes on the two bills were provided:

The first of these bills reflects the policies of the Government as stated by the Prime Minister in the Throne Speech debate on October 24, 1969, on the need for legislative action to protect the delicate ecological balance of the Canadian Arctic by laying down stringent anti-pollution measures. The second bill would extend Canada's territorial sea to 12 miles and provide for the establishment by the Government of new fisheries zones.

The Prime Minister stated, on October 24 last year, that Government policy "will reflect Canada's proposed interests not only in the preservation of the ecological balance ... but as well in the economic development of the North, the security of Canada and our stature in the world community". The two bills are directed towards the maintenance of these interests and together form a part of a comprehensive approach to the Canadian North, the protection of the Canadian environment and the conservation of the fisheries and other living resources of the sea.

These bills are evidence of Canada's determination to discharge its responsibilities for Canada's offshore marine environment. The Canadian Government has for some time been concerned about the inadequacies of both international law and domestic law to give adequate protection to the environment and to ensure the conservation of fisheries resources. The two bills are part of a series of related measures to cope with these problems.

The effect of this new legislation would be to make clear that the Northwest Passage is to be opened for the passage of shipping of all nations subject to necessary conditions required to protect the delicate ecological balance of the Canadian Arctic.[77]

Canada seeks to preclude the passage of ships threatening pollution of the environment. Commercially owned shipping intending to

---

[77]For background, see *1st Report*, December 16, 1969, House of Commons Standing Committee on Indian Affairs and Northern Development. See also House of Commons, April 16, 1970, for a comprehensive outline — with historical background — of the Arctic Waters Pollution Prevention Act by Mr. Sharp.

7 — The Environment

enter waters of the Canadian Arctic designated by the Canadian Government as shipping safety control zones would be required to meet Canadian hull, construction and navigation safety standards. These zones may extend up to 100 miles offshore. The owners of shipping and cargoes would be required to provide proof of financial responsibility and will be liable for damage caused by pollution. This liability would be limited but would not depend upon proof of fault or negligence. In the case of shipping owned by another state the necessary safety standards would be given effect by arrangement with the state concerned. Similarly, protective measures would apply to exploration and exploitation of the submarine resources of Canada's northern continental shelf.

The main provisions of the Arctic Waters Pollution Prevention Bill are set out in the attached summary. The second bill, amending the Territorial Sea and Fishing Zone Act of 1964, would have the effect of replacing the three-mile territorial sea and nine-mile exclusive fishing-zone by a 12-mile territorial sea. (Over 50 maritime states now claim a territorial sea of 12 miles or more.)

The bill would also enable the Government to draw fisheries closing lines across the entrances to bodies of waters in special need of fisheries conservation protection. Canada pioneered in the development of the concept of exclusive fishing-zones distinct from the territorial sea and this proposed legislation takes a step further Canada's attempt to contribute to the development of international law both by state practice and by multilateral negotiations.

State practice, or unilateral action by a state, has always been accepted as one of the ways of developing international law. There have been many such instances; for example, the 1948 Truman Proclamation on the Continental Shelf, which became established in international law a few years later.

The proposed anti-pollution legislation is based on the overriding "right of self-defence" of coastal states to protect themselves against grave threats to their environment. It is widely accepted that existing international law does not adequately recognize the need of coastal states to protect themselves against such dangers, which are real and present, as recent experience has shown. Traditional principles of international law concerning pollution of the sea are based largely on ensuring freedom of navigation to shipping states engaged in the large-scale carriage of oil and other potential pollutants. These principles are of little or no relevance to an area having the unique characteristics of the Arctic, where there is an intimate relationship between the sea, the ice and the land, and where the permanent defilement of the environment and the destruction of whole species could take place. There is an urgent need to develop both domestic and international law directly related to the special economic, social and environmental needs of the Canadian North.

These bills are the first of a series of related provisions with regard to the Canadian marine environment and offshore fisheries resources off Canada's East and West Coasts. Legislation now being prepared will protect that environment against the kind of pollution caused by the wreck of the oil tanker *Arrow* in Chedabucto Bay.

The Government is pledged to the development of the use of Canada's Arctic waters to encourage expansion of Canada's northern economy. The Government intends to open up the Northwest Passage as a waterway for innocent passage by ships of all states, by laying down conditions for the exercise of such passage; by establishing that the passage of ships threatening pollution will not be considered innocent; by ensuring against the Northwest Passage becoming, through the process of customary usage, an uncontrolled international strait; and by adopting a functional and constructive approach which does not interfere with the activities of others and reflects the Government's responsibility to its own people and the international community to preserve the ecological balance of Canada and its marine environment.

3. Overfishing

Overfishing, particularly in waters off the Atlantic Coast, has both domestic and international aspects. Until 1986, the allocations set by the North Atlantic Fisheries Organization (NAFO) had been generally accepted, but by 1988 quotas were no longer being respected and catches began rapidly to decline.

Both Canadian, as well as international interests, overfished and drastic measures had to be taken to prevent total depletion of the resource, particularly cod. Somewhat similar problems have also arisen affecting Pacific salmon, but less drastically.[78]

This section deals mainly with overfishing by European Union countries on the Grand Banks just beyond the 200-mile limit. The EU countries mainly concerned have been Spain and Portugal, but others have been involved as well, including Russia and some of its neighbours, as well as several Far Eastern states.

Few coastal states have such a prolonged continental shelf as Canada. A particular problem for Canada internationally is that overfishing has been occurring in waters just outside its jurisdiction and fish have no respect for international boundaries. The possibility of securing agreement to extend control beyond the currently-accepted 200-mile limit has little hope of support or success.

Another international fishing problem facing Canada much closer to home was the France-Canada maritime boundary dispute

---

[78]See Chapter III above (Canada/U.S. relations) for an account of this aspect of the question.

regarding jurisdiction over waters just south of Newfoundland, involving the French islands of St. Pierre and Miquelon. This dispute was settled in 1992.

European overfishing in Canadian waters

DFAIT NEWS RELEASE, OTTAWA, OCTOBER 6, 1988.

The Canadian Government is committed to stopping foreign overfishing. All NAFO country members, with the exception of the EC, have agreed once again to abide by NAFO conservation decisions and quotas. Canada wants to persuade the EC to accept its environmental responsibility.

The 1987 World Commission on Environment and Development (Brundtland Commission) issued a warning on the dangerous effects of overfishing and concluded that overexploitation threatens not only many stocks as economic resources, but also the communities and people who depend upon them.

Since 1986, the EC has consistently rejected NAFO conservation decisions and fished at levels far in excess of the quotas set by other NAFO members. This overfishing is a major factor leading to recent declines in key stocks.

The information campaign will be directed at European Fisheries Ministers, EC Commissioners, the EC Council, and the European Parliament. Others who will be contacted include members of national parliaments, European industry leaders, European environmental organizations, and the European media.

Europeans will be told about the damaging consequences of overfishing and the disastrous effects that this overfishing has had on fishermen on both sides of the Atlantic.[79]

3.1. The Fish War with Spain

EU countries, Spain particularly, continued to overfish off the Grand Banks between the late 1980s and mid-1990s. By 1995, a serious dispute between Canada and Spain — the so-called Fish War — had arisen. Matters reached a head in March 1995, when under the provisions of Bill C-29 (May 1994) Canadian officials boarded and arrested a Spanish ship: the *Estai*. Things calmed down after Spain filed an application against Canada at the International Court of Justice (ICJ) in The Hague, which declined jurisdiction in the case in December 1998.

---

[79]The DFAIT News Release comes with a *Backgrounder* outlining the problem in detail and providing a useful chronology of events.

Doc. 7.5   **[Canada, straddling fish stocks, and the ICJ]**

REMARKS BY FM L. AXWORTHY, DECEMBER 4, 1998, REGARDING THE INTERNATIONAL COURT OF JUSTICE DECISION.

The International Court of Justice is one excellent tool to resolve disputes between States, but we prefer it when we can negotiate a good settlement, as we have already done on the Northwest Atlantic fishery with the EU. Even better is to agree on a good set of rules to enforce conservation of straddling Atlantic fish stocks so that disputes don't arise in the first place. This we have done in negotiating a UN multilateral agreement of straddling stocks, which Canada hopes to ratify soon.[80]

Doc. 7.6   **[Fish dispute with Spain]**

MEDIA LINES, MARCH 27, 1995.

Canada's objective is to achieve an enforceable set of rules to protect endangered fish stocks.

To this end, we have concluded two rounds of negotiations (in Brussels and Vancouver) with the European Union and discussions are continuing.

To help these negotiations to succeed, Canada proposed a Canada-EU moratorium on fishing turbot until an agreement is reached. We are enforcing this moratorium against Canadian vessels and it is being honoured.

To give these negotiations the best chance of success, Canada chose not to enforce against Spanish vessels fishing in violation of Canadian law during the Vancouver Round.

In the face of continued and provocative overfishing by the Spanish fishing fleet, Canada took enforcement action on Sunday.

Given the disturbing evidence collected against the *Estai:* (illegal fish nets, undersized fish, dual log books, etc.) Canada cannot and will not sit by and talk endlessly while the last commercially viable fish stock on the Grand Banks becomes extinct like all the others before it.

This week the UN Conference on Straddling Stocks is meeting in New York. Canada will be taking a leadership role in seeking enforceable international agreement to protect fragile fish stocks.[81]

Doc. 7.7   **Canada-France fisheries dispute**

DFAIT NEWS RELEASE, OTTAWA, JUNE 10, 1992.

An International Court of Arbitration, established by Canada and France to resolve the Canada-France maritime boundary dispute, rendered a

---

[80]See DFAIT News Release No. 284, December 4, 1998. It carries a useful *Backgrounder* with a chronological summary of the issue starting in 1994. The *Ottawa Citizen*, March 10, 1995, has a chronology going back to 1979.

[81]The media lines were issued by DFAIT, along with the text of the statement to the UN Conference made on March 27, 1995, by Fisheries Minister Tobin (now Premier of Newfoundland), who led the campaign against Spain and the EU.

decision today in New York City confirming Canada's jurisdiction over disputed waters located south of Newfoundland and St. Pierre and Miquelon.

At issue were the fishing and potential oil and gas resources in a zone known as the 3Ps, as well as St. Pierre Bank, a large detached bank that is a part of the Grand Banks.

The Court awarded France very little of the area that it had claimed. France had claimed an area, outside the 12-mile territorial sea of 13,703 square nautical miles, but was awarded only 2,537 square nautical miles. A portion of this is in the deep waters of the Laurentian Channel, which contains virtually no fisheries resources.

To ensure an orderly implementation of the Court's ruling, Canada and France have agreed that fishing vessels will be given 45 days to adjust to the new boundary.[82]

4. Outer Space: Basic Policy — International Aspects

The Canadian Space Programme Plan for 1982–1985   Doc. 7.8

BOOKLET ISSUED BY THE MINISTRY OF SCIENCE AND TECHNOLOGY, OTTAWA, DECEMBER 1981. (EXTRACTS)

Cooperation with foreign partners in space activities, whether on a bilateral basis, for instance, with the United States or on a multilateral basis, viz., with the European Space Agency (ESA) is an integral part of Canadian space policy. All of the government's major space projects have been conducted jointly with other nations. This cooperation has permitted Canada to pursue its objectives in space at reduced costs and has provided access to important technology. This international involvement in space has become a significant element in Canada's foreign policy as space activities gain in international importance and as trade in space-related products increases at a rapid pace.

This policy is being extended through closer involvement with the European Space Agency with participation in several of its large-scale satellite programmes. By joining these programmes, Canadian industry will be able to develop commercial relationships with European industry. Substantial follow-on export sales are expected to result from our participation in these programmes.

Canadian cooperation with the United States, spanning two decades, has provided advantages to both Canada and the U.S. Prime examples are the joint space science programme, our participation in several large-scale satellite programmes, and *Canadarm* for the NASA Space Shuttle.

---

[82] A handy portfolio of documentation, with maps and a chronological survey of the question, was put together by DFAIT shortly after the Court issued its decision. It is available from DFAIT, Ottawa. It analyses both the French and Canadian positions on the subject. The maps are particularly good.

4.1. Protection of the Ozone Layer

Protection of the ozone layer from chemicals, especially chloro-fluorocarbons (CFCs), has become a major issue in the field of environmental diplomacy. Lack of ozone exposes the planet and its inhabitants to greater risks from cataracts, leukemia, skin cancer. It can also affect plants and plankton. In addition, the accumulation of carbon dioxide and methane in the atmosphere, which is trapping solar energy reflected from the earth, the so-called "green-house" effect, is a matter for international concern.

One of the basic documents on the protection of the ozone layer is the Protocol that emerged from the international conference held in Montreal in 1987, whereby it was agreed to set up a fund to help poor countries to deal with this problem; to tighten the timetable for phasing CFCs out; and to add two new substances to the list of restricted chemicals. In particular, it was agreed that rich countries would halve CFC use by 1998. It has now been accepted to phase CFCs out entirely by the year 2000.

Doc. 7.9 **The changing atmosphere**

SPEECH BY PM BRIAN MULRONEY, AT THE OPENING OF THE INTERNATIONAL CONFERENCE ON THE CHANGING ATMOSPHERE, TORONTO, JUNE 27, 1988. (EXTRACTS)

The world is coming to recognize what we believe in Canada to be self-evident — that economic development and environmental protection are mutually reinforcing, not mutually exclusive. Our economic activity must be increasingly compatible with today's environmental facts of life. We are faced with climate shifts, desertification, flooding, droughts, ozone depletion, acidification. These are major global issues. Consider the so-called "greenhouse effect". Carbon dioxide from fossil-fuel burning and methane from modern agricultural and industrial practices are accumulating in the atmosphere and trapping solar energy reflected from the earth.

Canada is committed to taking the necessary action to protect the environment. We endorsed the Brundtland Report at the United Nations. I am pleased to advise that our key legislative instrument required to implement all phases of the Montreal Protocol, the new *Canadian Environmental Protection Act*, will soon receive royal assent. We will then ratify the Protocol, becoming the third of the signatories to do so. Heeding the warnings of science that an 85% reduction is necessary, we will advance regulations to ban all non-essential uses of CFCs and halons.

Another plank in our international atmospheric legal framework, a protocol for the control of nitrogen oxides, will likely be signed by European and North American countries next fall. We need international legal mechanisms to forge global cooperation to protect and restore our atmospheric life-support system. Your deliberations on such international legal régimes will be crucial. The outcome of your work will form the basis for the follow-up meeting, to be hosted by Canada early next year, of international legal and policy experts on the law of the atmosphere — with particular focus on climate change.

I want to say a word about the threat of global climate change and the need to develop an equitable resolution of Third World debt. It is not just altruism. It is in our self-interest. If the debtor nations of the tropics stopped stripping their rainforests to generate export earnings to service their debts, the industrialized countries would benefit. The slowing of carbon dioxide build-up would give the developed world much needed flexibility in adjusting our energy mix to reduce reliance on fossil fuels.

Canada is committed to working with developing countries to find solutions to their staggering debt. Last year, we forgave $670 million in development assistance-related debt to the poorest nations of Africa. Structural adjustment programmes should be considered, along with debt-rescheduling and/or concessional financing undertaken with the goal of sustainable development in mind.

Canada is also supporting a feasibility study into a World Conservation Bank to work in concert with the World Bank. This innovative recommendation of the Brundtland Commission deserves serious consideration.

We, in Canada, believe that there are no limits to economic growth, but we do recognize that there are real limits to natural systems and resources. This is not just about the atmosphere, it is not just about the environment, it is about the future of the planet itself.

5. Earth Summit Conferences

[Rio de Janeiro]   Doc. 7.10

ADDRESS BY PM BRIAN MULRONEY, AT THE EARTH SUMMIT, RIO DE JANEIRO, JUNE 12, 1992. (EXTRACTS)

I am proud to sign both Conventions on behalf of Canada. These agreements are welcome additions to the growing body of international environmental law. Canada supports the extension of international environmental law to cover the world's forests.

Countries have a right to manage their forest resources and humanity has a right to expect that those management decisions will be ecologically wise.

Canada also supports the strengthening of international environmental law to prevent overfishing on the high seas. In Atlantic Canada overfishing beyond our 200-mile zone has created an ecological disaster. This is why for Canada a global agreement to prevent overfishing is quite simply crucial.

We have made good progress here, but the success of Rio will not be found in the minutes of this conference or the eloquence of its speakers. Success will come from converting our agenda, Agenda 21, into concrete accomplishments.

To capitalize on the momentum of Rio, Canada advocates five crucial steps:

- First, all countries need to develop their own plans for sustainable development, what we in Canada call our Green Plan. Canada's Green Plan is a $3 billion action plan with targets and timetables on a wide range of projects.

- Second, the agreements on climate change and biodiversity require urgent and constructive follow-up. For our part, we undertake to ratify both Conventions this calendar year.

- Third, the requisite resources are needed to ensure that developing countries can play their important roles. Canada has spent $1,3 billion for sustainable development in developing countries over the past five years.

- Fourth, multilateral institutions must be a part of the solution. Institutions that have a global perspective have a pivotal role to play. We will promote action on the results of this conference by the UN General Assembly this autumn and we will endorse the creation of a Sustainable Development Commission. With this in mind, the mandate of the acclaimed Canadian International Development Research Centre (IDRC) will be broadened so as to deal specifically with the environment and related concerns.

- Fifth, the idea of an Earth Charter of Environment Rights and Responsibilities, which has slipped beyond our grasp at Rio, should be revived. We propose 1995, the 50th anniversary of the United Nations, as a target date for completion of the Earth Charter.

Editor's notes: Five years after the Rio meeting, a follow-up Conference took place at Kyoto, Japan, reiterating much the same ideals but pushing the national greenhouse gas/fossil fuel emission targets from the year 2000 to 2010. Environment Minister Jane Stewart remarked, as reported on December 16, 1997, that: "Our intention is to ratify, but ratifying has important economic implications for us as a country. So it's important that we shall have to keep a close eye on what our major trading partners are doing as well." Natural Resources Minister Goodale also observed at the time that ratification of the Kyoto Treaty will come "when we believe it appropriate and in Canada's interest to do so."

Incidentally, apart from the economic, scientific, and technical challenges involved in the Treaty targets, the role and input of the provinces further complicates the Canadian position regarding both the targets and ratification.

8

Immigration and Refugees

ALL FEDERAL GOVERNMENTS SINCE 1945 have maintained the policy of encouraging migration to Canada, with ups and downs in the numbers received annually depending on economic conditions in the country.

The source and mix of immigrants changed a great deal during the period. Traditional immigration from Europe dropped substantially, almost to disappear towards the end of the century. It has been replaced largely by migration from Africa, Asia, the Caribbean, Middle America.

This has at times caused certain types of political problems internationally for Canada; some immigrant and refugee groups, with considerable grudges against political and at times religious opponents whom they left behind at home, have continued from Canadian soil to seek to achieve their political aims and ambitions in their countries of origin.[83]

Throughout the period, governments continued to provide humanitarian asylum, on an increasing scale, to large groups of refugees, reflecting the unsettled conditions prevailing in many parts of the world, e.g., Europe, immediately after the Second World War, and lately, Vietnam (the "boat people"), Sri Lanka (the Tamils), India (the Sikhs), Central America, Somalia, and others.

Recently, immigration and refugee matters have increasingly involved consultations and arrangements with the provinces, particularly since the 1970s.

1.   Basic Immigration Policy

1.1.   New immigration regulations

TABLED IN THE HOUSE OF COMMONS, OTTAWA, MARCH 8, 1978, BY EMPLOYMENT AND IMMIGRATION MINISTER BUD CULLEN. (EXTRACTS)   Doc. 8.1

---

[83]For details, see the *Report of the Special Senate Committee on Terrorism and the Public Safety*, Ottawa, June 1987. It goes into the question of terrorism in considerable detail and also analyses Canada's immigration policies and procedures in the context of terrorism. The report carries a useful bibliography.

Canadian Foreign Policy 1945-2000

Canada's new Immigration Act and Regulations will be tied to population and labour market needs. The new Act will link the number of immigrants to long-term demographic planning and the needs of the labour market through changes in selection criteria and the establishment of a closer working relationship with the provinces.

The new Act:

1) States for the first time in Canadian law the basic principles underlying immigration policy — non-discrimination, family reunion, humanitarian concern for refugees, and the promotion of national goals;

2) Links the immigration movement to Canada's population and labour market needs;

3) In consultation with the provinces and other groups, provides for an annual forecast of the number of immigrants Canada can comfortably absorb;

4) Establishes a family class allowing Canadian citizens to sponsor a wider range of close relatives;

5) Confirms Canada's commitment and responsibilities to refugees under the UN Convention and establishes a new refugee class;

6) Requires immigrants and visitors to obtain visas or authorizations abroad and prohibits visitors from changing their status in Canada;

7) Introduces security measures to protect Canada from international terrorism and organized crime;

8) Safeguards the civil rights of immigrants and visitors through an improved inquiry and appeal system;

9) Provides less drastic alternatives to deportation for cases involving minor violations of immigration law; and

10) States in specific terms the powers granted to the Government and its officers.

The selection criteria or point system will be revised whereby, in order to be admitted to Canada, every immigrant must achieve a minimum number of assessment points. For instance, entrepreneurs must have at least 25 points; assisted relatives must earn 25 to 30 points, depending on how they are related to the Canadian resident who has promised to help them. All other applicants rated under the point system must achieve 50 points, out of a possible 100, before they can be issued immigrant visas.

In addition, applicants must meet certain mandatory requirements regarding job experience and occupational demand.

8 — Immigration and Refugees

1.2. Revised selection criteria

SPECIAL REPORT TO PARLIAMENT, JUNE 27, 1985. (EXTRACTS)   Doc. 8.2

These revisions may be seen as the latest in a series of on-going measures which ensure that newcomers to Canada are selected against criteria which mirror the economic and social requirements of the day. At the same time, it has become necessary to introduce new elements into the system to meet changing circumstances, for instance, the decline in total immigrant landings from 143,000 in 1980 to just over 88,000 in 1984 and in selected worker landings from 21,000 in 1981 to 6,500 in 1984.

Five principles, or premises, guide the development of the changes required in the selection criteria:

1) The criteria should support the decisions of the Federal Government respecting the size and composition of future immigration levels;
2) All applicants are to be assessed against the same criteria and will be required to satisfy the same pass mark;
3) There should continue to be a preference accorded to applicants with relatives already in Canada, who are prepared to guarantee on-going support until the new arrivals are self-sufficient;
4) Occupational groups for which applicants would be eligible should be identified to ensure that Canada's labour market needs are met; and
5) The changes to the selection criteria should be clear and understandable to the Canadian public, potential candidates abroad, and those who are responsible for administering the programme.

1.3. The 1993 Immigration Act and Regulations: Summary

The 1993 Act and Regulations reflect the principles laid down in 1978, that is, non-discrimination, family reunion, humanitarian concern, and the promotion of Canadian social, economic, demographic and cultural goals. It too links the immigration movement to Canada's population and labour market needs.

However, in recognition of changed international circumstances, it introduces security measures to protect Canada from international terrorism and organized crime. It contains safeguards for the civil rights of immigrants, and provides short-term alternatives to permanent deportation for less serious violations of the immigration law.

In addition, under Section 108, it sanctions the provision for regular and closer consultations with the provinces with several of which immigration agreements have been concluded. The most comprehensive of these agreements has been with Quebec.

In essence, it maintains the provisions of the 1991 Canada-Quebec Accord that divides responsibilities for immigration to Quebec, whereby Canada continues to determine national standards and objectives and to have responsibility for family class and refugees, while Quebec is responsible for linguistic, cultural, and economic integration services for permanent residents and for the selection of independent immigrants. Similar agreements with other interested provinces, taking into account local circumstances, generally reflect these provisions.

The point system of selection criteria under the new Act remains basically the same as before, but in consultation with the provinces places greater emphasis on the selection of investor immigrants.

1.4. White Paper on Immigration 1998: Summary

Released in January 1998, it further updates the system by proposing a new selection model for choosing skilled immigrants; expanding the definition of spouse to include same-sex and common law partners; rejecting applications from criminals who have committed crimes against humanity and members of governments who have engaged in systematic or gross violations of human rights.

2. Basic Refugee Policy

Doc. 8.3   **Canada and Refugees**

STATEMENT BY SSEA MARK MACGUIGAN, TO THE NATIONAL SYMPOSIUM ON REFUGEE STATUS DETERMINATION, TORONTO, FEBRUARY 21, 1982. (EXTRACTS)

The refugee problem is of major interest to Canada for two reasons, both of which form a fundamental part of our foreign policy: first, our traditional humanitarian policy towards disadvantaged people; and, second, our interest in an international order that is stable and just.

Canada's response to the refugee situation covers a wide range of government activities. We play an active and leading role internationally through local integration and resettlement, humanitarian assistance, support for multilateral institutions, and initiatives in the United Nations.

Canada's overall refugee policy and response are developed through an on-going process of consultation within and outside the government. The process ensures an openness of the decision-making process to a range of views on these complex questions.

There is no hard and fast rule that determines Canada's approach to a given refugee situation. We generally follow internationally-accepted guidelines.

The ideal situation for refugees is voluntary repatriation to their homeland when conditions permit a safe return. In such situations, emergency relief and humanitarian assistance are usually the chief requirements. This is the situation, for example, of Afghan refugees, most Central American refugees, and the vast majority of African refugees. Should repatriation prove impossible, local integration is the next preferred solution. For example, the "boat people" of Vietnam.

The provision of humanitarian assistance to refugees is a major commitment for Canada. Such assistance is crucial in most refugee situations to provide basic necessities such as food, shelter, and medical aid.

I would not wish to characterize one refugee situation as worse than another, but the Government must establish priorities based on the finite financial resources at its disposal. In 1981, Africa — where there are presently 5 million refugees — was one of Canada's highest priorities. Elsewhere, we made contributions to Palestinian, Central American, and Indochinese refugees.

In these very serious cases of mass exodus, the refugee problem extends far beyond its humanitarian impact. Emergency aid is therefore not, in itself, enough. It is not enough to treat the symptom of the problem; if we wish to cure the disease, we must work towards preventing it.

What are the root causes of these refugee situations? How, if at all, can they be prevented? There are a variety of causes: natural disasters, for instance, such as earthquakes, floods, droughts; and also 'man-made disasters' such as wars, civil disturbances, human rights violations.

The question of refugees and human rights violations is of particular concern to Canada and I believe we are well-placed to raise this matter internationally. Canada has a long and close involvement with the UNHCR; we are a major contributor to humanitarian assistance; our local integration and resettlement record in the last few years is, on a per capita basis, the best in the world. Concern for human rights has been an element of our foreign policy for decades.

2.1. Arrangements with Quebec

Agreement between the Government of Canada and the Gouvernement du Québec (sic) with regard to cooperation on immigration matters and on the selection of foreign nationals wishing to settle either permanently or temporarily in Québec." Doc. 8.4

MONTREAL, FEBRUARY 20, 1978. (SUMMARY)

The Governments of Canada and Québec

CONSIDERING that Section 95 of the British North America Act recognizes the concurrent jurisdiction of the federal and provincial legislatures in immigration matters,

Have agreed to the following provisions:

I. Purpose

1) The contracting parties will cooperate fully in all areas relating to their migration movements and demography;

2) The contracting parties will participate jointly in the selection of persons who wish to settle permanently or temporarily in Québec.

II. Cooperation on Migration

1) A Joint Committee on migration is established in accordance with Article I.

2) The objective of the Joint Committee is to ensure continuing cooperation on the subject by the two governments.

The functions of the Joint Committee are: a) to harmonize the economic, demographic, and socio-cultural objectives of the parties with respect to the migration movement; b) to coordinate the application of the policies of the two governments with respect to the migration movement and immigration levels. (There follows at this point a series of clauses spelling out the details of the Joint Committee's coordination role, its membership, the frequency of its meetings, and so on.)

III. Selection

A. Independent immigrants

1) *Criteria*

   (a) The selection of foreign nationals who wish to settle permanently in Québec will be carried out on a joint and equal basis, according to separate sets of criteria for Canada and for Québec. (At this point, a series of technical clauses define the selection criteria.)

2) *Implementation*

   (a) The selection of immigrants destined to Québec will be the result of a joint process of decision, based upon the assessment of every applicant by each party according to its criteria.

   (b) The landing of an independent immigrant in Québec requires Québec's prior agreement. (The agreement then spells out the modalities of implementation, such as methods and procedures governing inter-communication and exchange of information by the parties, conditions of pre-selection of applicants, etc.).

Clauses B, C, D of Article III on the Selection of Independent Immigrants apply *mutatis mutandis* the foregoing principles and requirements to relatives, refugees, visitors such as seasonal workers, students, teachers.

8 — Immigration and Refugees

IV. Implementation committee

The purpose of the Implementation Committee is to coordinate the application by the contracting parties of the provisions of Articles III and V of the agreement and to carry out any other mandate assigned to it by the Joint Committee. (Its membership, frequency of meetings, and functions, which are largely administrative, are then given.)

V. General Provisions

This article deals with the date of entry into force of the agreement (1978), its term of validity (three years), its renewability unless terminated by either party on written notice of six months, its languages (French and English: both equally authentic).

The agreement carries two annexes. The first spells out the conditions and procedures governing the selection, arrival, and employment of temporary workers. The second lists in considerable detail the administrative and financial arrangements governing the status of agents abroad of the *Ministère de l'Immigration du Québec* (sic), as well as the provisions for the presence of Quebec officials in missions abroad of the federal government.

This agreement is known as the Cullen-Couture agreement, from the names of the federal and Quebec ministers of Immigration, respectively, who signed it in 1978. It has since been renewed.

Editor's note: The Immigration Act of 1993 further refines the process of selection and integration of immigrants to Quebec.

219

9

The Provinces and Foreign Policy

IN 1945, A CHAPTER ON THE INTERNATIONAL ACTIVITIES of the provinces in a book on Canadian foreign policy would have been extremely unlikely. Yet the provinces have played an important role in Canada's relations with the rest of the world for a long time. It is supremely ironical today to note that for thirty years (1882–1911) Quebec's representative in Paris handled Ottawa's interests in France![84]

Immigration, trade, investments — all subjects with foreign policy connotations — have been matters of provincial preoccupation virtually since Confederation. Every province at some point or other has maintained some form of representation abroad or has had dealings with foreign entities to foster its interests in these and other sectors going back at times well into the Nineteenth Century. Most provinces have long had bilateral trans-border arrangements with adjacent states to the south in areas of mutual concern, such as transportation, highways, forestry, hydro-electricity, with no direct Ottawa involvement.

It is mainly since the early 1960s that provincial thrusts into the foreign policy field have become stronger and more sustained, that provincial activity abroad has become more structured and widespread. Quebec and Ontario, notably, have maintained numerous posts abroad.[85] Official visits to foreign countries by provincial premiers, delegations, commissions, are now extremely common.

There are several reasons for this development, some domestic and some foreign, but one of the main ones is the evolving nature of diplomacy. Both the form and the content of foreign relations have changed a good deal. Gone are the days when

---

[84]Order-in-Council of July 12, 1882.

[85]The recession of the early 1990s occasioned a good deal of retrenchment in the presence abroad of all provincial governments. Indeed, Ontario — as an economy measure — closed its entire system of agencies abroad in 1993, while Quebec dropped some of its marginal ones and reduced staff in many others, as did most other provinces.

the art of negotiating, the fostering of trade, the reporting of political, economic, military trends and developments, were the main substance of diplomacy. They are still important but external relations now include the active pursuit of mutually advantageous cultural, educational, environmental, resource, scientific, social, and related exchanges, all of which either touch on or in some instances come exclusively under provincial jurisdiction. Today, in some sectors, Canada's external relations cannot be conducted without the provinces. In the field of education, for instance, only the provinces have the experience and expertise to represent Canada knowledgeably at international conferences on the subject.

While some Ontario external activities in the field of education go back as early as 1941, notably in the education sector,[86] the international activities of Quebec in this and in other fields have been more assertive recently and are consequently better known.

Quebec's influence and impact on Canadian foreign policy go back to the 1960s. They reflect the principles of the *Révolution Tranquille* launched by the newly-elected government of Jean Lesage in July 1960. However, the first step taken to establish Quebec's international presence was the Barrette government's decision in January 1960 to set up a *délégation générale* in Paris and one in London as well. The Barrette government was defeated in the provincial elections that year and it fell to his successor, Jean Lesage, to implement the decision.

La Maison du Québec, as the *délégation générale* in Paris is sometimes called, was inaugurated by Premier Lesage on October 5, 1961. His remarks on that occasion, and elsewhere in France during his visit, gave his conception of the role abroad of what he called *L'État du Québec* and also the rationale behind Quebec's growing interest in the rest of the world, especially the Francophone world.

Somewhat earlier, Minister of Youth Paul Gérin-Lajoie in the Lesage cabinet had voiced similar thoughts in Montreal at the inaugural session on September 8, 1961, of AUPELF (Association universitaire des pays partiellement ou entièrement de langue française). Later, as Education Minister, he became one of the most outspoken exponents of Quebec's right to independent representation and treaty-making powers with respect to matters under its direct jurisdiction. Under his impulse, Quebec negotiated and concluded with the not-unwilling government of President de Gaulle

---

[86]Direct teacher training arrangements with Bermuda.

accords or *ententes* on education and culture in February and November 1965.

The federal government was not, of course, merely a passive witness to these developments that were being closely monitored by the cabinet and DEA at the time. PM Pearson paid an official visit to France in January 1964. It gave its blessing to the France-Quebec *ententes* by placing them under a France-Canada "umbrella" treaty, thereby giving them official status. It also announced its readiness to cooperate with the government of any province in facilitating, in appropriate circumstances, the negotiation and conclusion of agreements (*accords* or *ententes*) not full treaties, between interested provinces and foreign governments. These agreements would, of course, require treaty sanction by Ottawa to be binding.

The foundations were laid at this time for the federal government's policy of bilingualism and biculturalism. Its aid programmes to the French-speaking countries were also stepped up. Thus, the battle lines between Ottawa and Quebec had been drawn and the effects are still being felt.

1. Quebec's External Relations

Doc. 9.1   **[Politique extérieure du Québec]**

ALLOCUTION PRONONCÉE À PARIS PAR JEAN LESAGE, PREMIER MINISTRE, LORS DE L'INAUGURATION DE LA MAISON DU QUÉBEC, LE 5 OCTOBRE 1961. (EXTRAITS)

Il existe une expression qui a de plus en plus cours chez nous. Je m'en suis moi-même souvent servi car je crois qu'elle symbolise l'éveil de notre population, non seulement à ce qu'elle représente dans la Confédération canadienne, mais aussi au rôle qu'elle peut jouer dans le monde qui nous entoure. Cette expression, c'est "L'État du Québec".

En l'utilisant, nous ne voulons pas nous faire collectivement croire, ni inciter les autres nations à penser que notre Province, par quelque "processus politique obscur", est devenue un pays distinct du reste de l'Amérique du Nord. Nos ambitions ne sont pas aussi étendues, mais elles n'en sont pas moins profondes. Pour nous, l'État du Québec, c'est le point d'appui commun, le levier dont nous pouvons et devons nous servir dans la poursuite des tâches que nous imposent notre présence dans la réalité canadienne et notre survivance au sein d'un monde américain dont la culture est étrangère à la nôtre. Il est devenu, par la force des choses et à cause des lois inéluctables de la démographie et de l'histoire, l'instrument communautaire d'une affirmation nationale s'appuyant, non pas sur un chauvinisme étroit, mais sur le souci bien légitime chez toute minorité de sauvegarder son mode de vie et les traits culturels qui la distinguent de la majorité dans laquelle elle risquerait de se fondre.

Notre conception du rôle de l'État — du rôle de *notre* État — ne s'inspire nullement d'un quelconque dogmatisme. Je dirais plutôt qu'elle provient d'un souci bien pragmatique. Nous n'avons tout simplement pas le choix de procéder autrement. Car il faut bien nous rendre compte d'une chose que l'histoire et la démographie nous dévoilent d'ailleurs brutalement. Comme groupe ethnique, nous formons environ 30 pour cent de la population canadienne. Nous ne représentons même pas un trentième de toute la population de l'Amérique du Nord: 6 millions, par rapport à 190 millions. Nous sommes collectivement un sujet d'étonnement pour les historiens. Il y a longtemps en effet que nous aurions pu être assimilés, mais en dépit des lois de l'histoire, nous avons survécu.

Quand je dis que nous voulons nous signaler à l'attention du reste du monde, je voudrais être bien compris. Il y a plusieurs façons de se manifester aux autres. Celle à laquelle nous pensons n'est nullement inspirée par un souci de vanité patriotique mal placé. Nous voulons tout simplement accéder au niveau culturel et économique auquel nous avons droit et auquel nous pouvons aspirer.

Jusqu'à maintenant noire situation historique et géographique nous a forcés de devenir ce que nous sommes: nous voulons désormais être ce que nous pouvons devenir. En d'autres termes, le peuple canadien-français a pris conscience de lui-même et de sa place dans le monde actuel. C'est pour mieux l'occuper que nous avons institué à Paris notre Délégation Générale. Et en nous installant à Paris, nous avons choisi d'être au centre des préoccupations de l'Europe.

Notre maison du Québec, dans la capitale de la France, aura des fonctions bien précises. Elle n'est, dans ce qu'elle signifie pour nous, que le prolongement de l'action que nous avons entreprise dans le Québec même. Elle résulte logiquement des attitudes nouvelles que nous partageons tous au Québec sur notre présence dans la réalité élargie qu'est pour nous le monde européen.

Nous désirons nous intégrer au fait français, mais nous ne voulons pas transformer le Québec en appendice nordique de la France. La richesse de la culture française à laquelle nous souhaitons nous abreuver intellectuellement est justement de permettre, chez ceux qu'elle influence, de demeurer eux-mêmes. C'est peut-être là un des plus grands hommages qu'on peut rendre à sa valeur universelle. Le lien de continuité que nous voulons établir avec la France ne sera donc pas un lien de dépendance; j'irai même jusqu'à dire que nous pouvons nous enrichir de nos différences mutuelles. Ce qui fait la force d'une communauté culturelle — comme celle à laquelle nous voulons appartenir — c'est sa diversité dans une saine unité, et non son uniformité.

Mais une nation ne vit pas que de l'esprit. Nous voulons également nous inscrire dans les nouveaux courants internationaux et prendre place dans l'univers économique européen où la France joue déjà un rôle si prestigieux.

Nous tenons plus particulièrement à vous dire, à vous et à tous les membres du Marché Commun, qu'il y a dans notre sol des richesses naturelles inexploitées et incommensurables. Nos délégués économiques seront maintenant sur place pour vous fournir tous les renseignements voulus et vous exposer clairement les nombreux avantages qu'il y a à investir chez nous, dans notre jeune économie.

Nous vous offrons, à vous Français d'abord, de collaborer avec nous à la mise en valeur de toutes les richesses dont, nous nous plaisons à le remarquer, notre Province est si abondamment pourvue. Nous voulons, en quelque sorte, que vos capitaux et que votre énergie créatrice s'ajoutent aux nôtres dans les tâches d'ordre économique auxquelles nous avons entrepris de nous attaquer. Nous désirons aussi que des échanges commerciaux plus nourris s'effectuent entre nos deux nations car, au seuil de l'expansion économique que nous connaîtrons bientôt, nous nous munissons déjà des moyens qui permettront à celle-ci de se poursuivre.

Nos initiatives culturelles, économiques et commerciales dans les autres pays — l'établissement d'une Maison du Québec à Paris en est un exemple — ne constituent nullement, à nos yeux, une concurrence que nous voulons opposer à nos ambassades à l'étranger, ni un dédoublement de forces. Le Canada est un pays fédératif formé de dix États distincts ayant chacun des pouvoirs législatifs étendus. L'éducation, par exemple, relève exclusivement des pouvoirs provinciaux. Vous saisissez dès lors l'importance et l'étendue de nos devoirs dans le domaine proprement culturel.

D'un autre côté, si la monnaie, les banques, les tarifs douaniers relèvent directement et exclusivement du gouvernement central, il n'est pas dit que le commerce extérieur soit de son ressort exclusif. Chaque gouvernement provincial a son ministère des Affaires économiques, de l'Industrie et du Commerce, et il appartient à chaque province de voir à l'expansion industrielle tant à l'intérieur qu'à l'extérieur de ses propres limites territoriales. Nos délégués économiques provinciaux apporteront en quelque sorte une aide précieuse au personnel de nos ambassades déjà sur place. Ce sera, de leur part, un complément de travail. Nous ne venons pas pour supplanter les agents fédéraux à l'étranger mais bien au contraire, pour travailler de concert avec eux.

De fait, plusieurs de nos ambassades ont réclamé notre présence à leurs côtés. Nous pouvons dire que nous arrivons sur place pour y recevoir des nôtres un accueil des plus favorables.

De toute façon, je pense bien qu'il ne faut pas interpréter notre présence ici — ou ailleurs dans le monde — comme une initiative en marge de celle de notre gouvernement fédéral. Il s'agit plutôt, si je peux m'exprimer ainsi, d'une présence conjointe inspirée beaucoup plus par un souci de collaboration que par un esprit d'émulation. La diversité naturelle du Canada implique souvent une variété dans son action. La puissance économique de notre Province et ses affinités culturelles avec certains pays, notamment la France, imposent à l'État du

Québec la nécessité d'assumer une responsabilité qui lui a toujours été implicitement reconnue par tous les Canadiens.

[Québec et la France]   Doc. 9.2

ALLOCUTION PRONONCÉE PAR PAUL GÉRIN-LAJOIE, MINISTRE DE L'ÉDUCATION, À QUÉBEC, LE 22 AVRIL 1965, DEVANT UNE DÉLÉGATION D'UNIVERSITAIRES BELGES, FRANÇAIS ET SUISSES.

Parce que l'éducation est un domaine en pleine croissance, en croissance presque explosive, c'est le domaine précis où le Québec a d'abord senti le besoin de dépasser ses frontières, de trouver à l'extérieur autant qu'à l'intérieur les moyens d'assurer son enrichissement et de participer, par le moyen d'échanges, à la vie intellectuelle du monde contemporain.

Tous les pays du monde traversent une crise de l'éducation; la science et la connaissance deviennent mondiales; la recherche est de plus en plus une activité internationale. Il était donc normal que le Québec allât constater ce qui se faisait ailleurs et sentît le besoin d'établir certains échanges avec les pays frères dont il partage en partie l'héritage commun.

Dans le domaine de la coopération en éducation, le premier geste du Québec a été de signer un accord avec l'Association pour l'organisation des stages en France, grâce auquel des ingénieurs et des techniciens de l'un ou l'autre pays peuvent faire de courts stages d'observation, d'information, de perfectionnement et de recherche, dans les domaines technique et économique.

Tout récemment, la signature d'une entente générale entre les gouvernements du Québec et de la France, pour l'échange d'étudiants, de professeurs et de chercheurs, a illustré encore davantage la détermination du Québec de collaborer avec les autres membres de la communauté culturelle française, et de faire connaître son vrai visage au monde contemporain.

Ce sont là les premiers actes que pose le Québec sur le plan international, et ce n'est pas un hasard qu'il les ait posés dans un domaine où la libre circulation des idées et la liberté du commerce intellectuel sont essentiels à un développement culturel et scientifique normal.

Vous vous demanderez peut-être comment le Québec, état membre d'une fédération, peut ainsi négocier et conclure lui-même des accords avec l'étranger. Il faudrait plutôt s'étonner qu'il ne l'ait pas fait avant aujourd'hui. Car cette activité nouvelle du Québec s'inscrit dans le processus de sa personnalisation et dans la dynamique de notre régime fédératif au moment où nous songeons à redéfinir le Canada en fonction du principe de l'égalité des deux communautés qui le composent.

En réalité, le Canada et le Québec, et ceci vaut pour toutes les autres provinces, se trouvent, en ce qui concerne les relations internationales, dans une situation très particulière. Le gouvernement fédéral, certes, possède le droit incontestable de traiter avec n'importe quel pays étranger et de conclure les accords qu'il juge bon, dans les domaines de sa convenance. Par contre, le gouvernement fédéral est totalement impuissant à assurer la mise en oeuvre et l'application de ces accords s'ils touchent à la compétence des états provinciaux. Seules, en pareil cas, les provinces disposent des moyens de procéder à la mise en oeuvre de traités, qui, sans leur participation, resteraient lettre-morte et s'avéreraient totalement inutiles.

Il se peut que plusieurs provinces canadiennes préfèrent laisser l'État fédéral signer des accords qui relèvent de leur juridiction, quitte à collaborer, sans discussion, à la mise en oeuvre de ces accords.

Le Québec, cependant, ne peut qu'assumer la position particulière que lui impose sa vocation d'instrument collectif des Canadiens-français. Il entend négocier lui-même directement avec les autres pays les accords qu'il sera appelé à appliquer. Si le Québec adopte cette attitude, ce n'est d'ailleurs pas uniquement pour des raisons constitutionnelles et pour des raisons de politique interne, mais aussi pour des motifs d'efficacité

Le Québec, en effet, n'est pas une simple province parmi d'autres, et les Québécois entendent bien se comporter comme un peuple maître de son destin: les Canadiens de langue française considèrent à juste titre le gouvernement du Québec comme l'instrument premier de leur épanouissement collectif, la garantie de leur permanence et le symbole de leur unité, bref, ils ont résolu de lui assigner le rôle d'expression politique de leur société.

Il va de soi que les Canadiens-français considèrent le gouvernement du Québec, où ils sont majoritaires, comme l'instrument par excellence de leur épanouissement collectif.

Pas plus qu'un peuple ne saurait confier à un autre le soin de fixer ses priorités pour la formation de sa jeunesse et l'épanouissement de sa culture, les Québécois ne sauraient davantage s'en remettre exclusivement, pour l'organisation de leurs rapports culturels avec l'univers Francophone, au gouvernement fédéral. Celui-ci dans le passé s'est toujours montré des plus circonspect en ces matières et n'a d'ailleurs manifesté que très peu d'intérêt sous ce rapport jusqu'à ces tous derniers mois. Son administration est peu familière avec la mentalité, les méthodes de travail, la langue, les cadres et les institutions d'enseignement et de culture du Québec.

Bien sûr, personne ne saurait mettre en doute la responsabilité du gouvernement fédéral dans l'établissement d'une politique étrangère du Canada. Dans cette perspective, nous devons souhaiter, dans l'intérêt même du Canada, qu'il s'ouvre davantage aux ressources intellectuelles, morales et matérielles que représentent les valeurs de la civilisation française.

Mais il nous faut prendre garde de tomber dans l'illusion que des liens avec le gouvernement fédéral permettent automatiquement à l'étranger d'avoir un contact étroit avec la communauté francophone du Canada. Pour des raisons démographiques et historiques, le gouvernement fédéral représente une entité plus anglophone que Francophone. La situation géographique de notre pays, les liens économiques étroits qui l'unissent à son puissant voisin du sud, sa participation soutenue aux activités du Commonwealth contribuent à orienter son action politique plus naturellement en fonction des préoccupations du monde Anglo-Saxon. Aussi est-ce surtout par le seul gouvernement francophone d'Amérique continentale, celui du Québec, que l'on peut établir un contact réel et fécond avec la collectivité qu'il représente.

L'action du Québec n'est pas seulement conforme au régime constitutionnel canadien, elle est aussi indiscutable sur les plans de l'efficacité et de la logique.

Dans ces domaines où le Québec est compétent pour agir, seul le Québec est muni des structures administratives et entretient des rapports réguliers avec les groupes et les institutions dont la coopération est nécessaire à la mise en oeuvre des accords internationaux. De plus, dans ces domaines, les intérêts et les aspirations du Québec sont généralement trop différents de ceux du Canada anglais, pour ne pas dire parfois même divergents sinon opposés, pour que l'État fédéral puisse prétendre négocier dans le meilleur intérêt de chacun des partenaires canadiens. Que ces intérêts et ces objectifs soient différents et même incompatibles, la répartition des compétences entre nos deux ordres de gouvernement le démontre amplement.

Enfin au plan de la logique, il faut bien reconnaître qu'on négocie et conclut une entente dans le but essentiel de l'appliquer et de demeurer fidèle à son esprit; c'est pourquoi il revient à ceux qui doivent l'appliquer et en bénéficier d'en préciser d'abord les termes.

Que le Québec n'ait pas, dans le passé, utilisé pleinement tous ses pouvoirs ni assumé le rôle de partenaire qui lui revenait, n'implique nullement que ces pouvoirs aient disparu et qu'on puisse aujourd'hui lui refuser le droit de s'en prévaloir.

À mesure que le Québec, dans le processus d'autodéfinition qu'il traverse, assumera son identité, il occupe progressivement tous les champs d'activité qui engagent son avenir et dont la responsabilité lui incombe. L'éducation ne constitue qu'un seul de ces champs d'activité. On pourrait tirer nombre d'autres domaines où le Québec entend exercer, soit seul soit en collaboration avec ses partenaires canadiens, une activité conforme à ses intérêts et à ses priorités, conforme aussi à son vrai visage.

Je citerai, à titre d'exemple, le domaine de la recherche, qui touche à la fois à l'éducation, au développement industriel, au développement économique et social équilibré de son peuple. Il s'agit plus que jamais d'une activité qui déborde les frontières, et où la collaboration et les échanges au niveau international sont indispensables.

Dans des cas comme celui-ci, qui dépassent de diverses façons le cadre strict de la répartition des tâches, le Québec, comme État membre de la fédération canadienne, désire être présent comme partenaire à l'élaboration des politiques et des programmes, tout autant qu'à leur négociation, puisqu'il sera, pour une large part, responsable de leur application et bénéficiaire de leurs résultats.

L'entente que le Québec vient de conclure avec la France est une preuve de l'intérêt que nous portons nous aussi à ce domaine. Évidemment, des ententes comme celle-ci n'empêchent pas et ne peuvent pas remplacer les contacts individuels qui ont toujours existé entre universités et institutions de natures diverses. Le ministère de l'éducation n'a pas l'intention de se substituer à des réseaux d'échanges qui existent déjà: au contraire, il entend favoriser leur extension et leur insertion dans un ensemble cohérent, et leur prêter le concours de son appareil administratif.

C'est dans cet esprit que le Québec envisage les échanges d'étudiants prévus dans l'entente de caractère général qu'il vient de signer à Paris. C'est aussi dans cet esprit que votre visite ici, messieurs les délégués, prend une signification particulière.

1.1. The Provinces and Treaty-Making Powers

Doc. 9.3   **[Canadian constitutional position]**

STATEMENT ISSUED BY SSEA PAUL MARTIN, OTTAWA, APRIL 23, 1965, REGARDING THE PROVINCES AND TREATY-MAKING POWERS. (EXTRACTS)

The constitutional position in this country on the question of treaty-making is clear. Canada has only one international personality in the community of sovereign states. There is no doubt that only the Government of Canada has the power or authority to enter into treaties with other countries.

It is, nevertheless, true that, under the Canadian constitution as it has been interpreted, there is a lack of harmony between treaty-making and treaty-implementing powers. This creates special problems for Canada in respect of treaties concerning subjects of provincial legislative jurisdiction. The problem is not unique. Other federal states have adopted various approaches to the task of harmonizing treaty-making and treaty-implementing powers, but there is no federal state in the world whose constitution allows its members to make treaties freely and independently of the federal authorities. The reason for this is obvious. Independent treaty-making powers are the prerogative of sovereign states. A federal state whose members actually possess such powers would neither be a federal union nor a state. It would be an association of sovereign powers.

The Federal Government has exclusive responsibility for the conduct of external affairs as a matter of national policy affecting all Canadians. The policy of the Federal Government in discharging this responsibility is to seek to promote the interest of the entire country and of all Canadians of the various provinces within the overall framework of our national policy.

9 — The Provinces and Foreign Policy

In respect of matters of specific concern to the provinces of Canada, it is the policy of the Canadian Government, in a spirit of co-operative federalism, to do its utmost to assist the provinces in achieving the particular aspirations and goals which they wish to attain. This was done, for example, in the case of the negotiations relating to the Columbia River.

It is clear that Quebec is the custodian of special cultural values and that this unique heritage cannot be developed in isolation from the French community. The Canadian Government recognizes that it is in the interest of Canada as a whole that this should be done. The pursuit of this objective is not in question. On the contrary, the Federal Government, for its part, is prepared to do all it can to assist Quebec in this regard. It recognizes that Quebec will play a major role in the achievement of these fundamental objectives.

The Canadian Government is ready and anxious to use its powers in the foreign-affairs field, within the framework of our national foreign policy, to assist Quebec and all the other provinces in furthering matters of special concern to them. The attitude of the Federal Government has recently been illustrated by the *entente* signed by representatives of Quebec and France in the field of education in February 1965. The Quebec and federal authorities co-operated actively in a procedure which enabled the Province of Quebec, within the framework of our constitution and our national policy, to participate in international arrangements in a field of particular interest to that province.

Thus, under existing procedures, the position is that, once it is determined that what a province wishes to achieve through agreements in the field of education or in other fields of provincial jurisdiction falls within the framework of Canadian foreign policy, the provinces can discuss detailed arrangements directly with the competent authorities of the country concerned. When a formal international agreement is to be concluded, however, the federal powers relating to the signature of treaties and the conduct of over all foreign policy must necessarily come into operation.

The approach of the Canadian Government to the question of Canadian representation in international organizations of a social, cultural, or humanitarian character reflects the same constructive spirit. We recognize the desirability of ensuring that the Canadian representation in such organizations and conferences reflects in a fair and balanced way provincial and other interests in these subjects.

2. "Vive le Québec Libre"

Discours de Charles de Gaulle   Doc. 9.4

LE 24 JUILLET 1967, À L'HÔTEL DE VILLE, MONTRÉAL.

C'est une immense émotion qui remplit mon coeur en voyant devant moi la ville de Montréal française. Au nom du vieux pays, au nom de la France, je vous salue de tout mon coeur.

Je vais vous confier un secret que vous ne répéterez à personne. Ce soir, ici, et tout le long de ma route, je me suis trouvé dans une atmosphère du même genre que celle de la Libération.

Et tout le long de ma route, outre cela, j'ai constaté quel immense effort de progrès, de développement et par conséquent d'affranchissement que vous accomplissez ici, et c'est à Montréal qu'il faut que je le dise, parce que s'il y a eu au monde une ville exemplaire par ses réussites modernes, c'est la vôtre. Je dis: c'est la vôtre, et je me permets d'ajouter: c'est la nôtre.

Si vous saviez quelle confiance la France, réveillée après d'immenses épreuves, porte maintenant vers vous! Si vous saviez quelle affection elle recommence à ressentir pour les Français du Canada! Et si vous saviez à quel point elle se sent obligée de concourir à votre marche en avant, à votre progrès! C'est pourquoi elle a conclu avec le gouvernement du Québec, avec celui de mon ami Johnson, des accords pour que les Français de part et d'autre de l'Atlantique travaillent ensemble à une même œuvre française. Et d'ailleurs, le concours que la France va tous les jours un peu plus prêter ici, elle sait bien que vous le lui rendrez parce que vous êtes en train de vous constituer des élites, des usines, des entreprises, des laboratoires qui feront l'étonnement de tous et qui un jour-j'en suis sûr-vous permettront d'aider la France.

Voilà ce que je suis venu vous dire ce soir, en ajoutant que j'emporte de cette réunion inouïe de Montréal un souvenir inoubliable. La France entière sait, voit, entend ce qui se passe ici et je puis vous dire qu'elle en vaudra mieux.

Vive Montréal, vive le Québec, vive le Québec libre, vive le Canada français, vive la France!

3. Canada, Quebec, and France

Doc. 9.5   **The provinces and foreign policy**

STATEMENT BY PM PEARSON, HOUSE OF COMMONS, NOVEMBER 28, 1967.

Mr. Speaker, I should like to make a short statement commenting on one made yesterday in Paris by General de Gaulle.

I said in my statement of July 25, 1967, Mr. Speaker, commenting on some earlier remarks of the President of the French Republic, that Canada had always had a special relationship with France, which was the motherland of so many of its citizens. I said we attached the greatest importance to our friendship with the French people; that it had been and remained the strong purpose of the Government of Canada to foster that friendship. I should like to confirm those words today.

I do not propose to deal in any detail with General de Gaulle's statement of yesterday, a statement very carefully prepared and made to the press. General de Gaulle's statement will obviously arouse discord in Canada. I am sure the people of this country will be restrained in their response to it, as I am in mine today, so as not to serve the purposes of those who would disunite and divide our country.

I believe the statement distorted some Canadian history, misrepresented certain contemporary developments and wrongly predicted the future. This statement was not merely a commentary on Canadian domestic or foreign policies, which could have been ignored; it was an intervention in those policies by the head of a foreign state. As such it remains unacceptable. Indeed, Mr. Speaker, in this case it is intolerable that a head of a foreign state or government should recommend a course of political or constitutional action which would destroy Canadian Confederation and the unity of the Canadian state.

The future of Canada, Mr. Speaker, will be decided in Canada, by Canadians.

I have confidence, and I know all members of this House have confidence, in the ability and good sense of all Canadians, French- or English-speaking, to make the right decision. They will do it in their own way and through their own democratic process. I believe this decision will require further constitutional changes to bring our federalism up to date and to ensure, among other things, that French-speaking Canadians who form one of our two founding cultural and linguistic groups, or societies if you like, will have their rights accepted and respected in Canada.

I agree also that the Federal Government — any Federal Government — should encourage and promote special and close cultural relations between French-speaking Canadians and France and other French-speaking countries. Indeed, Mr. Speaker, we are doing that. There should be no argument on this score, except with those who wish to use these relations to destroy the Federal Government's responsibility for foreign affairs and who do not accept Canada is a free country and its people govern themselves.

Canadians in Quebec and elsewhere in Canada have the right to exercise fully their political rights in federal and provincial elections. This determination is no new discovery for us.

We do not need to have it offered to us. To assert the contrary is an insult to those who discharge their democratic privileges as Canadian voters and to those who serve their country in this House and in provincial legislatures. To those who would set us free, we answer: "We are free". To those who would disunite us, we answer: "We remain united, in a federal system which is being brought into line with the requirements of time and of our origins and history".

On April 19, 1960, the great and illustrious head of another state, speaking in Ottawa, had this to say.

I quote from his speech:

And now, how do you Canadians appear to us? Materially, a country, of vast size, mighty resources, inhabited by a hardworking and enterprising people. Politically, a state which has found it in itself to unite two societies, very different in origin, language and religion, which exercises independence under the British Crown and as part of the Commonwealth, which is forging a national character though spread out over three thousand miles alongside a very powerful federation; a solid and stable state.

Mr. Speaker, I agree with those words of General de Gaulle in 1960. I disagree with his words in 1967.

Editor's notes: Matters between Ottawa and Quebec came to a head in January 1968, when Quebec received and accepted an invitation to attend a meeting of the French-speaking Education Ministers at Libreville, capital of Gabon, on the west coast of Africa. The federal government was not invited. Quebec was present with all the trappings of an independent state. Ottawa proceeded to suspend diplomatic relations with Gabon, but these were resumed later after things had quieted down. Canada's aid programme in Gabon was maintained. Quebec participated in the second phase of the Education Ministers' meeting, which took place in Paris in April 1968. Again, Ottawa was ignored. Concurrently, France's cultural activities among the French-speaking minorities in New Brunswick and Manitoba were stepped up. The French Government's official presence in Quebec, through increased consulate strength and activity, was greatly intensified.

Ottawa's suspension of relations with Gabon was essentially a warning, partly to France which was believed to be behind the Gabonese invitation to Quebec, but also to the other French-speaking African states, to tread warily in this area. If the federal government had ignored the matter, it would have implied that it was prepared to countenance repetitions of the incident. This would have served as an encouragement both to Quebec and to others to continue. Acceptance of participants at international conferences constitutes a form of diplomatic recognition. A series of precedents established by Quebec participation in intergovernmental meetings of the Francophone states could have led to eventual recognition of its independence: hence the importance of a federal response to the Gabonese gesture.

Ottawa was determined that Canada and not just Quebec should be invited to the next meeting of the French-speaking Education Ministers, scheduled to be held at Kinshasa, The Congo, in January 1969. It was also determined that Canada should be present at the international conference where the foundations of a French-speaking Commonwealth — *la Francophonie* — were soon to be laid. This conference was slated to take place at Niamey, capital of Niger, in February 1969.

These developments constitute the political backdrop to the two White Papers published by the Federal Government during the first half of 1968.[87] Basically, they reiterate the federal position on the constitutional demarcation line in this sector, as given in SSEA Martin's statement and, in addition, convey suggestions regarding provincial participation at international meetings.

Meanwhile, changes of government had occurred both in Quebec and in Ottawa, as well as in France, that changed things a good deal. The Trudeau government was a good deal tougher in its approaches both to France and Francophone Africa. The French government under Presidents Georges Pompidou and Giscard d'Estaing turned out to be more flexible than under General de Gaulle, who left office in 1969. The new Premier of Quebec, Jean-Jacques Bertrand, and his Liberal successor, Robert Bourassa, were also more flexible.

New federal approaches to the countries concerned — particularly in Francophone Africa — ensued. Urgent consultations with the provincial authorities in Quebec were undertaken. These measures were accompanied by increased Canadian aid activity in Francophone Africa, of which the Chevrier Mission during the late winter and early spring of 1968 is an example. It was authorized to approve aid projects and to commit funds on the spot.

Both the federal and Quebec governments received invitations to the next Education ministers' meeting at Kinshasa, where a co-chairmanship arrangement between the federal and Quebec governments was organized. These steps were successful.

Attention is drawn, in particular, to the voting procedures and to the evolution of arrangements for the chairmanship of Canadian delegations agreed upon by the federal government, Quebec, and other interested provinces for the two types of meetings concerned. In essence, for the Education Conferences, when a vote is called for and the Canadian delegation cannot agree on an issue, it abstains. In addition, delegations to such meetings are headed by the Quebec Minister of Education (with federal advisors in the foreign policy field). For the *Francophonie* conferences, where the mandate is broader than for the Education Conferences (aid, cultural exchanges, etc. are also included), only when disagreement occurs within the delegation on a matter affecting strictly provincial jurisdictions is abstention to take place.

---

[87] *Federalism and International Relations*, Ottawa, February 1968, and *Federalism and International Conferences on Education*, Ottawa, May 1968. See A.E.B. II, pp. 310–315 for details.

Canadian delegations to *Francophonie* Conferences are chaired by the federal government, the Vice-Chairman being from Quebec as detailed below. Other interested provinces are also represented at *Francophonie* meetings.

These arrangements tend to make Canadian delegations to such conferences by far the largest and most colourful of all, since Ottawa and each province have the right to be identified by plaques, flags, etc. These manifestations of Canadian tribalism are said to amuse the Africans no end.

As a result of the second conference of Niamey, held in March 1970, *la Francophonie* came into official being. It took the form of an international organization called the *Agence de Coopération Culturelle et Technique*, with some 30 member states. Its headquarters are located in Paris. France contributes 45% of its budget; Canada 35%, of which slightly more than 2% comes from Quebec; Belgium 12%, the remainder coming from the other member states. The *Agence*'s activities are concentrated mainly in the technical assistance and cultural exchange fields.

With the departure of President de Gaulle from the political scene and the two electoral victories of Premier Bourassa in 1969 and 1973 respectively, relations between Ottawa and Quebec as well as between Ottawa and Paris improved. Participation in the programmes of the *Agence* at the federal and provincial levels became less politicized, more pragmatic and routine.

By virtue of the *Agence*'s constitution, notably article 3(3), Quebec became — with Ottawa's blessing — a *gouvernement participant* in the *Agence*.

Doc. 9.6 **Conférence des Ministres de l'éducation: Paris, 1 au 4 décembre 1969.**

ÉCHANGE DE LETTRES ENTRE LES PREMIERS MINISTRES BERTRAND ET TRUDEAU.

Ottawa, le 26 novembre 1969.

Monsieur le Premier ministre,

Vous êtes déjà au courant que le gouvernement du Canada enverra une délégation à la deuxième session de la Conférence des Ministres de l'éducation d'expression française, qui se tiendra à Paris du 1er au 4 décembre 1969.

À la suite d'entretiens qui ont eu lieu récemment entre nos représentants respectifs au sujet de cette Conférence, les fonctionnaires québécois concernés ont transmis à mes représentants le texte d'arrangements *ad hoc* qui se rapporte à la participation du Québec à la délégation canadienne à cette Conférence. Je crois savoir que ce texte, qui nous est parvenu le 24 novembre, a déjà reçu votre assentiment.

Je me félicite que ces arrangements *ad hoc*, dont je joins copie pour mémoire, permettront une présence québécoise importante au sein de la délégation canadienne. Je demande donc au ministère des Affaires extérieures de prendre des dispositions immédiates en vue d'une réunion de la délégation avant son départ. Des agents du ministère se mettront sans délai en rapport avec vos représentants à cette fin.

Veuillez agréer, Monsieur le Premier ministre, l'assurance de ma haute considération.

(P.E. Trudeau)

le 21 novembre 1969

Sommaire des arrangements *ad hoc* concernant la deuxième session de la Conférence des ministres de l'éducation d'expression française à Paris, du 1er au 4 décembre 1969.

1) Le Québec déléguera à la Conférence de Paris son ministre de l'éducation qui agira comme président de la délégation canadienne.

   Celle-ci comprendra, en outre des délégués du Québec, des délégués des autres provinces s'il en est, et des conseillers en affaires étrangères de l'administration fédérale.

2) Une réunion des participants aura lieu avant le départ pour Paris.

3) Le ministre de l'éducation du Québec parlera au nom du Québec sur toute matière du domaine de la compétence constitutionnelle du Québec. Les délégués des autres provinces parleront de même. La délégation canadienne s'exprimera par la voix de son président, ou à défaut, celle de son vice-président.

4. La présence du Québec pourra être identifié de la façon suivante:

   — lors de la séance solennelle d'ouverture de même qu'à la séance de clôture, le président de la séance, ou les autres orateurs, pourront identifier le Québec au sein de la délégation canadienne par une mention appropriée;

   — la voiture des délégués québécois portera une plaque avec la double mention Canada et Québec, et des fanions consistant en des drapeaux miniatures du Canada et du Québec;

   — le drapeau du Québec pourra flotter sur l'hôtel où logera le ministre québécois;

   — à la salle de conférence ou à l'extérieur de cette salle, si l'on fait flotter les divers drapeaux, celui du Québec sera déployé pourvu qu'il le soit en association avec celui du Canada, la préséance étant donnée à celui-ci.

4) Dans le cas d'un vote éventuel à la Conférence, la délégation canadienne n'aurait qu'un seul vote. Si les membres de la délégation ne s'entendaient pas, le Canada s'abstiendrait.

5) Dans la salle de conférence, la délégation canadienne sera identifiée par une plaque se lisant "Canada". Des plaques placées derrière la plaque "Canada" identifieront les provinces représentées au sein de la délégation comme suit: "Canada-Québec", "Canada-Nouveau Brunswick", etc. Les lettres indiquant les noms des provinces seront de dimension comparable à celles indiquant le nom du Canada.

235

6) La liste officielle de la délégation canadienne sera présentée
à la Conférence selon le format suivant.
Délégation du Canada
Québec: Honorable Jean-Marie Morin, Président

_____

_____

Québec, le 27 novembre 1969.

Monsieur le Premier ministre,

Je réponds aux lettres que vous m'avez transmises par télex
hier et aujourd'hui. L'une portait sur la conférence des ministres de
l'éducation et l'autre sur la conférence des ministres de la Jeunesse et
des Sports. Ces deux conférences ont lieu à Paris la semaine prochaine.

Je suis d'accord avec les arrangements *ad hoc* auxquels nous
en sommes arrivés à la suite des consultations qui ont eu lieu entre
les représentants de nos deux gouvernements. Ces arrangements sont
en substance semblables à ceux qui ont prévalu à Kinshasà en janvier dernier, et j'estime qu'ils permettront une collaboration heureuse
de la délégation québécoise avec les délégations des autres provinces
intéressées ainsi qu'avec les conseillers de l'administration fédérale
qui seront sur les lieux, constituant tous ensemble la délégation canadienne.

J'ajoute toutefois que cet accord étant fait de nuances et de choix
de termes, j'aurais souhaité que la correspondance échangée sur le sujet reflète avec autant de précision que possible l'esprit qui y préside.
Vous dites dans votre lettre concernant la conférence des ministres de
l'éducation que "le gouvernement du Canada enverra une délégation"
à cette conférence. Dire plutôt qu'il y aura une délégation canadienne
composée des délégations d'un certain nombre de provinces et de conseillers en affaires étrangères de l'administration fédérale me paraîtrait
plus conforme au texte des arrangements conclus et au concept re-
cherché.

Je vous prie d'agréer, monsieur le Premier ministre, l'expression
de mes sentiments les meilleurs.

(J.J. Bertrand)

4. Canada and La Francophonie

Doc. 9.7   **[Canadian participation]**

STATEMENT BY PM PIERRE TRUDEAU, ON THE OCCASION OF THE SIGNING OF AGREE-
MENTS WITH THE PRESIDENT OF NIGER, MR. DIORI HAMANI, OTTAWA, SEPTEMBER 19,
1969. (EXTRACTS)

Canada, with six million French-speaking citizens, is naturally a part
of the francophone family. For Canada, the active participation in *la*

9 — The Provinces and Foreign Policy

Francophonie that is being organized is a necessity. In the North American setting, our country intends to reinforce its French characteristics and to spread their influence far afield. To that end, Canada must enter into close relations with all the peoples of the world who express themselves and assert themselves in the French language.

This is true for the French-Canadian people in the Province of Québec, which is the home *par excellence* of French culture in Canada. It is also true for the one million French Canadians in other Canadian provinces.

This participation in *la Francophonie* is, moreover, an extension of Canadian bilingualism on an international scale. It is thus a fundamental element, and a permanent one, in our policy. I say further that our bilingualism should be expressed not only through co-operation among French-speaking people but also in all of our foreign policy, especially within international organizations.

Co-operation with the French-speaking world has existed for some time through a whole network of bilateral relations, first of all in Europe, then in Africa and Asia. We shall continue to further systematically these relations as new prospects for multilateral co-operation open before us.

You are especially known in Canada, Mr. President, as one of the most important builders of *la Francophonie*. You will succeed, I am sure, in providing it with the structures envisaged at the Niamey Conference.

The Niamey Conference marked a turning-point, because it was decided at the time to study the possibility of establishing an agency for "cultural and technical co-operation". Co-operation among French-speaking nations will thus be placed on an organized basis — multilateral and intergovernmental. Canada has promised its full support in this project; we have already made a financial contribution to the agency's provisional secretariat. We shall maintain our support.

We view this agency not as a political community but as an instrument for multilateral aid in cultural and technical matters between French-speaking countries. We are prepared to recognize it as an agency for coordination, promotion and implementation, an agency that will evolve and expand in the light of experience. The agency will have to pioneer in unexplored or neglected areas. In short, Mr. President, we hope that the agency will play a major role in the organization of *la Francophonie*.

The Canadian Government intends to support African efforts towards economic expansion and social development. Considerable sums have been devoted to this end. Since 1960 it has been promoting a program of aid to French-speaking Africa by means of a fund that has almost doubled each year, reaching a total of $30 million in 1969. And this is only a beginning. Canada wants to see a strong, prosperous Africa, whose peoples are truly forging ahead.

Doc. 9.8 **La Francophonie: Conférence de Niamey, mars 1970**

COMMUNIQUÉ. MINISTÈRE DES AFFAIRES EXTÉRIEURES, OTTAWA, 24 MARS 1970.

Article I: Sommaire des Arrangements Ad Hoc pour la Deuxième Conférence des Pays Francophones

A. Un Ministre ou Haut Fonctionnaire du Gouvernement Québécois sera désigné pour faire partie de la délégation canadienne dont il sera le Vice-Président. La délégation comprendra des membres du Gouvernement et de l'administration fédérale et des délégués en provenance des provinces.

B. La délégation se réunira en temps utile, avant son départ, pour coordonner la participation canadienne à la conférence;

C. La délégation canadienne s'exprimera par la voix de son Président ou, à défaut, de son Vice-Président. Le Ministre ou Haut Fonctionnaire du Gouvernement Québécois pourra parler au nom du Québec sur toute matière de la compétence constitutionnelle du Gouvernement Québécois. Les délégués en provenance des autres provinces pourront faire de même. Il y aura consultation préalable sur les points de vue à mettre de l'avant à la conférence.

D. Dans le cas d'un vote éventuel à la Conférence, la délégation canadienne n'aura qu'un seul vote. Si les membres de la délégation ne s'entendaient pas sur une matière relevant de la compétence législative exclusive des provinces, la délégation s'abstiendrait.

E. La signature du Canada sera apposée comme suit: À la place qui lui est réservée et sous la signature du Président de la délégation apparaîtront immédiatement la signature du Ministre ou Haut Fonctionnaire du Gouvernement Québécois ainsi que celles d'un délégué en provenance de chacune des autres provinces. On s'en tiendra pour ces signatures à la formule suivante: "Gérard Pelletier, Secrétaire d'État du Canada"; "Julien Chouinard, Secrétaire Général du Gouvernement du Québec".

F. La présence du Québec pourra être identifiée comme suit, à la lumière des usages locaux. Il en sera de même des autres provinces.

1) Lors de la séance solennelle d'ouverture, de même qu'à la séance de clôture, le Président de la séance, ou les autres orateurs, pourront identifier le Québec au sein de la délégation canadienne par une mention appropriée.

2) La voiture des délégués québécois portera une plaque avec la double mention Canada et Québec, et les fanions consistant en des drapeaux miniatures du Canada et du Québec.

3) Le drapeau du Québec pourra flotter sur l'hôtel où logera le Ministre Québécois.

4) À la salle de conférence ou à l'extérieur de cette salle, si l'on fait flotter les divers drapeaux, celui du Québec sera déployé

pourvu qu'il le soit en association avec celui du Canada, la préséance étant donnée à celui-ci.

5) Dans la salle de conférence, la délégation canadienne sera identifiée par une plaque se lisant Canada. Une plaque placée derrière la plaque Canada identifiera le Québec au sein de la délégation, comme suit: Canada-Québec. Les lettres indiquant le nom du Québec seront de dimension comparable à celles indiquant le nom du Canada.

G. La liste officielle de la délégation canadienne sera présentée à la conférence selon le format suivant:

"Délégation du Canada

M. Gérard Pelletier	Secrétaire d'État du Canada Président et Chef de la Délégation.
M. Julien Chouinard Québec:	Secrétaire Général du Gouvernement du Québec et Vice-Ministre du Conseil exécutif; Vice-Président de la délégation.
Ontario:	M _____
Nouveau-Brunswick:	M _____
Manitoba:	M _____
Conseillers:	M _____ "

Article II: Arrangements Relatifs au Rôle du Gouvernement Québécois dans la Participation canadienne à l'Agence

A. Conférences Générales

Un membre ou haut fonctionnaire du Gouvernement Québécois sera normalement Vice-Président de la délégation. On pourra s'entendre sur la présidence d'un Ministre ou Haut Fonctionnaire du Gouvernement Québécois, selon les circonstances et la nature des intérêts en cause à chaque conférence. Pour que la délégation comprenne un nombre satisfaisant de représentants québécois et autres, on proposera que le nombre de délégués par pays ne soit pas limité à cinq. Cependant, les frais de délégués supplémentaires pourraient ne pas être à la charge de l'agence.

Il y aura une présence adéquate de représentants québécois dans les commissions et comités, compte tenu des règlements de la conférence générale.

Les arrangements *ad hoc* pour la conférence constitutive s'appliqueront aux conférences générales en ce qui concerne les réunions de la délégation avant les conférences, l'expression des points de vue fédéraux et provinciaux, l'identification du Québec et la liste de la délégation. Si des modifications étaient requises par les circonstances, les autorités fédérales et provinciales intéressées verraient à s'entendre à ce sujet.

B. Conseil Exécutif

Le Québec occupera un des postes disponibles pour le Canada au conseil exécutif.

C. Secrétariat Général

Il y aura consultation à l'intérieur de la délégation au sujet d'une candidature canadienne au secrétariat général.

D. Finances

La contribution canadienne aux frais de l'agence sera présentée de la façon suivante dans les rapports de l'agence: "Contribution du Canada: $ _____, dont le Gouvernement Central a contribué $ _____, le Québec $ _____, l'Ontario $ _____, etc."

Tout en notant que les contributions nationales seront versées globalement au budget général de l'agence, le Québec entend computer sa participation à la contribution du Canada sur les bases suivantes.

(A) Frais d'opération du Secrétariat:

— participation du Québec jusqu'à concurrence d'un montant égal à celui que contribuera le Gouvernement fédéral;

(B) Programmes d'action de l'agence:

— la contribution canadienne au coût des programmes de l'agence sera en principe fournie par le gouvernement fédéral, mais le Québec pourrait accroître sa participation à la contribution canadienne selon l'intérêt qu'il portera à ces programmes.

Les autres provinces peuvent évidemment participer à la contribution si elles le souhaitent.

Doc. 9.9 **Modalités selon lesquelles le Gouvernement du Québec est admis comme Gouvernement Participant aux Institutions, aux Activités et aux Programmes de L'Agence de Coopération Culturelle et Technique, Convenues le 1er octobre 1971 entre le Gouvernement du Canada et le Gouvernement du Québec**

COMMUNIQUÉ, MINISTÈRE DES AFFAIRES EXTÉRIEURES, OTTAWA, LE 8 OCTOBRE 1971.

L'article 3.3 de la Charte de l'Agence de Coopération culturelle et technique prévoyant que:

Dans le plein respect de la souveraineté et de la compétence internationale des États membres, tout gouvernement peut être admis comme gouvernement participant aux institutions, aux activités et programmes de l'Agence, sous réserve de l'approbation de l'État membre dont relève le territoire sur lequel le gouvernement participant concerné exerce son autorité et selon les modalités convenues entre ce gouvernement et celui de l'État membre,

240

les modalités suivantes selon lesquelles le gouvernement du Québec est admis comme gouvernement participant aux institutions, aux activités et aux programmes de l'Agence sont convenues.

Participation aux Institutions

Article 1
Le gouvernement du Québec participe aux institutions de l'Agence:
    Conseil d'Administration
    Comité des Programmes
    Conseil consultatif
    Autres comités et commissions
    Secrétariat général
    Groupe d'experts en gestion administrative et financière
    Conférence générale
Des modalités sont prévues à cet effet pour chaque institution.[88]

Editor's notes: All Quebec governments have maintained close relations with France since General de Gaulle's famous *Vive le Québec libre* speech in Montreal in 1967 and the election of the *Parti Québécois* to power under Premier René Lévesque (1976-1984) intensified Quebec's push towards France, both culturally and economically, as well as towards Francophone Africa in the aid field. Its return to power in 1994, with its near win of the sovereignty referendum of 1995, did not — somewhat unexpectedly — result in any great changes of outlook or approach.[89]

The relationship between the federal government and the provinces as regards international relations and the arrangements agreed upon earlier by the two levels of government has also remained pretty much unchanged. However the tone of the relationship towards the end of the Trudeau years had become a good deal harsher, owing not so much to provincial activity abroad as to the constitutional climate at home.

One of the first priorities of the Mulroney government in this

---

[88]There follow here the articles of the agreement (two to nineteen inclusive) describing the precise way in which Québec participates in the activities of each body mentioned in Article 1, as well as the manner in which Québec takes part in the programs and activities of the Agency. By virtue of Article 17, the Government of Québec contributes 50% of the Canadian share of the operating costs of the Agency's secretariat, headquartered in Paris. Canada's overall contribution to the Agency's total annual budget (staff and other administrative and operating costs, programs, and related development activities and assistance) amounts to 35%, of which Québec pays 2%.

[89]In 1996, the Bouchard government published a lengthy *Plan Stratégique du Ministère des Relations Internationales 1997-2000*, outlining its approach to international affairs. The *Plan Stratégique* develops in considerable detail, but does not alter, the policy established by earlier governments.

sector was to soften the tone of the relationship between Ottawa and the provinces and to seek to improve the dialogue generally.

It is worth noting here that it is France that has since become more correct in its relations with Ottawa through its policy of *non-interférence/non indifférence*. Another factor to be taken into consideration in this shift of outlook was the Mittérand government's tendency to concentrate on matters closer to home during its long years in power. The Chirac government has maintained this basic approach.

5. Recent Policy Developments

Doc. 9.10   **Ottawa and the provinces**

LETTER FROM SSEA JOE CLARK TO THE PROVINCIAL PREMIERS, DECEMBER 7, 1984. (EXTRACTS)

Among the most important objectives of the new government is the improvement of the atmosphere of federal-provincial relations so as to facilitate a more useful and productive process of consultation and dialogue between the two levels of government. To this end, the government has addressed itself to a series of measures to reduce the number of irritants in federal-provincial relations. Some of the measures taken have been announced by the Ministers concerned or will be in due course.

Approval has also been given to several important steps to reduce irritants in the area of foreign relations.

These relate to the following subjects:

1) Federal-provincial consultations on development of a National Trade Strategy.

    Discussions have been initiated at the senior official level with all provinces. It is my hope that they will lead to the formulation of a viable trade strategy with the full support of all eleven governments.

2) Contacts between provincial premiers and foreign dignitaries

    There is a general view that there have not been satisfactory procedures to facilitate contacts between provincial leaders and foreign governments. It has been decided to acknowledge that private meetings between visiting dignitaries, such as a head of state or government, and provincial premiers may be held in Canada, in return for a commitment from provincial authorities to provide an account of such meetings to the Department of External Affairs. Abroad, in keeping with accepted practice, premiers will be accompanied by Canadian heads of mission when making courtesy calls on foreign heads of state or government.

3) Preparation of visits to the provinces by foreign dignitaries

I have asked my officials to involve provincial authorities in the preparations for such visits as early in the administrative planning cycle of such visits as possible.

4) Visits of Ottawa diplomats to the provinces

Since I continually urge Ottawa diplomats to get out and visit the country, I would not wish to require that the established practice which has arisen of direct contacts been High Commissions, Embassies, and the provinces be re-routed through the Department of External Affairs. On the other hand, I know that some provinces appreciate the screening function provided by the Department for such visits and that many smaller foreign missions which do not have consulates in other Canadian cities prefer to coordinate their visits through External Affairs. My intention is to streamline the processing of such visits and I would welcome your comments on further improvements which you feel could be made.

5) Provincial participation on Canadian delegations to international conferences

The Federal Government is responsible for the designation of Canadian delegations to international conferences, including the UN specialized agencies, dealing with issues of interest or concern to the provinces. It pays the expenses of delegates to such meetings, many of whom are of course employees of provincial governments. It is my desire that the Department of External Affairs be as forthcoming as possible in including provincial representatives on delegations of this sort. At the same time, I would ask for your cooperation in seeing that Canadian delegations do not become so overloaded with provincial representatives as to occasion logistical difficulties, unnecessary expenses or protocol embarrassments for conference organizers.

In outlining these measures, I wish to emphasize that the government recognizes that provinces have legitimate interests in areas of international relations and that there is an increase in discussions at the international level of social issues which fall within provincial jurisdiction. At the same time, I should also mention that provincial participation on the international scene must be coordinated so as to avoid a diffusion of the image of Canada abroad, with adverse consequences for all Canadians.

5.1. Ontario

Ontario's international objectives and priorities   Doc. 9.11

SUMMARY OF A BOOKLET ISSUED BY THE INTERNATIONAL RELATIONS BRANCH, MINISTRY OF INTERGOVERNMENTAL AFFAIRS, TORONTO, APRIL 1986.

Jurisdiction over international affairs, being an essential attribute of sovereignty, is primarily the responsibility of the Government of Canada.

A province cannot, therefore, enjoy a full international personality in the legal sense.

The Canadian federal system, however, allows provinces to play a significant role in defining and pursuing their international interests, to the extent that those interests do not conflict with Canada's foreign policy directions and objectives.

Ontario's role

Ontario's role in international affairs is motivated by three main factors:

1) The responsibility to pursue internationally activities which fall under provincial jurisdiction, either exclusively, i.e., education, or partially, e.g., trade, culture, environment.

2) The need to protect and promote Ontario's particular interests. Ideally, the federal government, in its conduct of foreign relations, should represent the national interests of all Canada. In fact, in a country as diverse as Canada, it would be difficult, if not impossible, for the federal government to define "a national interest" which would take into consideration all the particular interests of each province or region. As a result, Ontario has to pursue its own international interests, as a necessary complement to federal efforts.

3) The need to participate more actively in the formulation of Canadian foreign policy. Ontario, as the industrial heart of the country, is more likely to be affected by federal policies than any other province. Consequently, Ontario must influence those foreign policy directions with a view that they take into consideration its interests. A current example of this need can be found in the context of the Canada-U.S. negotiations for trade enhancement between the two countries.

For these reasons, effective coordination of federal and provincial activities is required to ensure that the international interests of provinces can be expressed without compromising Canadian sovereignty.

Although the system has proved satisfactory in certain areas, there is still a lack of adequate information from the federal level regarding some directions of Canadian foreign policy, such as the crucial field of relations with the United States.

Ontario's objectives

The main goal of Ontario's involvement in international relations is the enhancement of the province's economic and social development. To achieve this goal three main factors should be taken into consideration: a) economic interests; b) role of supporting activities; and c) need for a corporate approach.

9 — The Provinces and Foreign Policy

Editor's note: Since elected to office, the Harris government has continued to emphasize this approach, indeed rather more than its predecessors, particularly in the trade sector. In a speech given in Cleveland, Ohio, on October 15, 1999, Premier Harris stressed that the boom in cross-border trade has made neighbouring states more important to Ontario than many parts of Canada; that what happens in Newfoundland or British Columbia economically does not affect Ontario as much as what happens in Michigan, Ohio, New York, Pennsylvania, and Illinois.

5.2. Quebec

Le Québec et l'Indépendance: Le monde pour l'horizon—   Doc. 9.12
Éléments d'une politique d'affaires internationales
BROCHURE DU MINISTÈRE DES AFFAIRES INTERNATIONALES, GOUVERNEMENT DU QUÉBEC, 1991. (RÉSUMÉ)

Les principaux objectifs

La présente politique d'affaires internationales du Québec poursuit cinq grands objectifs;

Premier objectif: Conduire les affaires internationales comme un instrument important de développement économique et socio-culturel.

Pour atteindre cet objectif, le gouvernement verra à: 1) développer sa capacité d'analyse de la scène internationale et de son impact sur le Québec; 2) faire connaître et valoir à l'étranger les principales caractéristiques économiques, socio-culturelles et institutionnelles du Québec actuel; 3) favoriser la participation des Québécois aux débats sur les enjeux internationaux; 4) poursuivre, dans le cadre de la francophonie multilatérale, l'objectif central du renforcement du potentiel des pays membres; et 5) établir, dans le cadre des relations bilatérales et en priorité avec les principaux interlocuteurs avec lesquels le Québec partage des intérêts géopolitiques, économiques et socio-culturelles, des rapports suivis centrés sur les principaux enjeux communs.

Deuxième objectif: Établir un ordre de priorité dans les activités internationales, soit, le développement économique, la coopération scientifique et le développement technologique, le développement des ressources humaines et le développement culturel.

Troisième objectif: Favoriser sur *le plan interne* le partenariat comme mode d'action préférée, en privilégiant: 1) une concertation suivie entre le gouvernement, les institutions publiques et parapubliques, les entreprises et les universités; 2) en associant de façon plus systématique les différentes institutions régionales; et 3) en stimulant la participation des communautés culturelles aux relations du Québec avec l'étranger.

Sur *le plan externe*, dans sa recherche de partenariat, le gouvernement du Québec voudra: 1) au sein de la Francophonie multi-latérale, consacrer des efforts soutenus au travail en commun au sein des réseaux de coopération reliant les institutions de divers pays membres; et 2) développer des rapports bilatéraux suivis avec l'Amérique et l'Europe, certains pays d'Asie et certains pays en développement, notamment francophones.

Quatrième objectif: Développer une approche intégrée dans la conduite des affaires internationales du Québec en établissant sous la l'égide du ministre des Affaires internationales un plan d'action annuel intégrant les activités internationales convenues avec les divers ministères et organismes concernés.

Cinquième objectif: développer une stratégie axée sur la recherche de l'effet multiplicateur en favorisant: 1) le respect de l'autonomie des intervenants; 2) l'identification d'objectifs partagés par les divers intervenants; 3) la recherche de la synergie des efforts soutenus; 4) l'appui aux leaders, aux percées; et 5) la recherche d'un effet d'entraînement. Il faut aussi: a) soutenir le renforcement de l'action internationale des chefs de file québécois capables d'affronter la concurrence et d'entraîner d'autres entreprises et institutions dans leur sillage; et b) renforcer le rôle international du Grand Montréal.

Le rôle du gouvernement fédéral

Dans le cadre constitutionnel actuel, les Québécois versent des impôts et des taxes à Ottawa qui, de son côté, consacre quelques $3,8 milliards à ses ministères et organismes ayant une vocation internationale explicite (Affaires extérieures, ACDI, SEE, etc.), ce qui ne comprend pas les activités internationales des autres ministères et organismes fédéraux.

Le gouvernement du Québec cherchera d'une part à s'assurer que ses intérêts, tels qu'il les définit lui-même, sont dûment pris en compte dans les politiques et programmes de ces ministères et organismes et lui assurent des retombées réelles appropriées; et, d'autre part, qu'il est à même de jouer son rôle d'acteur international en pouvant compter sur la collaboration effective du gouvernement fédéral.

6. La Francophonie

The bases of Canadian participation in *la Francophonie*, as set in the early 1970s, have remained substantially unchanged. Quebec and New Brunswick, the two provinces most interested in *la Francophonie*, continued to have the special status of *gouvernements participants* in the *Agence de coopération culturelle et technique* (ACCT), the operating arm of *la Francophonie* with headquarters in Paris. Ontario and Manitoba also take part in meetings as members of federal delegations. The budget shares determined at the time to defray Canada's participation in the *Agence* still prevail.

Its budgets continue to be relatively small.

Reflecting the expansion of *la Francophonie* — now nearly 50 countries and growing — as well as its usefulness to member states, particularly in the fields of language and culture, but recently the environment also, the Heads of State and/or Government of *la Francophonie* have — since 1986 — been meeting regularly (in theory, every two years). The first such meeting took place in Paris; the second in Quebec. In 1999, one was held in Moncton, New Brunswick. Substantively, like most *Francophonie* conferences, it was heavier on rhetoric than on substance. However, a new element appeared outside the meeting halls in Moncton, where vehement and large-scale manifestations took place against the political and environmental abuses prevailing in many *Francophonie* countries. This will likely continue to be a feature of *Francophonie* summits in coming years.

Le Canada et la Francophonie
Doc. 9.13

ALLOCUTION DU PM BRIAN MULRONEY, LORS DU SOMMET DE CHAILLOT, PALAIS DE CHAILLOT, PARIS, LE 19 NOVEMBRE 1991. (EXTRAITS)

Le Sommet de la Francophonie revient à Paris, d'où il a jailli il y a à peine cinq ans. La France qui nous accueille est le berceau de la liberté, la mère-patrie des droits de la personne. Et ce retour aux sources devrait nous être d'autant plus salutaire que nous prenons de plus en plus conscience que, sans démocratie véritable, il ne peut y avoir de développement durable et que, sans développement soutenu, il ne peut y avoir de démocratie solide.

Démocratisation: Nous devons faire en sorte que la Francophonie exprime, défende, et approfondisse les valeurs démocratiques. Nous devons nous donner les moyens à Paris d'appliquer nos convictions. Nous aurons l'occasion au cours de ce Sommet d'adopter une déclaration sur la démocratisation et le développement. Pour l'appuyer, le gouvernement du Canada, de concert avec le Québec et le Nouveau-Brunswick, proposera également la création d'une unité de soutien de la démocratisation et de l'information sur les droits de la personne.

La Francophonie et la condition de la femme: Nous présenterons aussi un projet visant à combattre les injustices et éliminer les obstacles que rencontrent encore trop de femmes dans le monde. Les femmes, par exemple, forment la moitié de la population mondiale, mais elles fournissent les deux tiers des heures de travail. Elles produisent la moitié de la nourriture de la planète mais ne reçoivent qu'un dixième de la rémunération et ne possèdent qu'un pour-cent des biens. La Francophonie est une famille et si un seul de ses membres est brimé dans ses droits, toute la famille s'en trouve appauvrie. Les droits de la personne, ce n'est pas une notion juridique abstraite ou une théorie politique en vogue dans les pays industrialisés. Ce n'est pas un produit de luxe, mais un outil essentiel de développement.

Droits de la personne et développement: Le Canada estime logique et juste que son aide au développement doit être de plus en plus canalisée vers les pays qui s'efforcent de respecter et qui travaillent à développer les droits de la personne chez eux. Ce qu'il nous faut donc viser, ce qu'il faut absolument atteindre, c'est la justice et le développement, la démocratie et le progrès.

L'endettement des pays en développement: En même temps que nous recouvrons avec fierté l'universalité des valeurs fondamentales, nous devons assumer aussi des responsabilités communes. L'endettement croissant des pays en développement, par exemple, nous appauvrit tous et nous devons ajuster nos politiques et nos objectifs pour corriger cette grave distorsion des rapports économiques. Le Canada fera bien sa part.

L'environnement: La dégradation de l'environnement est aussi un problème mondial qui appelle des solutions.

Nous avons les instruments appropriés à ces tâches. Nous en tenons présentement un entre nos mains: le Sommet de la Francophonie, qui mobilise nos ressources, inspire notre solidarité, et canalise nos efforts. Nous sommes à pied d'oeuvre sur le chantier de l'avenir.

6.1. Provincial Agencies Abroad

In 1977, there were 35 provincial agencies abroad. By 1992, the total had grown to 73. This number was considerably reduced in 1993, when Ontario closed all its offices abroad as an economy measure and Quebec discontinued some of its marginal ones while reducing the staff of many others. Most other provinces have also reduced or abolished posts abroad recently.[90]

7. Alberta and OPEC

Western Canadian oil producers became very active in the Middle East beginning in the late 1970s and early 1980s, especially in Libya after Colonel Moammar Khadafi expelled the American oil companies that had been working there for many years. The Libyans sought replacement equipment and personnel in Western Canada, owing to our knowledge of American oil technology. Currently, Canadian oil interests are also active in Sudan and, on a more modest scale, elsewhere in the Middle East.

When the editor of this volume was on posting to Tunisia and Libya in the early 1980s, the number of oil men in the area from Alberta rose substantially, from virtually nil in the late 1970s to

---

[90]See A.E.B. II, page 302, and A.E.B. III, pp. 147-148, for a list of such offices abroad in the 1970s and 1990s, respectively.

some 1,200 a few years later. There are many more there now. He recalls that in Tunisia, Western Canadians in the oil business were known as *les Arabes aux yeux bleus.*

Relations between the Federal government and Alberta have not always been smooth as regards energy matters, particularly exports. At one point, Alberta threatened to open a "listening post" in Washington, D.C., in order to better monitor Alberta's energy interests, but did not follow through on the threat.[91]

Alberta and OPEC — Crude oil   Doc. 9.14

REPORTED OFFER TO CUT PRODUCTION IN ALBERTA, HOUSE OF COMMONS DEBATES, MARCH 20, 1986.

Mr. Russell MacLellan (Cape Breton-The Sydneys): My question is directed to the SSEA. Premier Don Getty of Alberta in a telephone conversation with the Saudi Arabian Oil Minister, Sheik Yamani, has suggested a cut in the production of Alberta oil to try to halt the world decline in crude oil prices. Was this telephone call made with the prior approval of the federal government, and what is the federal government's position with respect to the offer Premier Getty has made?

Right Hon. Joe Clark (SSEA). Mr. Speaker, I spoke to Premier Getty this morning after I had seen those reports. Premier Getty fully understands that the Government of Canada speaks for Canada on international questions. It may be, Mr. Speaker, that members of the Liberal and the New Democratic Party think that someone else should speak on international policy for Canada.

We believe it is the responsibility of this government, and we do it. I want to assure the Hon. Member, and through him others who are interested, that Canada will continue to coordinate our approach to international energy issues with other members of the international energy agency.

Mr. Russell MacLellan (Cape Breton-The Sydneys). I would like to ask the SSEA if Canada has received any requests from any of the OPEC countries to cut oil production, and what Canada's position would be if such a request were received.

Mr. John McDermid (Parliamentary Secretary to the Minister of Energy, Mines and Resources). In reply to the Hon. Member, the answer is "no", we have not had that request.

Editor's note: Later, Opposition Leader John Turner, in comments outside the House of Commons, observed that the correct procedure for Alberta would have been to proceed through the Federal government. The production of oil is a provincial matter, he said, the international sale and market price are a federal matter. He did

---

[91]See A.E.B. II. pp. 327-328, for Premier Lougheed's statement about this.

not think that Canada could exert much influence on the market, Canada — in his view — being somewhat marginal among world oil producers.

Appendix
The Reorganization of the
Department of External Affairs: 1982

A FORMER UNITED STATES SECRETARY OF STATE, Dean Acheson, once said that "reorganizing the State Department was like performing an appendectomy on a man carrying a piano up a flight of stairs!"

While the reorganization of External Affairs, which stemmed from legislation in 1982, was perhaps somewhat less nerve-wracking, it did produce some extremely complicated and cumbersome results.

The Act originated with the government's decision to apply the strategies for national economic renewal outlined in *Economic Development for Canada in the 1980s*, issued with the budget on November 12, 1981. It reflected the general reorganization of the major economic departments that the government had decided upon.

This restructuring entailed the creation of a new super-Ministry of State for Economic and Regional Development (abolished by PM Turner just before the elections of 1984). A Cabinet Committee on Economic and Regional Development was established and a new department, Regional Industrial Expansion (the result of the amalgamation of the former Department of Trade and Commerce with that of Regional Economic Expansion), was set up. The mandate of External Affairs was radically altered by the restructuring, whereby it absorbed the Trade Commissioner Service of the former Department of Trade and Commerce. As a result of this amalgamation, External Affairs came to resemble the Department of State in Washington in structure.

The idea behind the changes affecting External was not a bad one, at least on paper, that is, to bring under one wing all matters with a foreign policy impact or external implications, whether cultural, political, trade, or other. For a while, the departmental mandate included Immigration, but this was hived off in 1992 to return to its former home.

Initially, as a result of the centralization process, it was hoped that in terms of power and influence in the governmental apparatus the Department might become a Central Agency in the foreign affairs field, like the Treasury Board in the administrative and financial sectors, or the Privy Council Office, but this did not come to pass.

The new Act created two new Ministers reporting to the SSEA, one of whom would have responsibility for international trade and the other for international development and *Francophonie* affairs.

Also to be appointed were three Associate Under-Secretaries, reporting to the Under-Secretary of State for External Affairs. One of these would become Deputy Minister for International Trade and the other would be Deputy Minister for Political Affairs. A Coordinator, International Relations, with the rank and status of Deputy Minister, was to be appointed as well. This triangular structure at the top was accompanied by a panoply of Assistant Under-Secretaries (15, at one point, heading the Department's area and functional bureaux) and, on occasion, Senior Assistant Under-Secretaries. A corresponding complement of Directors General, Deputy Directors General, Directors of Division, Deputy Directors of Division, Special Advisors, etc., shored the structure up.[92]

Incidentally, it should not be thought that this inflation of hierarchies and structures was exclusive to External Affairs. It was not. Similar developments were taking place in other government departments as well, but not to the same extent.

One result of the reorganization was built-in delay in the Department's work as memoranda, telegrams, recommendations, originating as drafts in a division moved through this array of hierarchical barricades on their way up to the Minister. It could sometimes take three or four days before an agreed text reached the Minister. At a time when the pace of international relations and telecommunications was rapidly expanding, this was rather incongruous. As a result, the SSEA would seek quicker advice from his or her own staff, which (for reasons other than strictly departmental) grew considerably during the 1980s, particularly under the Mulroney government, which created the function of ministerial Chiefs of Staff, who begot staffs of their own. The one in External was quite large and duplicated many departmental services and functions.

Another result of the reorganization was a built-in complexity in the Department's decision-making and policy-recommending

---

[92]Recently the titles Under-Secretary of State for External Affairs, Associate and/or Assistant Under-Secretary, became Deputy Minister, Associate and/or Assistant Deputy Minister, in order to conform with the nomenclature used by other government departments.

processes, since such a large number of senior officers, including the two new ministers (depending on the subject), were involved or had to be consulted before recommendations or decisions could be finalized. Also, the process became enmeshed in a growing number of advisory committees and special committees, task forces, study groups and working groups, buttressed by advisors, special advisors, and senior advisors, who had to be consulted along the way when concerned with a particular question or problem.

A third result was the lack of cooperation or smoothness manifest at times in the trilateral relationship among the ministers concerned, as turfs and personalities became involved in the process.

Some departmental clients, businessmen especially, viewed the changes with a considerable degree of scepticism. In particular, they believed that, buried in a much larger unit, the Foreign Trade Service would no longer be able to serve their interests as effectively as in the past or provide the tailored services to which they had become accustomed. There was some truth to this, at least at the outset, but less was heard about it following the appointment of senior cabinet ministers to the International Trade portfolio.

The upshot of all this, however, was that the power and influence of the Privy Council Office and the Prime Minister's Office in the foreign affairs field continued to expand at External's expense.

An Act Respecting the Department of External Affairs   Doc. 1

(EXTRACTS)

. . .

2. (1) There is hereby established a department of the Government of Canada called the Department of External Affairs, over which the SSEA shall preside.

   (2) The SSEA, referred to in this Act as the "Minister" has the management and direction of the Department in Canada and abroad.

3. A Minister of International Trade shall be appointed to assist the Minister.

4. A Minister for External Relations may be appointed to assist the Minister.

. . .

7. The Governor in Council may appoint an officer called the Under-Secretary of State for External Affairs as deputy head of the Department.

8. (1) The Governor in Council may appoint three Associate Under-Secretaries, each of whom shall have the rank and status of a deputy head of a department.

(2) The Governor in Council may designate one of the Associate Under-Secretaries to be Deputy Minister for International Trade and one to be Deputy Minister for Political Affairs.

. . .

10. (2) In exercising his powers and carrying out his duties and functions under this Act, the Minister shall:

   (a) Conduct all diplomatic and consular relations on behalf of Canada;
   (b) Conduct all official communication between the Government of Canada and the government of any other country and between the Government of Canada and any international organization;
   (c) Conduct and manage international negotiations as they relate to Canada;
   (d) Coordinate Canada's international economic relations;
   (e) Foster the expansion of Canada's international trade and commerce;
   (f) Have the control and supervision of CIDA;
   (g) Coordinate the direction given by the Government of Canada to the heads of Canada's diplomatic and consular missions;
   (h) Have the management of Canada's diplomatic and consular missions;
   (i) Administer the foreign service of Canada;
   (j) Foster the development of international law and its application in Canada's external relations; and
   (k) Carry out such other duties and functions as are by law assigned to him.

11. The Minister may, with the approval of the Governor in Council, enter into agreements with the government of any province or any agency thereof respecting the carrying out of programmes related to the Minister's powers, duties, and functions.

Editor's note: All this brings to mind the observation made by the first-century Roman satirical writer, Petronius Arbiter:

> We trained hard, but it seemed that every time we were beginning to form up into teams we would be reorganized. I was to learn that later in life we tend to meet any new situation by reorganizing, and a wonderful method it can be for creating the illusion of progress while producing confusion, inefficiency, and demoralization.

Appendix

Envoi

The continuity in Canadian foreign policy since the enunciation of principles in the Gray Lecture by SSEA St. Laurent in January 1947 is striking.

Over the years, the principles put forward in his lecture have been characteristic of all subsequent foreign policy reviews: national unity and security, political liberty and social justice, the rule of law in national and international affairs, the projection of our values against the backdrop of Christian civilization, the economic development of Canada and the world, acceptance of international responsibility in accordance with our interests and our ability to contribute to world peace. This approach to the world still characterizes our foreign policy as we enter the 21st century.

Suggested Reading

THE EXTENSIVE BIBLIOGRAPHIES MENTIONED UNDER *Suggested Reading* in A.E.B. I, II, and III cover most of the period dealt with in this volume and should be consulted by interested readers. The footnotes in R.A.M. also carry many bibliographical references.

R.A.M.: R.A. MacKay, *Canadian Foreign Policy 1945-1954.* Carleton Library Series 51. Ottawa: Carleton University Press, 1971.

A.E.B. I: Arthur E. Blanchette, *Canadian Foreign Policy 1955-1965.* Carleton Library Series 103. Ottawa: Carleton University Press, 1977.

A.E.B. II: Arthur E. Blanchette, *Canadian Foreign Policy 1966-1976.* Carleton Library Series 118. Ottawa: Carleton University Press, 1981.

A.E.B. III: Arthur E. Blanchette, *Canadian Foreign Policy 1977-1992.* Carleton Library Series 183. Ottawa: Carleton University Press, 1994.

- The Norman Patterson School of International Affairs at Carleton University, Ottawa, publishes a valuable periodical, *Canadian Foreign Policy/La politique étrangère du Canada*, regarding current international issues.

  In addition, its excellent annual series *Canada Among Nations* is a basic source of information on Canadian foreign policy during the last two decades. The references at chapter ends offer a wide-ranging bibliography of current literature on recent Canadian foreign relations.

- *Bout de papier*, a quarterly published for many years by the Professional Association of Foreign Service Officers (PAFSO), Ottawa, carries engaging and timely accounts of many aspects of Canadian foreign policy and diplomacy. It is available in libraries across Canada and at Canadian posts abroad or from PAFSO, at 412-47 Clarence Street, Ottawa, K1N 9K1; tel. (613) 241-1391.

- The *Canadian Military Journal*, a DND bilingual publication, is worth consulting on the defence side of foreign relations. It is available from DND through its Web Site given below.

- *Esprit de corps, CANADIAN MILITARY, then and now*, is an interesting magazine that provides news and views of the Armed Forces past and present. For information: 1-800-361-2791.

- *Canada World View*, published in French and in English by DFAIT, is available free of charge either through 1-800-267-8376 or its website, given below.

The following websites and telephone/fax numbers should also be kept in mind:

Department of Foreign Affairs www.dfait-maeci.gc.ca/
1-800-267-8376 (toll free)
InfoCentre Fax: (613) 996-9709 from a fax machine

Canadian International Development Agency www.acdi-cida.gc.ca/

Department of National Defence www.dnd.gc.ca/

To those sources might be added:

- *Pirouette* (University of Toronto Press, 1990), by Granatstein and Bothwell, who provide a detailed and lively analysis of Canadian foreign policy during the Trudeau years.

- *Special Trust and Confidence* (Carleton University Press, Ottawa, 1996), edited by David Reece, is a series of engaging essays by former Heads of Mission that explore the challenges confronting Canadian diplomats abroad during the period covered by this book.

- *Does Aid Work?* by Robert Casson and associates (Oxford University Press, 1986) is essentially a report to an Inter-Governmental Task Force on the subject. It was commissioned by 18 member governments of the World Bank and the International Monetary Fund and is probably the most comprehensive study of aid ever undertaken. While it does not deal with Canadian development policy or programmes as such, it presents a good analysis and discussion of aid generally, its impact, shortcomings, problems. Its answer to the question posed in its title is far from positive: Aid does work, but not as well as it might or, conversely, without aid things would be much worse.

- *Aid and Ebb Tide: A History of CIDA and Canadian Development Assistance* (Wilfrid Laurier University Press, 1998) by David R. Morrison, who traces the evolution of Canadian aid starting in 1950, when Canada joined the Colombo Plan, down to the 1990s.

- *Canada's Department of External Affairs*, published in two volumes by McGill-Queens University Press, covers the history of DFAIT from its early years down to 1968. Volume I (to 1946) is by John Hilliker; Volume II (1946-1968) by John Hilliker and Donald Barry. Both are very well done. They are also available in French.

Index

Index

www.ingramcontent.com/pod-product-compliance
Lightning Source LLC
Chambersburg PA
CBHW061719270326
41928CB00011B/2045